Government
That
Works

Government That Works

Works

The Results Revolution
in the States

JOHN M. BERNARD

★ RESULTS AMERICA ★

INSPIRING AND ENABLING EFFICIENT AND EFFECTIVE STATE GOVERNMENT

Government That Works: The Results Revolution in the States
By John M. Bernard
Copyright © 2015 by John Bernard. All Rights Reserved

Editors: Michael Snell, Libby Koponen, and Erin Bernard
Cover Design: Bobbi Benson
Interior Design: Bobbi Benson
Research: Paul Aljets

Printed by Thompson-Shore
Published in the United States by Results America
ISBN 978-0-9907265-1-7

Library of Congress Cataloging-in-Publication Data:

Bernard, John M.
    Government that works : the results revolution in the States / by John M.
    Bernard.
    p. cm.
    ISBN 978-0-9907265-1-7
    Includes bibliographical references and index.

1. Government productivity --United States. 2. Government accountability --United States. 3. Public administration --United States. I. Title.

JF1351 .B473 2015
352.3/5 --dc23   201495679

To my departed father, Joseph Martin Bernard, Jr., a man of boundless generosity and profound humility, who spent his life in service to his community. Never a paid public servant, he won tremendous love and respect because he always spoke what he believed.

CONTENTS

Governor O'Malley's Foreword   *xiii*

Governor Snyder's Foreword   *xv*

Acknowledgments   *xix*

Introduction   *xxiii*

CHAPTER 1: The Results Revolution   **1**
Delivering on the Promise of Social Good

Joining the Revolution   3
Fixing the Process   6
Improving Societal Outcomes   15
Learning a Lesson from New York City   21
Applying the New Management
    Philosophy to Government   25

CHAPTER 2: Models for Change   **27**
Understanding the Mechanisms of Transformation

Fearing Fear Itself   30
Applying the Antidote   34
Learning from Three Case Studies   37
    New Mexico Motor Vehicles   37
    Oregon Youth Authority   44
    Colorado's Lean Commitment   51

CHAPTER 3: The Complexity Challenge 59
Setting Goals and Measuring Results

Restoring Simplicity 60
Determining What We Want 65
Focusing on Results 70
Capturing Data 77
Defining Outcomes 80

CHAPTER 4: The Missing Link 89
Redesigning the Management System

Managing on the Edge of Change 92
Putting People Front and Center 101
Seeing the Organization as a Set of Processes 109

CHAPTER 5: The Fundamentals 119
Connecting the Work to the Results

Getting the Fundamentals Right: Michigan 124
Launching Results Washington 133
Adopting a Bottom-Up Strategy: Oregon 141
Creating a Fundamentals Map 145
Going Bottom-Up and Top-Down 150

CHAPTER 6: Big Breakthroughs 155
Planning and Managing the Game Changers

Achieving Breakthroughs: Colorado 158
Investing in People: Lead Tennessee 162
Setting Bold Targets: Washington's Target Zero 169
Designing Innovative Solutions:
    New Mexico Healthcare 174
Sponsoring Large-Scale Change 177

CHAPTER 7: True Accountability   **185**
Using Business Reviews to Drive Action

Structuring Stat Reviews: Lessons from Maryland   189
Doing it the Washington Way   193
Oregon's Retirement System: Thinking in
    Terms of Process   200
Best Practices for Business Reviews   204
Taking Seven Sure Steps to True Accountability   207

CHAPTER 8: Creativity on the Frontline   **211**
Engaging Employees in Removing Waste

Creating a Safe Improvement Zone   214
Ridding the System of Waste   217
Learning the Vocabulary of Waste   220
Living the Lean Life   227
Building Internal Capacity   232
Making Magic on the Frontline   237

CHAPTER 9: The Results Leader   **239**
Turning Resistance into Opportunity

Sharing the Vision   243
Describing the Gap   244
Teaching the New Thinking, Modeling
    the New Behavior   245
Removing the Resistance   248
Mastering the Five Steps of Transformation
    Leadership   251
Mastering Resilience   266

CHAPTER 10: A Results Legacy   269
Sustaining a Hard-Fought Shift

    Building a Positive Business Alliance   271
    Turning Big Data into Large Opportunities   276
    Passing Results-Driven Legislation   282
    Creating a Sustainable Management System   286
    Automating Performance Management   290
    Taking Time to Get it Right   296

CHAPTER 11: Recommendations   297
Winning The Results Revolution

    Implementing Your Own Results-Driven System   300
    Implementing Your Transformation in Phases   302
    Eight Best Practices of Results-Driven Government 304

CHAPTER 12: Conclusion   309
Joining the Voice for the Common Good

    Reclaiming Our Voice and Our Common Interest   310
    Meet Governor Rick Snyder of Michigan   312
    Meet Governor Martin O'Malley of Maryland   317
    Choosing Results Not Sides   321
    The Results Pledge   323

    Appendix A: New Mexico MVD Customer
      Bill of Rights   325

    Appendix B: Governor's Map   326

    Appendix C: LEAD Tennessee Competencies   328

*Appendix D: NOW Management System
  Leadership Requirements*   330

Appendix E: Links of Interest   332

Appendix F: Recommended Reading   333

About Results America   335

About the Author   337

References   339

Index   345

FOREWORD

We must be willing to make better choices. And we must embrace a new, more entrepreneurial, more collaborative, more performance- and results-driven style of leadership.

Things that get measured are things that get done. The ultimate test of any public policy is whether it works. Spare me your ideology. Does this work for me and my family? That's the question states seek to answer by measuring all these separate but connected inputs, outputs, indicators, and outcomes because it is impossible to steer or speed a ship without a compass or controls. Therefore, we must set public goals, measure government performance, and put our findings online for all to see. We have within our power as states, as communities, as individuals, the ability to achieve rising standards of living, better-educated children, more affordable college, a more highly skilled American workforce, safer neighborhoods, a more resilient homeland, healthier people, and a more sustainable balance with nature.

But none of this will happen on its own.

It is not a question of whether we are moving our states left or right, but whether we are moving our states forward or back. In this search for answers, John Bernard's *Government That Works: The Results Revolution in the States* offers an important path toward a better future for our states. This new Information Age has given us the ability to measure with insight and accuracy never before dreamed of. But acting upon this intelligence will require all of us to embrace a new type of leadership.

Ideological, hierarchal, bureaucratic leadership — these are the old ways of organizing human endeavor. Our times call for leadership that is entrepreneurial. Collaborative. Accountable. Performance measured. Relentlessly inter-active. Leadership which is willing to open-source information in order to unlock individual community-based solutions — on a massive scale. Leadership which understands the power of human dignity and the strength of our diversity. With greater collaboration than ever before, we can use technology to create common platforms, facilitate and coordinate and catalyze thousands of individually responsible actions. Actions that can advance the common good of progress and prosperity for all.

~ MARTIN O'MALLEY (D)
Governor
State of Maryland

FOREWORD

G overnment that works.

Now there's something you don't hear every day. And, yet, the insights and real-world examples that John Bernard so capably captures within these pages prove it's not an oxymoron.

Government *can* work. Indeed, it must work. And, in states like Michigan, it does work.

Government That Works is an excellent guide on both the why and how of results-oriented government. Government exists to provide citizens with effective and efficient services. To do that, we must move from looking at inputs, such as budget dollars, to measuring tangible results for citizens.

I won my first election in 2010. As a career businessman and the nation's only governor with a background as a Certified Public Accountant, I was struck by the lack of self-evaluation within state government. Whereas success in the business world demands long-term vision and meaningful benchmarks to guide the way, government too often operates in a polar-opposite universe.

Billions of dollars were spent each year, and state programs came and went. But little attention was paid to gauging whether any of this delivered the best value for taxpayers. Even lower on the priority list was any real effort to keep our talented state employees engaged, enthusiastic and innovative.

Michigan needed a reinvention, the heart of which had to be a culture change in which "value for money" and "real results for real people" became our yardsticks.

Job One was to tear down internal silos. We determined the

areas in which we wanted to measure our performance — such as economic growth and public safety — and organized our Cabinet into a group executive structure to enhance coordination between related program areas.

Next, I instructed Cabinet members to design scorecards that would convey their organization's mission and objectives. Accountability and transparency were not going to be mere buzzwords. They would become words to live by.

We also created a Michigan Dashboard that would show everyone how state government actually delivers on key metrics. I conveyed the idea of a dashboard to the public in my first State of the State address. The address itself put the Lansing establishment on notice: The old ways of doing business are gone. We will focus on our 10 million customers across Michigan and use facts to make decisions.

We didn't play it safe. We selected meaningful metrics so each and every taxpayer could clearly see our accomplishments or failures. In every annual State of the State address since that first one, I have shared dashboard highlights as a "report card" to the people of Michigan.

In short, we reorganized government from one based on functions to one based on results.

We then turned our attention to our internal customers — the more than 47,000 state government employees. These frontline men and women too often felt disenfranchised when it came to recommending and implementing improvements that might deliver better results.

Our "Good Government" initiative not only gave these dedicated, hardworking public servants a voice, it also empowered them to lead change. Each department appointed a "champion" who serves as the lead for driving government reinvention — or Good Government — within their respective departments.

The response has been overwhelmingly positive, not only internally, but also across the entire state of Michigan as this initiative helps shift the way the general public views state employees.

Government leaders can measure results in many different ways, and this book provides a good guide to those options. Also, as you read the following chapters, you will see the importance of culture change across government. Success comes only when you empower the capable and dedicated people working at all levels of state government. Entrepreneurship and innovation *can* happen in the public sector.

Government That Works shows how states serve as the "laboratories of democracy." As such, our states are leading the charge at bringing results-based leadership to the public sector. I greatly enjoyed reading this book because it helps define best practices that can benefit our entire country. As a governor, I am always looking at how we can make our state the best in the country. But, I am also looking for great ideas that I can borrow from other states and bring to Michigan.

Government That Works gives us a firsthand look at some of the bold, creative changes sweeping America. It's more than a good read. It's a blueprint for success at every level of government.

~ RICK SNYDER (R)
   Governor
   State of Michigan

ACKNOWLEDGMENTS

Countless people made this book possible. Some provided inspiration, others helped develop and prove ideas, and still others shared the stories of their personal journey toward government that works.

My work with state government began when two forward-looking agency leaders in Oregon, Colette S. Peters and Fariborz Pakseresht, engaged my consulting firm Mass Ingenuity to help them install our results-driven system of management. Their successes inspired many others around the country to follow suit. Thanks Colette. Thanks Fariborz.

We owe a debt of gratitude to many other Oregon state leaders as well, among them Patrick Allen, Lindsey Capps, Paul Cleary, Dr. Nancy Golden, Joni Hammond, Suzanne Hoffman, Ken Jeske, Dacia Johnson, Erinn Kelley-Siel, Mitch Morrow, Larry Niswender, Joe O'Leary, Dick Pedersen, Sarah Pope, Greg Roberts, Jack Roberts, Steve Rodeman, Clyde Saiki, Rob Saxton, Jim Scherzinger, and Jean Straight.

My heartfelt thanks also go to Michael Jordan, Sarah Miller, and Barry Pack for becoming our partners in expanding our efforts across the great state of Oregon.

Many people beyond the borders of Oregon displayed great vision and courage by joining the ranks of the results revolutionaries. These friends and colleagues include Claire Allard, Rich Baird, Jon Clontz, John Fitzpatrick, Marcie Frost, Dr. Mary Alice Heuschel, Steve Hill, Trish Holliday, Rebecca Hunter, Wendy Korthuis-Smith, Julia Lanham, Phyllis Mellon, James Ross, Lisa Spencer, and Zak Tomich.

A number of agency leaders in Washington State also joined the cause. I deeply appreciate the insights and contributions of all these dedicated public servants: Teresa Berntsen, Brian Bonlender, Pete Dawson, Mark Feldhausen, Dorothy Teeter Frost, Marcie Frost, Bill Hanson, Pat Kohler, Susan Lucas, Dan McConnon, Dan Pacholke, Jim Warick, and Bernard Warner

I must also extend my deepest appreciation to all of the state employees, managers, and leaders around the country who ardently believe in the need for government that works. They include Melissa Aerne, Cyndee Baugh, Jeannine Beatrice, Sharon Beck, Jody Becker-Green, Jean Bergen, Jennifer Black, Perrin Damon, Darrell Damron, Joe DeCamp, Bob Gebhardt, Cathy Iles, Bryan Irwin, Hollie Jensen, Michelle Johnson, Nathan Johnson, Kari Leitch, Heidi Loveall, Sue MacGlashan, Julie Martin, Sharon Pette, Rebecca Stillings, Angela Toussaint, and Janet Zars.

Russ Kuhn deserves special mention. He opened doors to many influential people in the world of state government, including Governor John Hickenlooper of Colorado, who, as Chair of the National Governors Association, invited me to serve in an advisory capacity. His *Delivering Results* initiative provides a shining example of leadership in the campaign for more effective and efficient government.

To the more than 50 people who granted interviews for this book, I can never fully express how much I benefitted from your insights.

A couple of wordsmiths helped shape this book. The leader of my editing team and my longtime writing partner, Michael Snell, added value to every page. Thanks, Michael, for helping improve the clarity and the flow of my prose. Every writer needs a stern editor like you to support the work when it goes well and snarl when it doesn't. Sincere thanks also go to Libby Koponen, who painstakingly edited the whole manuscript. She brought to the project a keen eye for detail and a knack for spotting gaps in my logic. Libby did her work in a shepherd's hut on the Isle of Coll, three hours by boat off the west coast of Scotland. Finally, I offer a hug of gratitude to my daughter Erin, an accomplished journalist, who helped edit and proofread the final manuscript.

Thank you, Bobbi Benson, for your visual creativity, marketing savvy and continuous brilliance in the creation of the book cover and interior design. Your husband, Joe Bernard, my brother, has always given me his calm and wise shoulder to lean on, helping me stay focused whenever my mind got frazzled. To my sisters Joan and Kathleen, who have always believed in me, and my other brothers, Jim and Ed, I love you and thank you for so many good memories.

I must also honor my wonderful team at Mass Ingenuity. I have never worked with a more talented group of people. Our consulting team contributed so much to this book: Ted Barber, Christine Barker, Beth Doolittle, Jim Clark, Jody Guy, Kelly Johnston, Barb Lloyd, and Tom Moore. Our support team, including Tim Dexter, Karen Grinnell, and Wally Glausi, kept us all on track. Aaron Howard and Kelly Ferguson, my business partners, played a critical role in shaping my thinking. But most importantly, I thank them for believing in me and investing a critical part of their careers in my vision for results-driven government.

Special thanks goes to supporters David Giuliani, Beverly Stein, Fred King, Scott Harra, Clif Finch, and Isaac Kastama, each of whom broadened my perspective and offered a lot of wise counsel along the way.

No single person has been more bold in his support of my efforts to help move government to a results focus than my dear friend and entrepreneur Mark Cleveland. His advocacy and the willingness to spend personal relationship capital on my behalf is second-to-none. You are an amazing man, Mark. Thank you.

Paul Aljets conducted a tremendous amount of research, transcribed hours and hours of interviews, and worked side-by-side with me on every aspect of writing, designing, and producing this book. I could not have done it without you, Paul.

Thanks to Lou Lovas, whose love and support during the trying times of life that ensued as I wrote this book, kept my head in the game. I owe her more than I can say.

When people ask how I developed my passion for improving government, I often say that I do it for the children. In my case, that's my lovely adult daughters, Ryann, Erin, and Ashley, and my two grandchildren Sawyer and Emery, and their loving father Alex. And of course I do this work for the two most recent joys of my life, my eight-year-old twins, Jacqueline and Christian. I love you all so much.

INTRODUCTION

Joining the Results Revolution

"I hold it that a little rebellion now and then is
a good thing, and as necessary in the political
world as storms in the physical."
~ THOMAS JEFFERSON

Were he alive today, Thomas Jefferson would vigorously support The Results Revolution in state government. After all, he championed the dispersal of power to the states and knew the newborn union would survive only with effective and efficient government, government that works.

Ironically, the founding father helped write the Declaration of Independence in 1776 but did not participate in drafting and ratifying the US Constitution, the document that united the states under a federal government. During that crucial point in American history he was serving his country as the US Ambassador to France, where he watched as that country entered its own revolution against a heartless, controlling monarchy.

When Jefferson returned to the United States, he joined President George Washington's cabinet as Secretary of State and almost immediately engaged in a contentious and famous argument with Treasury Secretary Alexander Hamilton over the debt the newborn United States had incurred financing the Revolutionary War. Jefferson maintained that the states must have their own, substantial power. The exercise of that power was essential to thwart establishment of a virtual monarchy by a burgeoning federal government. In the end, he and James Madison formed the anti-administration party, a move that eventually led to our contemporary two-party system.

Jefferson's actions so angered Washington that the president was rumored to be ready to fire him when he resigned from the cabinet in 1793. The two men never spoke again. Jefferson continued his pursuit of states' rights because he feared that centralized power would lead the United States down the same path that had ended in the French Revolution and the rise of Napoleon.

The debate rages to this day. Does the country need a strong federal government to take care of the nation's citizens, or should that job fall to the states? Many people are grateful for Jefferson's insight. Regardless of your personal opinion in the matter, you cannot argue against more efficient and effective state government. Jefferson wouldn't. Nor would I.

In 2008, I pitched a consulting project to Colette Peters and Fariborz Pakseresht, who had been asked by their governor to turn around Oregon Youth Authority. As I have done with leadership teams hundreds of times before, I routinely ran through all the reasons for using scorecards and engaging employees in process improvement. After all, I had sold our state-of-the-art management system hundreds of times before. Little did I know that this experience would be the spark of a new passion, propel me on a new mission in life, and change the direction of Mass Ingenuity, the consulting company I founded.

I have always thought of myself as a management junk collector, a backward way of saying that my real strength comes from being a systems thinker. I see management as a system.

The most effective leaders create and operate a system that aligns their people and resources in order to achieve their desired results. Think of the system that keeps a supersonic jet aloft. It drives toward a singular destination (results); it involves a lot of moving parts (employees, customers); it requires fuel to reach its destination (money), it has to be flown skillfully (the full engagement of the crew with the power to make decisions that keep the plane safe and on course), and it needs a good pilot (leadership). I was surprised and delighted to discover that Peters and Pakseresht were taken by the concept that management is a system. Their passion to deliver exceptional results to their customers, Oregon's troubled youth, inspired me.

That deep connection to social good started me and my team on our current path. Today we are doing all we can to help those entrusted with the welfare of our states' citizens transform their management systems in a way that fulfills their deep dedication to public service.

Many from both inside and outside government have tried to introduce business best practices to government, but most have failed, largely because they could not fully account for the enormous complexity of contemporary government. While the management system that drives a Fortune 100 firm functions like the power train in a supersonic jet focused on profits, a state government's system works more like a complex series of warp drives serving not one result but as many as 50.

When talking to people in state government I describe the structures and processes that have evolved over the decades as the equivalent of a series of violent earthquakes that have formed a city. It just happened; nobody planned it. The earthquakes are a metaphor for the fact that government's basic organizing system is events, not goals. The event may be a disaster, an act of fraud or negligence, a lawsuit, a front-page news story, a project gone bad, an emerging trend, or of course, legislation. Some force creates a reaction. Government today is the sum total of all the reactions over many, many decades. Governor Rick Snyder of Michigan calls it a "spaghetti bowl."

Most governors sense the need for a sea change in how government works. Department heads feel the endless pressure to get more and more done with what in all practical reality is less and less money. Middle managers are dealing with angry citizens every day because things take forever to get done and the left hand doesn't know the right hand even exists, let alone what it is doing. Frontline public servants work in processes that might have made sense 20 years ago, but today are senseless. There's waste everywhere, the goals are unclear, and nobody is happy about it.

But in fact across the nation an answer to the complexity and dysfunction is emerging. That's why I wrote *Government That Works: The Results Revolution in the States*. The new organizing principle is results. The idea is simple: if we have a clear set of commonly held goals, and a set of measures that show progress toward those goals, government can organize its work around these goals.

While you could dismiss my optimism and this solution as naive, I am among a growing number of people who see focusing government on results as the most viable solution for remaking our government. In this book you will meet many of them; their stories offer proof that The Results Revolution offers hope for us all.

The idea is simple, but the shift is not easy. That's why it has taken a whole book to show you how to do it. In my previous book, *Business at the Speed of Now* (published by Wiley in 2012), I documented the best management practices businesses can use to develop powerful, results-driven management systems.

In *Government That Works*, I extend those best practices to the complex world of state government, and mix in the emerging best practices being developed by results revolutionaries across the nation. In the pages ahead you will learn about these state-of-the-art practices, practices that are delivering results that matter to this nation. All of these initiatives aim at improving everything from the waiting time for a driver's license to the quality of education and child welfare.

You will also meet many dedicated, hardworking public servants who have already joined The Results Revolution by putting these and other best practices to work in Oregon, Washington, Colorado, Tennessee, Michigan, New Mexico and Maryland. I am sure there are many more results revolutionaries driving results in the other 43 states.

Soon after I began pursuing my new passion to promote The Results Revolution in state government, I met Howard Behar, who had recently retired from his job as the number two executive at Starbucks. The Results Revolution had had some early successes in Oregon, and I hoped Howard would help by opening doors to well-connected friends and colleagues in Washington state. Graciously, he spent 3½ hours listening to and challenging our vision for better government. At the end of the meeting he said something that took me by surprise: "John, I will support you in this work under one condition. You cannot stop once you get to three states; you have to keep going until you get to 15. If you do that, you will change the course of the nation."

Behar's words sent a huge warm electrical charge down my spine. I was stunned by the audacity of his vision. It took me nearly a year to fully embrace its boldness.

I don't accept that this nation's good years are behind us. That's not a legacy I want to leave my children, nor do I suspect it is one you want to leave yours. America's best years are yet to come. But that bright future is only possible with a government that works.

Revolutions are about people. People who care enough to take action to change the status quo.

We are the people. We are the change. And we have our work cut out for us.

Let's begin . . .

CHAPTER ONE

The Results Revolution

Delivering On the Promise of Social Good

"The best way to find yourself is to lose
yourself in the service of others."

~ MOHANDAS GANDHI

Heather Adams went to work for the Department of Health Services shortly after graduating from the State University. Now, several months later, she finds herself in the middle of her first training session with over 80 co-workers from her division's 38 branch offices. Discussion has turned to the issue of the highly variable workload in various offices around the state.

Heather, eager to show off her recent education, offers a creative solution to the problem: "We could create a simple checklist app that would quickly identify people whose workload has gotten out of hand. Then anyone with some time to spare could jump in and help out."

That suggestion elicits a grimace from the discussion leader and a lot of eye rolling from the more seasoned people in the room. As Heather walks down the hallway to join a small-group breakout a half-hour later, her colleague Bob Tomkins, a 22-year veteran of the agency, pulls her aside.

"Why the long face, kid?" he asks. "A little fatherly advice: you're smart and you want to do a good job. In fact, you remind me of myself at your age. But you need to take it easy, keep your head down. Once you get used to the way we do things around here, you'll see that it's better not to mess with the status quo. Look around you. Most of these people have died inside."

"I just want to see us deliver better results!"

Bob just shakes his head and mutters, "You'll grow out of it."

Heather could not believe her ears. She had taken this job because she believed this agency could make a big difference in the lives of the people it served, and she had seen almost immediately that some rather simple and inexpensive changes could go a long way toward helping her co-workers deliver services more efficiently and effectively. Basically, Bob was telling her to sit down, shut up, and shrivel up inside. That was not in Heather's nature.

However, working in government *was* in her nature. As the daughter of a single mom who had engaged in the social unrest of the late 1960s and eventually became a career social worker for a county youth corrections agency in Washington state, Heather had seen firsthand the need for services that would help create stable living conditions for troubled young girls. Her mother's passion to help others became a guiding beacon for Heather, who had worked hard to get her degree in public administration at the University.

An inspiring professor had taken her under his wing, encouraging her to master the latest technology and to develop her communication and leadership skills.

He told her, "We need more people like you in government."

She had followed his advice, and now she felt as if she had

made the biggest mistake of her life. Why hadn't she gone to work for Google?

While we have changed the names and details of this story to protect the "Dead Inside," it really happened. In state agencies throughout the country, many Bob Tomkinses, once as energetic and enthusiastic as the Heather Adamses of the world, have grown jaded as the bureaucracies that have taken over public institutions have steadily eroded their once-vibrant idealism.

Studies such as the one conducted by James L. Perry (1996) reveal that public sector workers bring high ambitions to their jobs. They really do want to serve their fellow citizens. They feel:

- An attraction to public policy-making
- A commitment to public interest
- A belief in civic duty
- A desire for social justice
- An attitude of self-sacrifice
- A sense of compassion

How can a Heather Adams fulfill these desires? How can she avoid the "death inside" that Bob Tomkins suffered from after 22 years of service? Fortunately for both Heather and Bob, a new breed of results-focused government leaders has begun to make sweeping changes in the way states serve their citizens. If their initiatives take hold around the country, we can look forward to a level of governmental reform unprecedented in modern American history.

Joining the Revolution

A growing number of those who work in state government and their advisors outside of government are taking steps to make *meaningful* and *measurable* progress toward solving our society's most critical problems. Rather than sitting down, shutting up and dying inside, they are passionately committed to installing practices that can actually improve education, create better jobs, ensure the safety of our communities, clean up and sustain our environment, update a decaying infrastructure, and make all government workers efficient and effective.

Signs of change have been springing up in almost every state, from Alaska and Oregon to Tennessee, Michigan, Maryland, Washington, Colorado and Rhode Island. This new breed of leaders has been emerging in every corner of government, from the Department of Motor Vehicles to Child Welfare Services, and their ranks include both Heathers and Bobs, both elected and appointed officials, both Republicans and Democrats, both liberals and conservatives, both political activists and conservative businesspeople, and even ordinary, everyday citizens. Going beyond the rhetoric of change, they have embraced the practical benefit of results. You can see it in such down-to-earth everyday practices as establishing clear measures and targets, creating scorecards, improving underlying processes, and posting results on government websites. It comes down to making government more accountable for results and truly respecting the people who make government work. You can't spell "accountability" without "count," and you cannot hold yourself and others accountable for results if you cannot measure those results.

Football, basketball, academic tests, weight loss, job performance, customer satisfaction, productivity, profitability, efficiency, blood pressure, you name it — success in every human endeavor requires some means of keeping score. Keeping score ensures focus on a purpose, inspires innovation, and monitors progress toward a defined goal.

State government focuses on critical goals in many areas:

education, health and public safety, the environment, and the state's economy, among others. The measures of success a state adopts both reflect and greatly influence public policy direction. As we at Mass Ingenuity, the consulting firm I founded and where I serve as chairman, conducted extensive research for this book, we compiled more than 50 measures across all 50 states (available at www.resultsamerica.org). The measures range from high school graduation rates, to murder rates, to levels of obesity and reliable access to food, to the number of people living in poverty, as well as the number of new-business startups and other measures of economic prosperity.

The successful, results-oriented efforts underway around the country inspire everyone involved in government to learn, to raise the bar for best practices, and to join the movement. The movement depends heavily on the underlying motivations, experience, innovations, and engagement of the millions of people who work in government. They know that solutions to government's problems do not come about after some Big Bang explosion of change, but through hundreds of thousands of incremental, measureable improvements and innovations by the people who do the work: people like Heather Adams and that younger version of Bob Tomkins. The Results Revolution is rooted in releasing the talent, passion and energy of the people who serve in government.

A focus on measurable outcomes organizes logical thinking, engenders innovation, and reveals what works and what doesn't work. Of course, results-driven government demands major changes in management practices to continually stimulate the vital, incremental cycles of improvements that eventually achieve The Results Revolution. Those changes in management practice begin with engaging the people who work in government and examining the processes with which government delivers results.

Fixing the Processes

As the editors of *Governing* (2013) magazine wrote recently, "Most public sector workers are amazing people who came to their careers in hopes of making a difference in the lives of the people in their counties, cities, and states."

These bright-eyed Heathers want to help the needy, protect the environment, and ensure the welfare of children. What goes wrong?

According to the editors, "Often what demotivates us are the same things that upset our customers — paperwork, red tape, long lines, endless bureaucracy."

They go on to say that improvement efforts too often focus on money, communication, and training rather than on removing the obstacles that get in the way of delivering results: "The reason so few of those efforts truly motivate our peers is because we come with our motivation built in, it's our work processes that beat it out of us, and until we remove the thorns, no amount of financial salve is going to help long term."

It's a lose-lose proposition: the broken and waste-ridden processes that rob public servants of the results they want to deliver also rob citizens of the results they need. Only a results-driven approach to government reform can create a win-win situation for both those who deliver services and those who benefit from them. That ultimately depends on process improvement — the incremental improvement of routines people follow as they work. Who can best fix those processes? The people on the frontlines who do the work day in and day out.

The reality is that public employees like Heather encounter numerous obstacles as they walk carefully through bureaucratic mazes. They need ways to move from long-standing patterns of passivity to a strong *desire* to share their expertise and drive process improvement.

Back in 1980, many dominant American manufacturers found themselves under fierce attack by Japanese competitors. Much of Japan's success had come about due to the insights and efforts of one American, Dr. W. Edwards Deming, who helped advance General Douglas MacArthur's efforts to rebuild Japan after World War II. Quality, preached Deming, would get Japan back on its feet. It did. What we've come to know is that Deming taught more than quality — he taught a new management philosophy and system.

This new approach propelled Japanese electronics and automobile makers like Sony and Toyota to global dominance. In 1980, NBC TV aired a provocative whitepaper called *If Japan Can, Why Can't We?* That challenge so impressed American business leaders that they embraced America's "Quality Revolution," a new focus that helped many American businesses such as General Electric and Ford Motor Company compete more effectively with their overseas rivals. Today, the management philosophy underlying the quality revolution has evolved into "Lean." That approach argues that success requires a sort of organizational fitness, a "leanness" in which every employee focuses relentlessly on removing all waste from all processes — that is, on anything that does not add value for customers.

The vast majority of successful companies apply these management principles not out of idealism, but out of practical competitive necessity.

Think about that. How can government do the same — deliver better results for customers/citizens? The answer seems obvious: by ridding its processes of activities that add no value. Seems easy enough, right? Well, it is, and it isn't. Doing it takes more than the do-good intentions of public servants. It takes a lot of smart, hard effort at the grassroots level of government and dedicated effort by the men and women who do the work.

Otherwise, both those who deliver services and those who receive them will remain frustrated, dissatisfied, and disengaged.

Engage the People Who Do the Work

"The biggest victims of bureaucracy are the employees themselves," is a comment often repeated by Michigan Governor Rick Snyder(R).

Working in government is enormously frustrating, and increasingly public servants are often causally ridiculed in social settings for being part of the bloated bureaucracy. It's hard for public servants to be engaged in a system with so many broken pieces and over which they have so little influence. It is a fact that businesses that suffer from the disengagement of their employees suffer severe financial consequences. Despite all of the differences between business organizations and government agencies, all organizations court the same perils when it comes to disengaged workers. In its 2013 report, the Gallup Organization's ongoing *State of the American Workplace* study found 50 percent of American employees unengaged in their work; they just show up and never take the initiative to do work above and beyond the basic tasks they were hired to do. In addition to that 50 percent, another 20 percent actively attempt to sabotage performance.

In my book *Business at the Speed of Now* (2012), I explored in detail the consequences and causes of this debilitating dimension of American work life. I concluded with the bottom-line observation that traditional management practices have failed miserably at winning the hearts and minds of employees. Yet, largely, these practices continue to dominate public sector work life.

In contrast, engaged workers love their jobs, remain loyal to the organization, make fewer mistakes, suffer fewer accidents, experience less stress and burnout, and contribute to the organization's productivity and profitability. Engaged employees are far more open to change as well because they know they will have a hand in the change.

Government employees will more likely deliver the results they and their customers expect if they are fully engaged in their work — and to be engaged, they must have a significant degree of control over their work processes. They must feel free to point out process problems and propose creative solutions, without fear of repercussions. Blaming people when a process goes south simply causes a break between managers and staff and reduces staff willingness to assume responsibility. Yet blaming people for things that go wrong is common practice in government. A focus on processes, and on collectively addressing gaps in processes when they emerge, puts the energy into improving the process. The bottom line: a focus on processes rather than on people is better for people.

When Dr. Deming tackled the economic revitalization of Japan, he cited fear as the predominant force in the vast majority of businesses. Many leaders and managers rely on fear to get and keep their people in line. Their underlying beliefs about people are both disrespectful and dehumanizing, and so is their treatment of them. These managers view their people as parts of the machinery to get work done and intentionally use fear to hold them down.

But fear blocks initiative and creates dissatisfaction, disengagement, and even rebellion. Results-driven leaders are learning to replace fear with respect, encouraging their people to fix the processes that make it hard to deliver the results both they and their customers desire. That means giving them the authority to reduce or eliminate waste.

While for a long time management experts have espoused the connection between feeling safe and innovation, there's a huge body of work that's emerging on the human brain that backs the theory with facts. Thanks to new mapping technology, scientists now have a much clearer understanding of how both thinking and emotion shape behaviors.

Traditional Management

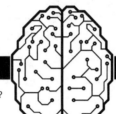

- Play by the rules
- Just do what you are told
- There's no use questioning

THINKING

- What does the customer need?
- How can we do this better?
- Facts reveal the truth

- Apathy, boredom
- Dread, disappointment
- Irritated, stupid

EMOTION

- Energized, excited
- Proud, confident
- Compassion, joy

Results-Driven Management

FIGURE 1.1: The thinking/emotional response to management systems from a neuroscience perspective helps explain the experience people in public service have when they work in two very different systems of management.

Using these ideas to make the transition from traditional public sector management practices to results-driven practices requires new thinking and will result in emotional engagement in the work environment. Engaging people in results requires moving people out of passive thinking into active thinking, which is no small shift. Teaching people to think about processes and waste, rather than simply doing as told, will engage the passion public servants have for serving the people of their state.

Go Lean or Go Home

In the late 1980s, IBM quality expert H. James Harrington published *Poor-Quality Cost* (1987), a book that popularized the idea that poor quality processes and products cost an organization a lot of time and money. Harrington described both direct costs, such as prevention, detection and rework; and indirect costs, such as business lost due to customers badmouthing the company.

For many technical reasons, especially the complex math needed to support the argument, the "Cost of Poor Quality" movement never gained much traction, but its basic premise did. It may remain difficult to quantify the true costs, but on average, waste costs:

- 20-25 percent of revenue in manufacturing organizations
- 30-40 percent of revenue in service organizations
- 40-50 percent of budget in government organizations

This does *not* mean people who work in these organizations are wasteful morons; it does mean every organization can find and remove waste from its processes.

Some common wasteful activities — so common that they are called "the seven deadly sins" — are:

Seven Deadly Sins of Waste

1. **Waiting** – time lost re-handling and re-starting work as you wait for things needed to complete it

2. **Inspecting** – checking work to try and catch errors

3. **Re-entering** – putting information in one place that already exists in another

4. **Searching** – trying to find data, materials, reports or whatever else is missing

5. **Moving** – routing things or moving people from one place to another, staging work, etc.

6. **Reworking** – doing work over again because it was incomplete or incorrect

7. **Over-processing** – doing work that serves no identifiable customer or purpose

FIGURE 1.2: The seven deadly sins of waste create a vocabulary for understanding the opportunities for improvement that exist within work processes.

Now, the opportunity to improve results becomes clear: (1) Government officials and workers can find a lot of waste to reduce or eliminate; and (2) The people who can do it best are those who work the waste-filled processes day in and day out. That's easy to say, but harder to do.

Sometimes, leveraging the connection between the opportunity and the people who can best act on it takes more blood, sweat, and tears than moving a mountain. That's because the public sector still relies predominately on management methods developed and perfected during the Industrial Revolution. The old era of mass production depended upon the frontline worker repeating the same process over and over again, putting Hexnut A on Brass Bolt B. Management viewed those workers as "hands" or "wrenches" — mere machines designed to perform one task over and over and over again until the factory whistle blew. Management did the thinking, engineering did the designing, and accounting did the number crunching. Whatever your job, you worked in a silo, isolated from all the other silos.

These mass production management techniques created the great American middle class and amassed more wealth for more people than any management approach in the history of the human race. They worked. Their logic eventually permeated how we managed everything. For over a century, they got results for every sort of organization, from a mom-and-pop corner grocery store to the State Department of Education.

However, we have moved beyond the age of mass production into the age of mass customization, in which the old management approach no longer works. Mass customization means delivering goods and services tailored to the needs of each unique customer. For government the net impact is that customer service expectations have gone through the ceiling and citizens compare their service experience with government to their service experience at the Apple store.

Service has begun to replace manufacturing in the US economy. As a result, manufacturing as a percent of US employment has declined steadily from 26 percent in 1953 to 8 percent in 2013. Service jobs have grown exponentially, and service jobs, whether in corporations or government, must address a new breed of customers who demand, *"I want it the way I want it, and I want it now."* Customers and citizens increasingly expect more from the organizations that serve them.

Only more agile, efficient, effective, and customer/citizen-focused organizations can meet those expectations. Such organizations require new management approaches that treat workers as much more than replaceable cogs in great big machines. Lean management offers the best path to that goal because it respects the desire and unleashes the ability of people to do their very best work.

Slice Through Complexity

This brings us back to processes. Basically, government processes provide the means whereby a government agency or department translates the laws passed by elected officials into the rules and regulations and procedures that deliver desired results. These rules, and in turn, the processes designed to implement them, tend over time to multiply to the point that they gum up the machinery of government. Rules pile on top of rules, and processes grow sluggish and unwieldy, until everyone inside and outside the walls of bureaucracy suffers. Workers die inside and citizens despair over a government that has turned into a tangled, convoluted, and often common-sense-defying mess. Simplicity has never been a goal of government, but it is a worthy one.

If you look closely at most government processes, you will quickly see the problem: a system bogged down with miscues, non-value-added steps, unnecessary handoffs, and double- and triple- and quadruple-signoffs. For example, one state agency received new phones that came without an essential accessory, a stylus. To obtain the 30-cent stylus a manager had to call the assistant to the agency director, obtain an account number, and then send the director an email asking for permission to receive the stylus. Once approved, the email request went to the information technology help desk, where someone finally issued the stylus. The cost of that simple transaction? Fifty dollars' worth of time for each person who needed a stylus, all but wasted by the well-intentioned but ultimately misguided effort *not* to waste taxpayers' dollars. It would have been far cheaper to have simply given every employee a stylus.

Another classic disconnect is contracts requiring more than a dozen signatures. In the end there is no real accountability because everyone sees that everyone else has reviewed the contract, so they sign it without reading it. The lesson is that excessive signoff steps actually reduce accountability.

Popular in government is the belief "that's not possible under statute." This is more often than not simply untrue. But to get past that belief requires both different thinking and a different emotional response to the challenge.

The design of many government processes looks a lot like the Rube Goldberg device that used an intercontinental ballistic missile to pull the cotton out of an aspirin bottle. They didn't start out that way; they just grew ever more complex as conscientious officials corrected mistakes, patched holes, and designed approval protocols to "cover their tails" if anything went wrong.

The state of most processes in government today could best be described as an accident. It would be akin to multiple people designing and building the parts of an automobile without ever sitting down in the same room together to talk about how the pieces fit together. In a government process, a one-time error that occurred 12 years ago might have caused multiple steps to be added, and no one doing the work today has any idea why they take those steps. You don't have to travel far to find a department where a form is automatically printed in duplicate while the standard operating procedure is to throw away the duplicate pages.

The only people who can simplify these processes in ways that will make them more efficient at delivering results are the very people who currently waste so much of their precious time dealing with them. They are in the best position to ask, "Why do we do this?" for every step in the process.

But one thing that is very different about the switch to Lean from most other changes in management, in particular for government leaders, is the need for leaders to both be trained and to personally engage in improvement activities. The reason is simple. Lean requires a new type of thinking and operates from a different emotional base. Until leaders have actually done this, they simply cannot understand the new results world.

Only these trained, engaged leaders can improve societal outcomes and fulfill the passion that attracted them to government work in the first place.

Improving Societal Outcomes

Those who join The Results Revolution do so because they want to improve societal outcomes. But what if working toward that goal means admitting that current practices fall far short of the mark?

Oregon's Chief Operating Officer, Michael Jordan, insists that you cannot solve a problem without making it public. He says: "Even if the results are poor, sharing the unvarnished truth builds credibility. No one wants to show his or her dirty laundry, but failure is not a sin. Not asking *why* is the sin. People respect that you are willing to look at the problem."

Jordan brought to public service a passion for turning policy into measurable results. You must, he believes, make the measurements transparent to all concerned. When you do that, you stand a much better chance of aligning the interests of all stakeholders, discovering creative solutions, and fixing what's broken. When you place measurements at the heart of the agenda, stakeholders can communicate and work together much more effectively.

In Chapter Two, we will look at how Mark Williams, director of the New Mexico Motor Vehicles Division, brought people together in the way Jordan recommends. Williams has found that in dealing with the press he gets much more favorable coverage when he acknowledges fault. "When government makes excuses it is like a red flag to a bull," he says.

"It's a dance," Jordan says about the relationship between politicians who set policies and the workers who must implement them. "When both partners are listening to the same music, it is a beautiful thing to watch, and when they are not, everybody's feet hurt."

Jordan's career began in the private sector, where he worked for a power company. However, at age 28, a longing for a greater challenge pulled him into public service at the "entry level" as a city councilman in his rural hometown of Canby, Oregon. From day one, he relished the complexity of public service and the opportunity to figure out ways to make government more efficient and effective. Four years later, he was contemplating a run for mayor when the city manager's position opened up. Driven by his interest in getting results, Jordan crossed over from volunteer politician to full-time city manager. It took guts for someone with so little experience in public administration to make such a huge leap, but it led to 10 fruitful years managing a city of 9,000 souls.

Looking back, he's glad he seized the opportunity to extend his service to his community: "I love to build things, and it is enormously gratifying to look back and see the many good things that have manifested themselves from those years," he says. Even today, from his much higher perch as Oregon's Chief Operating Officer, he still sees making a long-term difference in one small town — keeping businesses operating and providing good jobs in Canby's industrial park — as a highlight of his career.

Eventually, he left Canby to accept the job of first appointed Chief Operating Officer of Metro, the regional government for the Portland, Oregon, metropolitan area that is responsible for "creating a vibrant and sustainable region." Jordan served in that role from 2003 to 2011 before accepting Oregon Governor John Kitzhaber's invitation to become the State's first-ever Chief Operating Officer. As COO, he oversees the day-to-day operations of Oregon's executive branch.

Reflecting on the trajectory of his career from power company worker to top public administrator, Jordan says he's glad he moved from the private to the public sector: "In the private sector, the hardest thing we had to solve in a year was simple compared to the things we face every week in government. In government, we have to deal with the hopes, fears, and childhood baggage of everyone involved because as Americans we all believe we each know what is best."

As in any organization, be it a lone-wolf start-up, a multinational conglomerate, a small-town city council, or the United States Senate, the biggest challenges come not from the day-to-day work but from all the sticky, gooey, messy, and sometimes crazy "people stuff."

"As a nation, we are a collection of individuals — it's in the Constitution," Jordan observes. "And as a result, we are incredibly resistant to collective action. Yet, government *is* collective action."

To resolve that paradox, public servants must believe in their hearts that the path to the best solutions runs right through the combined wisdom and experience of the full collection of stakeholders. That's a lot of people. That's a lot of "people stuff." But Jordan attests that without involving them all, you can never slice through the complexity of the work and come up with creative solutions that have the support of those who must live with them.

Jordan makes the mandate clear: "In government we do have the power to **convene,** but that's only the beginning of bringing policy and implementation into alignment for the collective good."

A convention of stakeholders does not make anything happen unless you **engage** them all in hammering out a common problem statement, and then aligning everyone around a desired, measurable result.

"If you have effectively built consensus on the problem statement, solutions sets and the desired result, then the community will return the authority power to you to **implement,**" he adds. "You become a tool of the collective."

Great collective results are more than the sum of great individual results. Measures create a line of sight between strategic goals and everyone's daily work; employees can see how the work they are doing aligns with and supports the goals of the organization. Measures, as you will see in Part Two of this book, hold great sway in eliminating silos, driving communication, integrating processes and causing collaboration. Measures with improvement targets provide the impetus to collaborate.

Too frequently in government circles in our work we hear the story of a cabinet meeting with a governor where the standard report from agency leaders is, "We're doing the best we can with all the limits we're facing. Funding from the last cycle was insufficient. We have a study in place that will ensure that as we move forward we'll achieve X. But this study will achieve such and such great things, etc." And in one incident a governor, showing enormous frustration said, "The next person who talks about what they're doing with a blue ribbon study I'm going to fire. You're not here to spend all of your time doing studies that never seem to result in later results. You're here to get those results NOW. If any of you aren't up to that, I'll replace you."

The Results Cycle

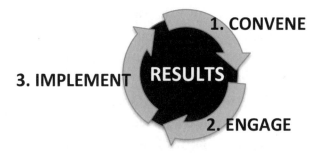

Convene: Bringing together the people who do and/or benefit from the work

Engage: Agreeing on the problem/opportunity, solutions sets and the desired measurable result

Implement: Delivering the solution set, monitoring the results (scorecards), and then reconvening the stakeholders to examine what has and has not worked

FIGURE 1.3: The results cycle demonstrates the cycle of improvement involving stakeholders in order to build a trusting relationship.

One clear and urgent goal sits at the center of the opportunity to make government work: RESULTS. Results for the politicians who set policies, results for the workers who must implement those policies, and results for the citizens who receive the fruits of the implementation of those policies.

In Jordan's view, "This only works if implementation credibility is built, and objective measures are the key to building credibility. Reviewing the progress with measures engages the community in asking, 'Why is it working? Why isn't it working?'"

Note the emphasis on engagement: shared responsibility and accountability for every stage of the cycle. If all stakeholders participate in defining the problem, developing the solutions *and* measuring successes and failures, they feel less tempted to play the blame game when results fall short of the mark. All too often, government workers accuse the politicians of creating bad policy, and policymakers bemoan the incompetence of the government workers who implemented it, not to mention the citizens, who think the whole bunch are complete idiots. Engagement creates a different cycle.

"The more power you give, the more power you have," says Jordan, and that principle holds true for all three constituencies. Government has a strong tendency to concentrate too much decision-making authority at the top. There is no way to run large organizations effectively without having a means to assess accountability and to empower staff with sufficient and level-appropriate authority. Measures create the performance framework necessary to appropriately frame delegation. Like in basketball, the scoreboard defines success.

It's easy to fall prey to victim thinking, warns Tennessee State Senator and emergency room physician Mark Green (R). Green authored the book, *A Night With Saddam, A Special Ops Flight Surgeon's Interview with Saddam Hussein on the Night of His*

Capture and The Missions which Led To Their Meeting. As the physician on the scene during Hussein's capture, Green administered the former Iraqi leader's post-capture physical exam.

"In medicine, we measure everything," he explains. "Doing so focuses the team on the patient and not on the healthcare worker. The lack of measures in government allows political leaders to play a blame game with no way to verify whose rhetoric is accurate. With a government scorecard, politician's incentives are aligned with the goals of 'the people,' and cooperation becomes essential to their survival."

Senator Green has gained national attention in his party partly because, like Oregon Chief Operating Officer Michael Jordan, he believes wholeheartedly in focusing on results.

Learning a Lesson from New York City

A December 30, 1990, *New York Times* editorial described the crisis playing out in one of the world's greatest cities:

> New York City is staggering. The streets resemble Calcutta, bristling with beggars and sad schizophrenics tuned in to inner voices. Crime, the fear of it as much as the fact, adds overtones of a New Beirut. Many New Yorkers now think twice about where they can safely walk; in a civilized place, that should be as automatic as breathing. And now the tide of wealth and taxes that helped the city make the streets bearable has ebbed . . . Safe streets are fundamental; going out on them is the simplest expression of the social contract; a city that cannot maintain its side of that contract will choke.

These deplorable conditions contributed to the 1993 election of tough-on-crime Rudy Giuliani to Mayor of New York. Almost at once, Giuliani took aim at street crime in his beloved city with a refreshing, results-oriented solution. He based his program on facts, accountability, transparency, and the engagement of the city's employees and the citizens. It worked.

Between 1990 and 2012, New York City saw across-the-board crime reduction never before seen in the United States:

- Murder down by 81.5 percent
- Rape down by 53.8 percent
- Robbery down by 79.9 percent
- Felony assault down by 56.1 percent
- Burglary down by 84.3 percent
- Grand larceny down by 60.8 percent
- Grand larceny auto down by 94.5 percent

The following two charts demonstrate the steep decline in crime that New York City has enjoyed. Because the scales are dramatically different, we separated out rape and murder to help better visualize the reductions in those two types of violent crime.

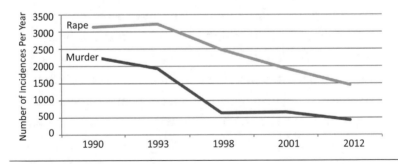

New York City CompStat Crime Statistics

FIGURE 1.4: New York City's most violent of crimes, rape and murder, have continued to decline in no small part demonstrating CompStat's effectiveness.
Source: New York City Police Department

The results-driven approach in New York began when Mayor Giuliani and NYPD Commissioner Bill Bratton discarded rhetoric in favor of reality. The roots of that approach sprang from the subway system. Transit police officer Jack Maple had developed the habit of sticking pins on a map to show where crimes had been committed. He then used these facts to predict where future crimes would most likely occur. Officer Maple set in motion what turned out to be one of the best examples in modern government of effective process management.

"I called them the Charts of the Future," explained Maple. "On 55 feet of wall space, I mapped every train station in New York City and every train. Then I used crayons to mark every violent crime, robbery and grand larceny that occurred. I mapped the solved vs. the unsolved."

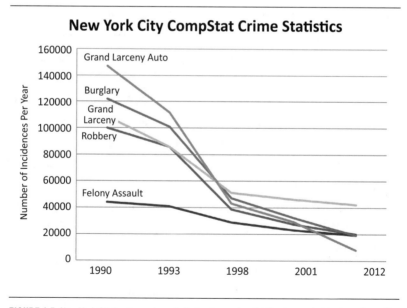

New York City CompStat Crime Statistics

FIGURE 1.5: New York City's other crime statistics have also declined remarkably since CompStat was instituted.
Source: New York City Police Department

The transit police recruited Bratton to cut crime in the "caves" (New York City subways). After Maple showed Bratton his charts, the department used that data and Maple's analysis to cut felonies in the caves by 27 percent and robberies by 33 percent between 1990 and 1992. In 1994, Mayor Giuliani appointed Bratton to head NYPD, with Maple his second-in-command.

Today, the system relies on detailed crime statistics to predict when and where crimes might occur so authorities can take action to prevent them. Those stats include weekly crime complaints, arrests, summons activity, written reports about major cases, crime patterns, and police activities, all recorded on a map of the city.

They came to be called the CompStat (computerized statistics) system and were developed into a statistical software package. But CompStat is much more than that. It reflects an underlying management philosophy not unlike the one embodied by Lean. In the pages ahead, we will apply a similar comprehensive, results-driven system of management to government. It includes all of the organizational and behavior elements that affect results.

As Heather MacDonald, a John M. Olin Fellow at the Manhattan Institute reported in a 2010 article, "The crime analysis and accountability system known as CompStat, developed by the New York Police Department in 1994, is the most revolutionary public-sector achievement of the last quarter-century" (MacDonald, 2010).

She goes on to note that CompStat had driven down crime in New York by an astounding 77 percent. Police officers who participated in the program went on to run police departments in other parts of the United States, and they used the same approach to get similar results. Even other government agencies around the country have adopted the CompStat model to analyze hard data and to hold managers accountable for results in everything from enhanced public health to decreased reliance on government handouts and road repairs.

Applying the New Management Philosophy to Government

Washington Governor Jay Inslee (D-WA) adds his voice to the chorus for change: "Holding ourselves accountable for results to the citizens of Washington isn't politically expedient," he says. "But it clearly is the right thing to do."

Governor Inslee offered this view to the state's agency heads in the fall of 2013 as he began rolling out one of the most comprehensive sets of results-oriented measures in the nation, less than a year into his first term.

Other state governors have also heeded the call to action, among them: John Kitzhaber (D) of Oregon, Martin O'Malley (D) of Maryland, Peter Shumlin (D) of Vermont, Lincoln Chafee (D) of Rhode Island, Mary Fallin (R) of Oklahoma, Sean Parnell (R) of Alaska, Susana Martinez (R) of New Mexico, Nathan Deal (R) of Georgia, Gary Herbert (R) of Utah, Mike Pence (R) of Indiana, Bill Haslam (R), of Tennessee, and Rick Snyder (R) of Michigan. Enthusiasm for results does not follow party lines; it follows the line of common sense. It follows a straight line from the governor's office through each and every state agency to the citizens who have voted the governor into office.

In the quest to select measures for results, these and other governors have set their sights on serving their state's citizens more effectively and more efficiently. If every state joins the cause, and if the cause finds its way into the federal government, the United States may finally deliver on the promise of a government capable of meeting modern society's needs.

While business measures results in terms of productivity and profitability, governments at all levels must measure hard-to-quantify variables, such as the quality of life, liberty, and the ability to pursue happiness. Compared to the complexity of government, business looks quite simple. But those immersed in complexity can often learn from simpler models. Wise governors know they can't let complexity excuse underperformance, and that to ensure high performance, they must find practical, sometimes simple, ways to quantify the degree to which state workers deliver services to the people.

The results revolutionaries understand that without measuring effectiveness, you're just wandering in the wilderness, hoping you will reach the right destination.

A close look at the states that have joined the results movement reveals that all of them are essentially pursuing **The Seven Goals of Good Government:**

- GOAL ONE: The best-educated people
- GOAL TWO: The most innovative and prosperous economy
- GOAL THREE: The safest place to live, work, and raise a family
- GOAL FOUR: The most responsible sustainability practices
- GOAL FIVE: The healthiest and fittest people
- GOAL SIX: A second-to-none infrastructure
- GOAL SEVEN: A government respected for its efficiency and effectiveness

In the chapters ahead, we will examine the ways in which a new, results-oriented philosophy and management system can help state governments — indeed, governments at all levels — to deliver on these vital goals.

CHAPTER TWO

Models for Change

Understanding the Mechanisms of Transformation

"A government ill-executed, whatever may be
the theory, in practice is poor government."

~ ALEXANDER HAMILTON

The staff at the Carlsbad branch of New Mexico's Motor Vehicle Division (MVD) decided to lock the front door of the office shortly after 3:00 p.m.

With a long line of customers waiting outside for service, the staff knew they couldn't possibly serve all of them before the 5:00 p.m. closing time. When a staff member tried to close the door, one customer refused to budge, saying, "No, we're not going to leave." Others joined the protest and started a minor scuffle, which ended when the police arrived.

Mark Williams, a former business executive turned public servant and Director of the state's MVD, learned of the incident from a couple of not-so-happy legislators.

Williams, who brought a no-nonsense business background and an MBA in finance from Cornell University to his job, immediately scheduled a Friday night town hall meeting with a number of legislators and concerned citizens.

More than one hundred people came to air their gripes. Williams listened carefully to the complaints: "That many people showing up to the MVD on a Friday night says just how frustrated the Carlsbad community was with the MVD. They all said how terrible our service was. One Carlsbad resident told us that this office had been a disaster since 1969—for more than forty years. We agreed to fix it."

He says: "The next morning MVD management went down to the Carlsbad MVD and there were people in lawn chairs lined up outside the office at 7:00 in the morning so they could get in when the office opened up at 8:00. And that suggested an obvious point: why don't we open earlier?"

It did not take an MBA to see the problem. Every stakeholder expressed anger and frustration: customers, legislators, and, of course, the MVD staff itself. Unfilled staff vacancies and poor management contributed to the problem. No matter how hard the overworked and stressed-out staff tried, they could not shorten the lines of dissatisfied customers, who waited an average of 96 minutes for service.

Williams, a certified Lean/Six Sigma black belt (professional certification in specific process improvement methods) and Rebecca Joe, MVD's bureau chief who oversees the Carlsbad MVD, took four sure steps toward a solution by:

1. *Listening* closely to customers in order to understand their needs
2. *Engaging* employees in the mission to satisfy their customers

3. *Showing* employees how to improve the processes they used to deliver services

4. *Teaching* employees how to use scorecards to track progress

Today, the Carlsbad MVD office opens at 7:00 a.m. It has solved its staffing problem. And, a friendly "MVD Ambassador" greets arriving customers, makes sure that everyone has the right documents, and then directs people to the correct counter. Customers wait a scant 3 minutes for service. Before they leave the facility, they complete an automated survey that immediately delivers any concerns or complaints to a manager. Before an unhappy customer can walk out the door, a manager steps in and has been empowered to resolve issues that previously required escalation to the MVD Director's Office. *See the MVD Customer Bill of Rights in Appendix A.*

Williams takes great pride in his staff's accomplishments. "The people who work in that office have been given the tools they need to deliver great service and are now totally motivated after years of not being motivated at all. When I got here, the biggest thing was that *no one* believed MVD could be any better than it was."

On Saturday, May 4, 2013, the Carlsbad MVD held a Community Appreciation Day to celebrate the end of a long history of all-around frustration and the start of a whole new era of *government that works*. Williams, his boss Taxation and Revenue Secretary Demesia Padilla, and Governor Susana Martinez joined the festivities. The community loved it. The press covered the event on the front page. Everyone who worked at the MVD shared William's pride in accomplishing their mission to provide superior service to their community.

"Once our Carlsbad staff was given what they needed to dramatically improve customer outcomes, our senior management had very little need to oversee their work," said Williams. "They vastly preferred being complimented and thanked rather than criticized by their customers and were willing to do what it took to maintain their exceptional level of performance. The more things improved, the more customers credited the staff, which provided additional motivation that kept the staff working to improve."

Almost everywhere in the US you hear complaints about the agency that implements the policies and laws concerning motor vehicle operation. Not in New Mexico, where the state has replicated the Carlsbad approach in office after office. No longer does the MVD serve as the poster child for inefficient government operated by disengaged bureaucrats.

This success came about because Williams and his people focused their attention on *results*, the *processes* needed to get results, and ways to *measure* progress toward results. They became soldiers in The Results Revolution.

Fearing Fear Itself

While many of the good people who work in government may have come to believe they that they can exercise little, if any, control over their work, those who have joined The Results Revolution know otherwise.

Before we look at how a government agency like New Mexico's MVD can make the shift to results-driven government, we need to back up a step and examine how government actually works. In the most simple terms:

1. The Legislative Branch passes a bill; the Governor signs it into law and passes it along to the Executive Branch for implementation.

2. The Executive Branch formulates regulations and rules

that will guide the interpretation, implementation, and enforcement of the law.

3. Agencies and Departments of the Executive Branch develop the procedures (what we will call "processes" throughout this book) that employees will use to implement the rules and regulations.

Over time, as people work with those processes, they learn a lot about what works and doesn't work. Of course, people pay less attention to a smoothly operating process than they do to one that runs off the rails like the Carlsbad MVD office did. You don't need to fix it if it ain't broken, but if it *is* broken, it can bring grief to anyone who comes near it.

Take, for example, reimbursing state employees for travel expenses. Suppose an audit discovers that the mileage traveled between Podunk and Timbuktu varies wildly on expense reports from various state employees. That's a problem. Let's make a rule that says all employees must always list 113 miles on their expense reports. That's the distance you get if you look it up on Google Maps. But what happens when Denise drives from the far side of Podunk to the far side of Timbuktu, while Jose travels from the near side of Timbuktu to the near side of the Podunk? Denise has driven 139 miles, while Jose has only driven 109 miles. Since both must report 113 miles, Denise gets shortchanged (and upset), while Jose chuckles over the extra pennies in his pocket. To solve that problem, the state adds the rule that to report a distance that differs from the Google Maps distance, the employee must fill out a form and get it signed by a supervisor. Pretty soon, people are spending hours on paperwork — time that could have been spent providing services to increasingly dissatisfied citizens. This piling rule on top of rule happens all the time in government.

One four-letter word drives this tendency to multiple rules: fear. Fear that someone will unfairly exploit the system. Fear that a reporter will air the dirty secret in public. Fear that someone up the ladder will punish the perpetrator. As we said in Chapter One: fear, more than anything else, sabotages higher quality, greater efficiency, and better results.

Government officials make thousands of big and little tweaks and changes to processes every year in every state in America as they try to fix and patch and mend the way they do business, mostly to keep themselves and government workers out of trouble. But what starts out as a sensible little mouse of a law born from perfectly good intentions can, over time, evolve into a long-necked brontosaurus with its head in the trees. A decade later, the processes used to implement the original law no longer get the results customers expect.

Inefficient processes breed employee turnover, which can further sabotage the system. As employees rotate in and out of jobs, experienced people pass the processes for getting work done to neophytes. It's like the children's game, "I've Got a Secret." Ten kids sit in a circle. Tom whispers a sentence to Sally: "The big, brown dog ate my algebra homework."

She whispers it to the next kid, and so forth, until it reaches the tenth kid, who says, "The pig in town came home late."

The message has become hopelessly distorted. In an organization, it takes only two or three hand-offs for those who work the process to lose sight of its reason for existence. Twenty years and a dozen secret-sharings later, no one remembers exactly *why we do what we do here.*

Employees who receive handed-down processes fear questioning or altering them, even if the processes seem unwieldy or poorly designed or even nonsensical. Rather than asking *why* they do what they do, they just follow orders: keep your head down, don't ask embarrassing questions, just fill out Form 501, get the necessary three signatures on it, and pass it along to another department with Form 501B attached. Don't buck the system in any way that would jeopardize your job. No wonder so many government workers seem so disengaged. Rather than engaging with their work and their customers and taking creative steps to solve a problem, they place all of their trust in a four-inch-thick book of policies and procedures.

Jackie Barretta, author of the book *Primal Teams: Harnessing the Power of Emotions to Fuel Extraordinary Performance* (2014), describes how the management philosophy behind this approach to work can damage an organization. Basically, management says to workers, "Since we don't trust you to do the right thing, we've put together this manual that tells everybody what to do, all the time, in every conceivable situation."

Add to that fact the reality that in government, some people have the job of enforcing rules; others enforce them by choice. They pride themselves on knowing the manual better than anyone else, lording it over their colleagues and using rules to embarrass or punish them.

If a problem pops up, consult the manual. As Barretta points out, "That message will make everyone feel distrusted, disrespected, resentful, and indignant. It motivates people to stop thinking creatively, to cover their tails, to avoid admitting mistakes, and, in the long run, to settle for lackluster results."

Today, most state government agencies operate in the culture of fear created by this approach. When management believes people can only do great work when they follow painfully detailed step-by-step how-to instructions, people grow fearful of asking the basic question, *"Why do we do this work in the first place?"*

It's dangerous to soar above all the complexities of the day-to-day job and see the larger picture. It's much safer to stay on the ground and wander through the thicket. Forget about sorting the crucial work from the trivial tasks. In the end, workers *major in minors*, fussing over teeny-tiny details rather than tackling the bigger issues.

People who work in a culture of fear dread that they will get in trouble if they do not:

1. Follow every policy and procedure to the letter of the law
2. Submit painstakingly complete and correct paperwork
3. Dot every "i" and cross every "t"
4. Suspend their personal judgment about the right thing to do
5. Check their brains at the door when they enter the office

"Oh my God, what if I screw up, and a reporter from *60 Minutes* ambushes me?" While an innocent mistake can lead to big trouble, just following orders and doing everything by the book can get people in even more trouble. Creativity takes a vacation, paperwork expands exponentially, problems go unsolved, customers get upset, the media investigates, and all hell breaks loose. Either way, after working at the MVD for a few months, you wish you could enter a witness protection program, change your name, and move to a small town where no one will ever find you. Fortunately, there's a surefire cure for that toxic feeling.

Applying the Antidote

A results-based management system provides the best antidote for fear, because it makes the *outcome*, not the process, the top priority. Shifting attention from how we do what we do to the results we deliver completely changes the game. However, few real game-changers come easily or without a certain amount of pain. That's the bad news. The good news: people who come to government work really do want to deliver results to their customers and clients. Given a choice, they would much rather solve problems with grit and imagination than keep their noses buried in those four-inch-thick manuals.

The hard work of shifting to a results focus involves four fundamental elements that have guided the successful change efforts at New Mexico's MVD and other state agencies across the nation:

- *Listening to Customers* – You must develop a deep understanding of customer expectations before you can design processes that will effectively and efficiently fulfill those expectations
- *Engaging Employees* – You must tap into the experience, knowledge, and passion of the people who know the work best: those who do it
- *Improving Processes* – You must learn exactly how existing processes work and then make use of a range of validated best practices to optimize them
- *Using Scorecards* – You must drive transparency, accountability, and improvement by measuring result

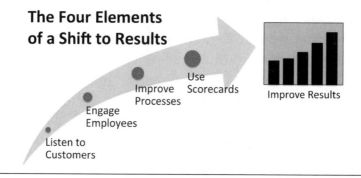

FIGURE 2.1: The four elements of the shift to results-driven government drive a focus on measurable improvement.

Listening to customers should always initiate the change effort because customers know best what they really want from government. Too often, government officials *assume* they know what's best for customers, but that attitude usually makes customers feel patronized, like unruly children who need a wise parent to tell them, "This gooey glob of spinach is good for you."

Whatever you learn from your customers, you can count on one thing: they never value waste. And what customers want and what is truly in the public interest often contradict each other.

Engaging employees ties those who do the work to customer needs and expectations. Employees engage by improving the way in which their work gets done. Since they will operate the processes that deliver services, they need to do it with commitment and enthusiasm. Fully engaged employees will keep the first fundamental element — listening to customers — in mind, constantly paying attention to customer feedback about what works and doesn't work. Without fully engaged employees on board, you cannot possibly move to the third fundamental.

Improving processes involves the use of proven, practical tools that can systematically eliminate waste from processes. We will look at many of these tools, such as basic problem solving, Lean techniques, and practical scorecards, in the pages ahead.

Scorecards provide the ruler with which you can precisely measure progress toward desired results. The best scorecards, like the one below, are clear and concise enough for anyone to use without getting bogged down in the onerous paperwork that, as we have seen, tends to flourish in government.

Each of these tools can drive real changes; in combination they transform agencies. Scorecards, using red, yellow and green, instantly communicate what performance is acceptable and what performance is problematic. Target lines show desired levels and timing of improvements.

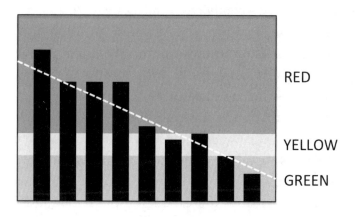

FIGURE 2.2: The use of red, yellow, and green backgrounds helps communicate whether or not the current level of performance needs to be improved.

Those four fundamentals, listening to customers, engaging employees, improving processes and using scorecards, sum up the results philosophy. How do they play out in real life?

Learning from Three Case Studies

To move from abstract principles to concrete applications, let's look at how two different government agencies and one state used the four fundamentals to transform themselves.

Case #1: Go for Quality

New Mexico MVD Director Mark Williams relishes the challenges he encounters in government, much as he did while working on Wall Street, and starting, running, and turning around companies in the world of entertainment and software. During his life as a business leader, he worked with such well-known organizations as *Playboy Magazine*, British Broadcasting Corporation, and American Express.

Why would a hard-charging, get-it-done corporate executive fall in love with the complicated and messy world of government work? He cites two reasons: a passion for effecting customer-centric, cost-effective better government, and an awareness that professional management, including the use of best practices in process management, is the missing link to government that meets public expectations. He drew inspiration to make the move from the words of Walter Annenberg, the founder of *TV Guide*: "He said something that resonated with me: that in your career you should make money, have fun, and accomplish some greater good. If you care about more than just making money, then the public sector is a good place to be."

It did not take him long to see the opportunity to apply his passion to government organizations, which had remained almost completely immune from the quality movement of the 1980s.

In his earlier incarnation as a business leader, Williams had served on the Board of Examiners for the Malcolm Baldrige National Quality Award, the prestigious prize for quality modeled after Japan's Deming Prize and given to the number one American company every year (National Institute of Standards and Technology, 2014).

Signed into law by President Ronald Reagan in 1987, the Baldrige Award challenged American businesses to respond to the quality threat from Japan. Today, the award includes not only businesses, but also governmental entities, including schools. Winners range from well-known businesses such as Lockheed Martin Missiles and Fire Control (2012), Nestle Purina Pet Care Co. (2010), and Honeywell Federal Manufacturing & Technologies (2009) to healthcare organizations such as Sutter Davis Hospital (2013), Henry Ford Health Center (2011), and AtlantiCare (2009). Governmental organizations that have recently won the prize include Pewaukee School District (2013), City of Irving, Texas (2012), and the US Army Armament Research, Development and Engineering Center (2007).

Many companies and agencies apply the Baldrige Award criteria to their organizations even if they do not intend to compete for it because the criteria provide an exhaustive method for judging performance. They have also helped state agencies in 34 states including Alabama, Colorado, Florida, Georgia, Iowa, Tennessee, New Mexico, and Washington win their own special awards for quality (Florida Advanced Technological Education Center, 2014).

Williams loves this trend: "In the past, process management hadn't made it into government's DNA, but that is now changing rapidly. Senior leaders in the public sector used to delegate operations management to mid management. The most effective public sector executives are now personally engaged in Lean, Six Sigma and related tools because we all know that it's the best way to improve operating performance without increasing resources or budgets. Lean initiatives are breaking out in state government all across the country," he observed as governments were coming under increasing pressure to drive down cost while simultaneously improving services.

When Williams took over New Mexico's MVD, he became the 11th director in 12 years. That series of handoffs deserves a spot in *The Guinness Book of Records*. As Williams explained, "MVD was widely regarded as a death march or a suicide mission, and the state had attempted to hire a bunch of people — all of whom turned them down. They offered it to me, and I thought, 'This is not unfixable.'"

Williams set to work applying Lean techniques to improve the quality of the services provided by the MVD. Within a year, the agency displayed such measurable improvement that it became a role model for other state agencies around the country.

Williams began the effort on the frontlines: "I started by acknowledging people. I thanked them."

"Some staff told me that in their long careers at MVD, they had never been thanked for their work," Williams said. "So the benefit in simply acknowledging their commitment and their service was probably greater than it would have been in an organization that had already learned the value in providing positive reinforcement."

This marked the dawn of a new era of engagement. Williams and his team surveyed employees, and they said that management had rarely sought their opinions, let alone thanked them for their service. "So not only did we try to create systematic means to hear what our employees had to say, we also tried to come up with ways to acknowledge the great things that everyone was doing on a daily basis. We created the MVD Stars program, which makes staff recognition democratic, since any staffer can recognize any other staffer. Instead of having only one employee of the month chosen by management, we now have scores of MVD Stars chosen by all of us. We asked our people if they wanted to make outstanding service our top priority — every customer, every transaction, every time," Williams said.

The response was overwhelming, with 80 percent saying yes. The statement about outstanding service — "Every customer, every transaction, every time" — became the agency's mission statement.

As he said, "In talking with some of our longer serving managers, they acknowledged that great customer service had never been a major priority here."

Now, under Williams's leadership, it has become THE major priority. Drawing upon his turnaround experience in the private sector, Williams initially set his sights on a handful of short-term gains. He then built a coalition of early adopters who could demonstrate and champion the practices that had so greatly improved service. Finally, he developed a two-year plan to make MVD a national role model.

As a key component of this strategy, Williams oversaw the training of 60 staff members in Lean techniques. These Lean practitioners implemented a program called CORE (customer outcomes reengineering), aimed at eliminating waste from processes. They wanted to cut customer wait times by 50 percent, raise the percentage of customers who rated the agency's service as "good" to 90 percent, and drop the number of those who rated it as "poor and unacceptable" to less than one percent.

The initiative quickly cascaded throughout an agency that employed 350 people in 91 offices and worked with 400 supporting entities. After a short 18 months, the MVD's employees and partners had fully engaged in the new mission. The results spoke for themselves:

- Complaints to the executive about MVD service were reduced to less than 50 per year over 2.5 million transactions — a tenfold reduction
- Customer satisfaction reached a 98 percent "good/ excellent" rating in MVD field offices — up from 60 percent in 2010
- Transactions online, which allow customers to skip a trip to the MVD, increased 300 percent
- Field office wait times were well below the official target of 20 minutes for three consecutive quarters; wait times were below MVD's internal target of 15 minutes in about 75 percent of offices
- Most call center wait times were below three minutes

- 91 percent of employees approved the department's strategy
- 80 percent of employees categorized themselves as engaged
- The MVD won the Quality New Mexico performance award for 2012 and 2013
- The department built an online license renewal system in 90 days with no budget increase
- The MVD introduced the first real-time motor vehicles department customer satisfaction tracking tool in the nation

That last accomplishment deserves special notice. Imagine strolling out of the MVD a mere 3-10 minutes after walking in the front door and pausing for three seconds to punch your level of satisfaction into a handy computer terminal:

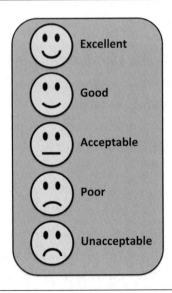

FIGURE 2.3: New Mexico's Motor Vehicles Division customers encounter a simple rating system as they exit a service center.

You grin as you hit the smiley button. Everyone's happy: you, the branch's employees, and their bosses. If you hit the frowny face button? A supervisor instantly receives that message and rushes to deal with your complaint before you can get to your car. No one who works in the branch will rest easy until they put a smile on that unhappy customer's face.

Traditionally, MVD did what many state agencies do — they surveyed their customers every two years. Williams dismissed that data as stale and worthless. He wanted immediate feedback.

"Governor Martinez, Secretary Padilla and MVD management picked this organization up, shook it and turned it inside out," said Williams. "The kinds of changes we have made have been extremely disruptive, and yet 90 percent of our staff [in a survey] support what we are doing."

Still, in 2014 the transformational journey for New Mexico's MVD has just begun. After the initial successes, MVD's leadership team did not sit back and congratulate themselves on a job well done; they looked for ways to do it even better. "We brought in Southwest Airlines when we were exploring how best to create the MVD of tomorrow," Williams said. "Southwest's focus on making air travel fun resonated with us, and we started thinking how we could turn MVD into the Southwest Airlines of motor vehicle agencies. So for example, we decided that when a 16-year-old comes into one of our offices for their first driver's license, we were going to celebrate it by announcing it to everyone over the PA system, applauding, giving that new driver a certificate of recognition and overall, making what is probably his or her first experience with government something positive. We're also exploring how we can do driver's license photos as glamour shoots. All in all, we're going to try to come up with something new every quarter to dramatically improve the experience of being in an MVD office — both for our customers and for our staff."

Case #2: Get Serious about Results

"The two most important days of your life are the day you are born and the day you find out why," says Fariborz Pakseresht, Director of Oregon Youth Authority.

Since assuming leadership of the agency responsible for some 1,250 young people whose lives have veered off course, Pakseresht has helped his agency deliver results by getting its people to ask two crucial questions: "Why do I exist?" and "What does it all mean?"

As Pakseresht put it, "Ultimately, when you open the veil and push everything else away, we are all trying to find the answer to these two questions."

He exemplifies the deep dedication to service that attracts so many people to government work: "Even when you talk to some of our most violent kids, kids who have transformed their lives and are now mentoring other kids, they say there is a reward in giving back that cannot be quantified in money or a Porsche or anything else in this world."

When then-director of OYA Colette Peters appointed Pakseresht as her deputy director, he found an agency in dire need of asking the two big questions: "Why does this agency exist?" and "What positive difference does it make in people's lives?"

In his previous role with Oregon's largest agency, the Department of Human Services, Pakseresht had asked the same questions, the answers to which led to a major transformation that relied heavily on the application of Lean tools, techniques and process improvement initiatives. He hoped he could transport the knowledge he had gained from that effort to OYA.

"Some of the folks in the organization were very anxious to implement Lean," he recalled, "but with the culture and mindset we had I did not believe we could successfully sustain a Lean effort."

Experience had taught him that real change depended on establishing the right context for change: "Something that I quickly realized was, as great as Lean is, and as many tools and opportunities as it has to offer, if you don't have a comprehensive framework in which Lean fits, and if you don't begin to change culture and mindset, then you will see this pendulum effect where you will see some areas improve, but they will begin to fall back because the culture cannot sustain the changes."

Having heard that 95 percent of Lean efforts fail within two years of their launch, Pakseresht and Peters started asking serious foundational questions about Oregon Youth Authority, including:

- Why are we in business (Mission)?
- What beliefs guide our actions (Values)?
- What reputation do we want (Vision)?
- What accomplishments will define our success (Key Goals)?
- How will we gauge our success (Outcome Measures)?

The answers to these questions help translate good ideas into the concrete reality of daily work. While most organizational leaders address these foundational questions at some point, most fail to keep asking and answering them as a routine habit. Two additional questions further close the gap between principles and action:

- What routine work must we do well (Core Processes)?
- How will we know that we are doing the routine work well (Process Measures)?

Peters and Pakseresht made *measurement* a top priority because they needed cold, hard numbers to guide change at OYA and, eventually, to prove that the agency was fulfilling its mission to provide exemplary service to Oregon's youth.

The transformation to a results-driven culture involved what Pakseresht calls a "framework" for change. The comprehensive framework ultimately linked all of the necessary ingredients into one strategic package: Lean/process improvement, employee engagement, customer focus, organizational change management, accountability, transparency, and performance management.

To illustrate the framework in action, the agency created a Fundamentals Map that hangs on Pakseresht's office wall in downtown Salem, Oregon.

"For a system to work, it needs a visual representation where everyone in the organization can see themselves," Pakseresht says.

To create this map, the OYA team spent months hashing out a shared understanding and language for the agency and its work. The structured process they used to build the Fundamentals Map included widespread and detailed conversations about all of the agency's core processes and how they interact with one another. It took a lot of time and effort to complete the map.

"I was very intentional about taking the time," explains Pakseresht, "because I had experience in my previous positions that if senior leadership doesn't understand what it is doing, then that work will end up on a shelf as another great idea that we paid a lot of money for but didn't get anything out of."

Pakseresht could finally see that the transformation would succeed when, five months into the project, one of the agency's senior leaders came to him and said, "I now get it, and I can now explain it." The Map had shown him the way.

Pakseresht smiles when he looks back on that turning point: "Three years into this effort, I can tell you I have been pleasantly surprised at how little resistance we have gotten from various layers of the organization."

In order to provide a role model for other agencies, OYA always plays host to a large gallery of observers who come to watch its Quarterly Target Reviews. The observers include leaders and staff from other agencies, citizens, legislators, and guests from out of state.

Again, the results speak for themselves:

- Outcome measures increased across the board by 27 percent (two years)
- Youth released from close custody and receiving transition services increased from 59.6 percent to 83.3 percent
- Close custody youth with active case plans within 30 days of post-intake assessment rose from 50.6 percent to 100 percent
- Agency culture became noted for transparency and openness between management and staff:
  - Employees who *Strongly Agree* or *Agree* that OYA's leaders generate high levels of motivation and commitment in the workforce rose 20 percent
  - Employee engagement (via a survey) increased by 17 percent
  - One OYA employee said, "Cascading information to people on the frontlines helps them make changes. They've moved past the fear of being beat up by the numbers."
- Problem-solving training sessions gave employee teams new decision-making skills that help them brainstorm and innovate solutions to processes that needed improvement:
  - By Q3 2013, 69 percent of agency measures met or exceeded targets

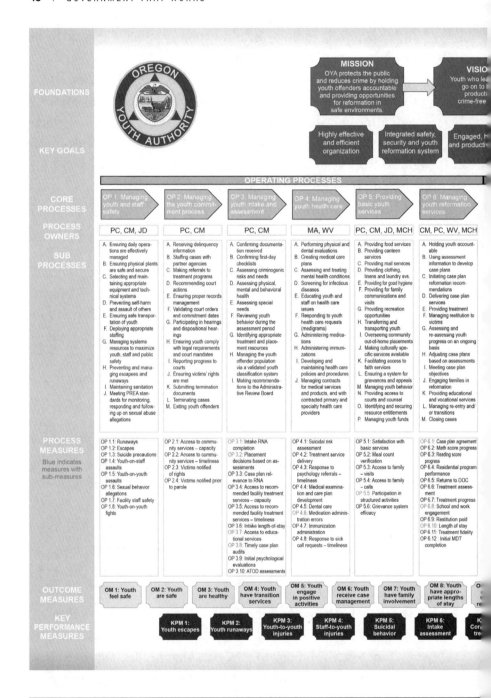

FIGURE 2.4: Oregon Youth Authority's Fundamentals Map, the first such map created in state government.

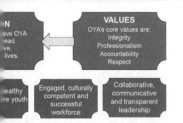

VALUES
OYA's core values are:
Integrity
Professionalism
Accountability
Respect

OREGON YOUTH AUTHORITY
PERFORMANCE MANAGEMENT SYSTEM
FUNDAMENTALS MAP
October 1, 2014

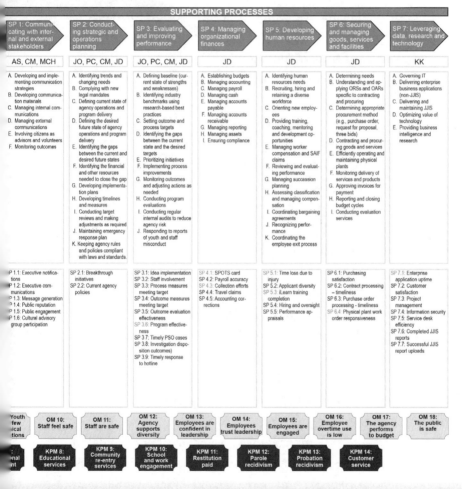

SUPPORTING PROCESSES

SP 1: Communicating with internal and external stakeholders	SP 2: Conducting strategic and operations planning	SP 3: Evaluating and improving performance	SP 4: Managing organizational finances	SP 5: Developing human resources	SP 6: Securing and managing goods, services and facilities	SP 7: Leveraging data, research and technology
AS, CM, MCH	JO, PC, CM, JD	JO, PC, CM, JD	JD	JD	JD	KK

SP 1
A. Developing and implementing communication strategies
B. Developing communication materials
C. Managing internal communications
D. Managing external communications
E. Involving citizens as advisors and volunteers
F. Monitoring outcomes

SP 2
A. Identifying trends and changing needs
B. Complying with new legal mandates
C. Defining current state of agency operations and program delivery
D. Defining the desired future state of agency operations and program delivery
E. Identifying the gaps between the current and desired future states
F. Identifying the financial and other resources needed to close the gap
G. Developing implementation plans
H. Developing timelines and measures
I. Conducting target reviews and making adjustments as required
J. Maintaining emergency response plan
K. Keeping agency rules and policies compliant with laws and standards.

SP 3
A. Defining baseline (current state of strengths and weaknesses)
B. Identifying industry benchmarks using research-based best practices
C. Setting outcome and process targets
D. Identifying the gaps between the current state and the desired targets
E. Prioritizing initiatives
F. Implementing process improvements
G. Monitoring outcomes and adjusting actions as needed
H. Conducting program evaluations
I. Conducting regular internal audits to reduce agency risk
J. Responding to reports of youth and staff misconduct

SP 4
A. Establishing budgets
B. Managing accounting
C. Managing payroll
D. Managing cash
E. Managing accounts payable
F. Managing accounts receivable
G. Managing reporting
H. Managing assets
I. Ensuring compliance

SP 5
A. Identifying human resources needs
B. Recruiting, hiring and retaining a diverse workforce
C. Orienting new employees
D. Providing training, coaching, mentoring and development opportunities
E. Managing worker compensation and SAIF claims
F. Reviewing and evaluating performance
G. Managing succession planning
H. Assessing classification and managing compensation
I. Coordinating bargaining agreements
J. Recognizing performance
K. Coordinating the employee exit process

SP 6
A. Determining needs
B. Understanding and applying ORSs and OARs specific to contracting and procuring
C. Determining appropriate procurement method (e.g., purchase order, request for proposal, three bids)
D. Contracting and procuring goods and services
E. Efficiently operating and maintaining physical plants
F. Monitoring delivery of services and products
G. Approving invoices for payment
H. Reporting and closing budget cycles
I. Conducting evaluation services

SP 7
A. Governing IT
B. Delivering enterprise business applications (non-JJIS)
C. Delivering and maintaining JJIS
D. Optimizing value of technology
E. Providing business intelligence and research

SP 1
P 1.1: Executive notifications
P 1.2: Executive communications
P 1.3: Message generation
P 1.4: Public reputation
P 1.5: Public engagement
P 1.6: Cultural advisory group participation

SP 2
SP 2.1: Breakthrough initiatives
SP 2.2: Current agency policies

SP 3
SP 3.1: Idea implementation
SP 3.2: Staff involvement
SP 3.3: Process measures meeting target
SP 3.4: Outcome measures meeting target
SP 3.5: Outcome evaluation effectiveness
SP 3.6: Program effectiveness
SP 3.7: Timely PSQ cases
SP 3.8: Investigation disposition outcomes)
SP 3.9: Timely response to hotline

SP 4
SP 4.1: SPOTS card
SP 4.2: Payroll accuracy
SP 4.3: Collection efforts
SP 4.4: Travel claims
SP 4.5: Accounting corrections

SP 5
SP 5.1: Time loss due to injury
SP 5.2: Applicant diversity
SP 5.3: iLearn training completion
SP 5.4: Hiring and oversight
SP 5.5: Performance appraisals

SP 6
SP 6.1: Purchasing satisfaction
SP 6.2: Contract processing – timeliness
SP 6.3: Purchase order processing - timeliness
SP 6.4: Physical plant work order responsiveness

SP 7
SP 7.1: Enterprise application uptime
SP 7.2: Customer satisfaction
SP 7.3: Project management
SP 7.4: Information security
SP 7.5: Service desk efficiency
SP 7.6: Completed JJIS reports
SP 7.7: Successful JJIS report uploads

OM 10: Staff feel safe	OM 11: Staff are safe	OM 12: Agency supports diversity	OM 13: Employees are confident in leadership	OM 14: Employees trust leadership	OM 15: Employees are engaged	OM 16: Employee overtime use is low	OM 17: The agency performs to budget	OM 18: The public is safe

KPM 8: Educational services	KPM 9: Community re-entry services	KPM 10: School and work engagement	KPM 11: Restitution paid	KPM 12: Parole recidivism	KPM 13: Probation recidivism	KPM 14: Customer service

To see this map in detail visit: www.resultsamerica.org/oyamap

- Overtime fell by 10 percent
- Program effectiveness improved from 44 percent to 90 percent, meaning that treatment plans were actually being followed with rigor
- Timeliness of case audits improved from 70 percent to 95 percent, ensuring the quality of case management

- Quarterly Target Reviews (QTRs) have evolved from a senior management exercise to a series of performance and improvement sessions that connected people at every level of the organization:
  - In Q1 2013, 60 percent of agency measures showed improvement
  - In Q2 2013, 35 percent of agency measures showed improvement
  - 90 percent of staff participated in the latest QTR
  - The Agency had conducted ten QTRs
  - Senior managers required all field offices to hold their own QTRs
- A total of 36 field QTRs contribute data to the enterprise QTR

In so many ways the changes at OYA have touched the lives of the youth in the agency's custody. One interesting one has been the involvement of two youth in research related to a set of measures we propose for the states that appear in Chapter Three of this book. The data they gathered on state performance can be found at www.resultsamerica.org.

OYA has adopted the management system explained in detail in *Business at the Speed of Now* (2012). The system provides an integrated set of tools and management practices that lead to these seven transformational changes:

1. **Everyone gets and stays on the same page**
   Every employee's efforts align with the organization's goals
2. **Everyone focuses on results**
   Every employee understands the definition of success and knows how to measure progress
3. **The voice of the customer drives improvement**
   Everyone studies their customers' needs and works relentlessly to fulfill them
4. **Employees keep fully engaged**
   People implement improvement ideas daily without management permission
5. **Everyone pays attention to improvement**
   Problems become opportunities for process improvement
6. **Fear evaporates**
   People feel safe to speak freely, always focusing on problems rather than people
7. **Silos disappear**
   People constantly collaborate and do not wage turf battles

Case #3: Go Lean the Right Way

Henry Sobanet, Director of the Office of State Planning and Budgeting for the State of Colorado, talked to us about his early experience applying Lean techniques in the state. "Sometimes, it's like a garage that's been piled into for years and you say, 'Look, this Saturday, we're going to do the garage,'" he recalled. "And then you're three boxes in and it's already lunchtime and you say, 'Oh my God! There is no way this is a one-day job.' And you give up."

He did not give up. Fortunately, his perseverance paid off when he received $5 million dollars in funding for the project, which enabled him to dive into a few initial Lean projects.

"We had a fixed amount of money and a fixed amount of

time," he explained, making it all the more imperative that he accomplish as much as possible as soon as possible.

Sobanet's interest in Lean began a few years earlier, when, in July 2011 the Denver Health Medical Center (DMHC) invited Sobanet and his Deputy Director to attend a Lean training session. DHMC had been applying Lean to the organization for several years under the leadership of its CEO Dr. Patty Gabow.

Sobanet brought a lot of skepticism to the visit. But by the second day he was already becoming a big fan of what the Toyota Motor Company had accomplished with Lean: "Waste is disrespectful of humanity because it squanders scarce resources; and waste is disrespectful of workers because it makes them do work that has no value."

Sobanet saw quite quickly that Lean meant far more than a collection of tools to improve processes. It represented nothing less than a whole new way of thinking about managing an organization. That new thinking offered a huge opportunity to design a great management system for his state. After all, in terms of revenue Colorado would rank in the upper third of the Fortune 500. "Most companies of our size have a management system, GE probably being the most famous," he explained.

Convinced that Colorado's citizens and public servants would benefit big-time from a Lean-based system of management, Sobanet began developing a seven-step process for turning Colorado into a results revolutionary.

Step One: *Align with the governor's vision*

Sobanet got the initiative off on the right foot. "Governor [John] Hickenlooper wants state government to be more efficient, more effective," he explained, acknowledging the governor's background as a business owner. "But, he added this other piece, more *elegant*. Wow, how are we going to be more elegant?"

By "elegant" Governor Hickenlooper meant, "Both sides of the transaction feel uplifted about the interaction, not demoralized or upset." In other words, design a system that delights both the customer and the employee. To fuel the effort, the Governor granted access to half of the State's remaining stimulus money. Otherwise, the economic crisis at the time would have killed the dream. With financing and strong support at the top, Sobanet could move forward with confidence.

Step Two: *Gain a deep understanding of Lean*

Sobanet and several allies became increasingly big fans of Lean as they attended additional training sessions. They appreciated what a valuable contribution it could make to a stronger public sector.

"Lean has this galvanizing magic of getting people to even acknowledge that they have a customer," he said. "That is a rare thing in government I think. We *don't* have factories, but we *do* have processes. We do have standardized work, and we certainly have customers. Not everybody is a taxpayer. We have the customer buying a hunting and fishing license; there's the student paying tuition; there's a person who needs a license to conduct business. If you shift your perception, you see more customers than taxpayers."

He shifted a lot of people's perceptions as he expanded the base of Lean knowledge until he had forged a sturdy foundation for the work ahead.

Step Three: *Think through the change*

Sobanet assembled a four-person team to design the new management system. That took a lot of deep thought. "We spent intensive time thinking about the ways we could minimize the issues that come up around change management."

It may seem obvious, but only a good change manager can change management. All of your good intentions will go for naught if you do not deal with people's natural inclination to resist change. (Read more about change management in Chapter Six).

The economic crisis, coupled with fears that Lean would lead to more layoffs, made people feel threatened by the initiative. Sobanet took steps to show skeptics and naysayers that Lean actually offered a way to minimize the threat because it would make better use of scarce resources without the burden of impossible workloads. "Learning new skills, finding efficiencies, and assuring everyone this wasn't a layoff exercise calmed everyone down."

Later on, when a particularly successful project prompted the elimination of some positions, department leaders got together and committed to finding positions elsewhere in state government. This proved their argument that Lean was not a scheme for getting rid of people but a way to make everyone's work more efficient and satisfying.

The launch team never demanded that an agency jump into the program, assuming that when department heads saw some impressive results they would leap at the chance to join the movement. And join they did. "We were invited in," Sobanet said with pride. "We were full up and had the cabinet eager to get their own efficient, effective, and elegant successes."

Step Four: *Contract external expertise*

Sobanet knew that he could use some outside expertise to help ensure the success of the Lean initiative. Any failure could set the state back to the old way of doing business. "There's a potential to fail. If we want to spend taxpayer money on something better, then we better become better as a result."

Colorado ended up hiring The North Highland Company, a consulting firm skilled at guiding agencies through their initial projects.

Step Five: *Launch a learning program*

You can most easily spread the word and teach new skills if you set up a "School for Lean." Colorado did just that, inviting a number of motivational speakers like Dr. Gabow to champion The Results Revolution. "Every cabinet member brought all or most of their leadership team," said Sobanet.

Students quickly began to think differently about their work and to learn the basics of Lean. The new way of thinking led the Department of Transportation to call a deputy director a process improvement person rather than just another deputy.

"People were enthusiastic, and I do think they appreciated that they got to choose their path," Sobanet recalled. Enthusiasm spread like wildfire. "We didn't just engage the executive director, we allowed the senior people who are the real leaders in those big divisions to come to the table and be acknowledged."

Step Six: *Set the scope of the mission and launch improvement projects*

With interest running high and the clock ticking on the dwindling stimulus dollars, Sobanet needed to move from thought to action by setting the scope for the mission and actually launching model projects.

"We have a cabinet-level committee called the Budget and Efficiencies Committee, and that became the board of directors for this project," he explained. "In the early days the Governor and the Chief-of-Staff came to every meeting."

The committee discussed which Lean projects should receive top priority during the early application of the Lean effort. They

developed a scope sheet that included important projects managers could successfully complete within 4-6 weeks. This allowed
for 4 weeks of data gathering and process mapping, followed
by 4-5 days devoted to developing implementation plans.

In the first wave of Lean, Colorado completed 80 projects.
Then it went on to add 200 more by the end of 2014.

Step Seven: *Measure improvement*

Sobanet talked about the most important final stage of Lean
implementation. "Keeping a culture of continuous improvement
in mind, we are now asking people to formally quantify the
outputs and outcomes that they are tracking." Colorado adopted a philosophy of measuring what you can truly measure,
bearing in mind that you want both good and bad numbers to
motivate people. Good results keep people passionate about
getting results; poor ones impassion them to do better. Colorado did that with a new accounting system that uses "performance
budgeting" as part of its comprehensive performance management system. The state even began building Lean into its long-
range strategic planning.

Colorado used Lean to drive results that matter to the state,
to its legislature, to its taxpayers, and to its customers. By adopting thoughtful change management practices and building,
rather than dictating, enthusiasm, the state has reduced customer wait times, shortened approval cycles, and taken waste out
of processes, thus reducing its operating costs.

In 2014, Colorado's measures showed such clear successes as:

- A redesigned process for key documents in the Departments of Revenue and Personnel and Administration
  that will save nearly $2.1 million a year.

- A 50 percent reduction in the cycle time for evaluating teacher license applications in The Department of Education.
- A threefold increase in identifications for prisoners released by The Department of Corrections.
- Colorado's Department of Licensing has gone from a mostly manual system for processing applications to a new process where customers determine license and registration requirements, calculate fees, and complete their applications electronically. The state processes 40,000 licenses a year and those who use the new system receive their approved licenses immediately.

Colorado's Lean initiative, New Mexico's Motor Vehicles Division, and the Oregon Youth Authority all serve as poster children for *government that works*. More will follow as states and agencies across the nation join the ranks of results revolutionaries embarking on their own missions of transformation.

CHAPTER THREE

The Complexity Challenge

Setting Goals and Measuring Results

"I didn't have time to write a short letter,
so I wrote a long one instead."

~ MARK TWAIN

Tom and Irene Barry dreamed of opening a little convenience store with a gas pump on a highway leading to the Oregon coast. In their minds, they could already smell the fresh-baked chocolate chip cookies and the extra-foamy mocha lattes. When Irene's father passed away, the couple invested her modest inheritance in a cozy little log-cabin-style store with living quarters in the back. Imagine their excitement when they moved into their dream business and began sprucing it up for the Grand Opening.

Eleven months later, Tom sported black saddlebags under his eyes, and Irene looked as ragged as a mother fox in a forest fire. Neither had slept well for months. Flat broke and nowhere near serving their first customer, they had fallen victim to a morass of Oregon laws and regulations, always complicated and often contradictory, involving no less than 12 different state agencies. Welcome to the world of government complexity.

How did it get so bad? When 39 men affixed their signatures to the newly minted US Constitution, they hoped they were launching a great government based on a few clear and simple principles: liberty, justice, freedom of speech, states' rights, and the unfettered pursuit of happiness. Paradoxically, they birthed what would grow, over the next 250 years, into a monster of complexity that could easily devour Tom and Irene Barry's dreams, not to mention their nest egg.

Modern American government has evolved into the most complex societal enterprise in the history of humankind. In the process, it has lost sight of the simple principles that inspired the nation's founders.

Restoring Simplicity

To refocus on the founders' ideals and help the Barrys enjoy the fruits of a dream come true, a government that has become a roadblock must, to a certain extent, get out of the way. Before it can smooth the path, however, leaders must deal with two problems that make it difficult for government to deliver timely and efficient services to citizens like Tom and Irene:

1. *Sheer size.* Government has grown so huge that the people it serves cannot quickly and easily access the services they need.

2. *Too many rules and regulations.* As we saw in Chapter Two, laws beget problems, problems beget new laws, and new laws beget even more new laws, until citizens who need answers and solutions find themselves mired in an impossible tangle of confusing and contradictory rules and regulations that have accrued over many, many decades.

The solution to both problems requires a greater focus on results. That focus encourages people who work in government to keep asking some fundamental questions: "Do we deliver services that make a difference, and do we do so in a timely and efficient fashion? If not, how can we become a leaner, speedier and more well-oiled machine?"

In the spirit of the Mark Twain quote that opened this chapter, *it will take a lot of time and hard work to make government simpler and more efficient.*

Imagine how Thomas Jefferson or Benjamin Franklin would react to the vast expanse of government that has welled up in the union they conceived:

- 22 million government employees (US Census, 2012)
- 89,004 unique governmental entities (states, counties, cities, transportation districts, water districts, school districts, etc.) (Politifact, 2013)
- An almost-infinite number of federal laws and regulations that no reliable source can begin to count, although they include:
  - A US Tax Code containing 3.8 million words (Carey, 2013)
  - Between 2,500 and 4,500 new federal regulations every year (Congressional Budget Office 2014)
- A 2014 federal budget of $3.78 trillion (Hoover, 2010)
- State budgets totaling $1.36 trillion

To put these rather mind-boggling statistics in perspective: the number of government workers in the United States equals the combined populations of Alaska, Delaware, District of Columbia, Hawaii, Idaho, Maine, Montana, Nebraska, Nevada, New Hampshire, New Mexico, Wyoming, North Dakota,

Rhode Island, South Dakota, Vermont, and West Virginia. The annual federal budget amounts to roughly $9,500 per living, breathing American citizen, and the national debt is $58,000 per person.

In every state in America, the government employs more people than any other enterprise. That's a lot of jobs. Yet size alone does not explain the complexity that besets almost all government activities. A lot of it grows out of the many conflicting responsibilities and often opposing constituents' needs it must accommodate.

From a citizen's point of view, government exists to serve the citizen's needs. Dylan pays taxes and expects the government to maintain safe highways for his commute to work. Rhonda also pays taxes, but she does not drive a car. Instead, she expects her tax dollars to fund an efficient and inexpensive public transportation system. Both want value for their dollars, but Dylan's and Rhonda's needs do not coincide. That's when the *public interest* comes into play.

What serves the public interest does not always match an individual's needs. But government must weigh both. Sure, Dylan may feel frustrated when he gets stuck behind a public transit bus on his way to work, but Rhonda, riding in that very bus, works as a maintenance supervisor in the building where Dylan keeps an office. Both benefit from the state's investment in roads and public transportation. However, dealing with the seemingly contradictory or conflicting needs of both inevitably breeds government complexity.

Consider another example. Dylan drives over the speed limit because he's late for work. A state highway patrolman pulls him over and gives him a speeding ticket. No matter how courteously and efficiently the officer issues the ticket, Dylan will not appreciate the excellent "customer service." He's going to get to the office even later now. Rhonda, sitting in a window seat on a transit bus passing this scene, will say a silent "thank you" to the cop for keeping the highway safe. The patrolman's service did not directly benefit Rhonda, but it did serve the public interest. And it may have saved a life or two.

What about the sacred right for every individual to pursue happiness? What if government intervention makes us *unhappy*? Well, we must accept the fact that sometimes the *collective will* must overrule our *individual will*. Back in the 1980s, the state of Oregon enacted tough environmental controls on timber harvesting. As a result, many once-flourishing Oregon mill towns eventually became almost ghost towns. Score one for the environmentalists. However, a lot of reasonably prosperous forestry and mill workers lost their jobs and ended up doing less-well-paid work. While some economists argued at the time that Oregon would replace the lost jobs with even higher-paying ones in the technology sector, not many middle-class mill workers from Lyon, Oregon, successfully made the transition. There were no former mill workers in Intel's wafer fabricating facility in Hillsboro, Oregon.

The need to accommodate the many possible conflicts between the *individual citizen perspective* and the *public interest perspective* adds a good deal of complexity to everything government does, and government must make tough trade-offs between the two every day. But no matter how hard it tries, no matter how many new wrinkles and nuances and rules and regulations it adds to the system, someone, somewhere, will get hopping mad. No wonder so many citizens feel disenchanted in and disappointed with their government.

According to the National Council of State Legislatures, the states produce some 22,000 new laws per year (not counting new rules and regulations). Many of those laws, and the wrinkles and nuances called "rules and regulations," creep into the system as government tries to serve both individual and community interests. That creates a burdensome by-product: miles and miles of red tape, otherwise know as paperwork. Anyone who has dealt with a state agency has probably come away with red stains on his or her hands.

Lawmaking superstars Texas and California create over 1,000 new laws every legislative session. Oregon passes about 912. Illinois lags behind with 471, while Washington weighs in at a measly 357, and Arizona at a mere 331. In Oregon, those 900-plus new laws will result in 25,000 pages of new regulations, which brings us back to Tom and Irene and their dream of running a cozy little convenience store on a scenic highway to the coast.

Tom and Irene's dream lasted just shy of two-and-a-half years. The Great Recession beat it up, but the incredible tangle of laws killed it. They ended up escaping foreclosure when they sold the property to someone else with a dream. But who ended up winning? Not the hungry customers driving to the beach for the day. Not the suppliers who would have happily stocked the store's shelves with magazines, candy bars and energy drinks. Not the bank that foreclosed on the property. Not the taxpayers of Oregon, who lost the benefits of the tax revenue the government would have collected from a thriving business. Not the state itself. Sadly, this lose-lose-lose-lose situation occurs countless times every year in every state in the country.

To change that unhappy outcome and enable all stakeholders to win, government needs to focus on delivering *measurable results* that serve both the individual and the public interests. It starts with figuring out what we really want from government.

Determining What We Want

Maryland Governor Martin O'Malley (D) says, "Governing by performance requires a willingness to openly set goals; to openly measure the performance of public institutions and efforts; to broadly share information rather than hoarding it; and to change course when necessary to move the graphs in the right direction."

You can't cross the finish line (i.e., get results) without a goal. That may sound painfully obvious, but nothing interferes with the efficient and cost-effective delivery of services more than a lack of concrete goals shared by all stakeholders — both those who must deliver services and those who need them. Our research into the accomplishments of results-focused state governors reveals these seven most frequently shared goals:

- GOAL ONE: Well-educated citizens
- GOAL TWO: Healthy and fit citizens
- GOAL THREE: An innovative and prosperous economy
- GOAL FOUR: A safe place to live, work, and raise a family
- GOAL FIVE: Responsible, sustainable practices
- GOAL SIX: A strong and durable infrastructure
- GOAL SEVEN: A government respected for its efficiency and effectiveness

Of course, leaders intent on achieving such goals must devise effective ways to measure progress toward them, a subject we will discuss in Chapter Five.

While business organizations define success with one simple measure — profitability — government, which plays so many different roles in contemporary society, requires many more yardsticks. Herein lies at least one clue to dealing with the complexity that beleaguers government at all levels. While both business and government aim to deliver what customers and citizens want, business executives, even those who run massive global operations, must deal with far less complexity than US government officials.

Take, for instance, the hypothetical International Micromachining Corporation (IMC). IMC's leaders can easily define the organization's purpose: *To make a profit in order to earn a return on the investment of those who fund the business.* Everything IMC does, from hiring and training skilled employees to designing and manufacturing and selling micro machines that delight customers, serves this one clear purpose. The company's leaders may adopt sustainable practices that promote the public interest, such as protecting the environment and setting high ethical standards that go beyond merely satisfying minimum legal standards, but they never lose sight of the bottom line. If they did, they would lose their jobs.

In her excellent book, *The New Corporate Facts of Life* (2013), sustainability consultant Diana Rivenburgh shows how sustainable practices can and do respect profitability. She makes a compelling case for "a new, emerging business model built on the premise that businesses, not government, can most effectively harness the forces of change to find innovative solutions to society's greatest problems and increase their profitability by doing so." If profits do not accrue, the business will die and never get a chance to help save the planet.

As I mentioned in my book *Business at the Speed of Now* (pages 196-197), Whole Foods demonstrates a strong social purpose represented by its motto, "Whole Foods, Whole People, Whole Planet." But make no mistake about it: the company securely connects the social good to its own financial welfare. Whole Foods' net profit margin soundly beats that of its national peers not in spite of but in part because of its commitment to give back to the world in which it earns its profits.

Setting business goals and measuring progress toward them does not require the IQ of an Einstein, but it does require knowledge, training, and skill. Businesses must keep ahead of the competition by developing new, innovative (though disruptive) products and services and ruthlessly improving every single process to deliver them. It's tough running and growing a successful business, but it's child's play compared to running a lean and efficient government.

Government leaders also set goals, but as we have seen, they must navigate the complexity of balancing the individual citizen's needs with the public interest, not to mention observing the tangle of laws created over the years. They also deliver products, in the form of services that fulfill those often-conflicting needs, and they must measure how well they do that. But what yardstick do you use to measure results in a vast sea of need? Profit never comes into play. Tax dollars keep flowing into the system, and not even the most burdensome deficit it seems will ever put government out of business, even if it fails to deliver the best possible results. Results. That's what it's all about, because only results can define in unambiguous terms what a government does for its people.

Let's look at an example of how government measures progress toward just one of the seven goals listed above:

GOAL FOUR: A safe place to live, work, and raise a family
As we saw in Chapter One, New York City measures results with respect to the rate of certain crimes:
- Murder
- Rape
- Robbery

- Felony Assault
- Burglary
- Grand Larceny
- Grand Larceny Auto

The lower the rate of crime, the safer families feel in their homes, schools, and workplaces. That seems like a pretty good yardstick, doesn't it? But hold on a second. A closer look opens a Pandora's box of complexity. These measures cover the kinds of crime that contribute to us feeling unsafe. But to fully represent the complexity of public safety requires even more measures. According to USlegal.com, the term "public safety" refers to the welfare and protection of the general public. It is usually expressed as a governmental responsibility. Most states have departments for public safety. The primary goal of the department is prevention and protection of the public from dangers affecting safety such as crimes or disasters. In many cases the public safety division will be comprised of individuals from other organizations including police, emergency medical services, and the fire force. "Public safety officer" includes corrections officers, fire service professionals, parole and probation officers, police officers, and youth correction officers. Add highway workers who design and build and maintain roads and highways and everyone who works for the Department of Motor Vehicles to this list of service providers, and you end up with a huge army of government employees.

Now you need another yardstick to measure progress toward the goal of a safe place to live, work, and raise a family: safer roads for all who use them, from commuters to vacationing families. These public-safety considerations add many possibilities to the measures of public safety, including:

- Number of accidents caused by potholes and other obstacles that need repair
- Rate of arrests for speeding
- Rate of arrests for driving under the influence
- Number of traffic accidents, injuries, and deaths
- The length of delays caused by traffic congestion
- Etc., etc., etc., ad infinitum

You get the picture. While the CEO of International Micro-machining Corporation quickly scans her company's one-page income statement, the Governor of Name-the-State gets a headache just looking at the 12-inch stack of statistical reports on her desk, covering everything from the recidivism rate in state prisons to the number of potholes in a three-mile stretch of Route 666. More goals and more measures naturally breed complexity, yet no matter how complex it gets, state government must try to get it all done with limited resources.

At IMC, micro machines and micro machine engineers and profit margins lend themselves to easy counting: "Last year, we sold 163,987 million micro machines, hired two new widget designers, and earned a 23 percent pre-tax profit."

But measures of social services get a whole lot messier because government must track hard-to-quantify human benefits such as education, health and welfare, and economic prosperity. What makes Tom feel healthy, wealthy and wise may fall far short of Irene's expectations, and vice versa. If you're the Governor of Illinois, how do you deliver and measure satisfactory results to the 13 million people living in your state? Hello, headache. Goodbye, sleep.

The results revolutionaries we have been discussing in this book understand that without measuring effectiveness, we cannot know to what extent government is effectively delivering results that satisfy individual and societal needs. Just like a runner trying to set a personal record, government needs to know its current level of performance and goal, but as it runs the race, government must make everyone else happy, too. That's why government is so much more challenging than a for-profit company.

Focusing on Results

A large body of literature has been written about managing change in the business world. Change scares people. Ever since we humans crawled out of the caves, our brains have been hardwired to react with "flee, fight, or freeze" to any threat to our well-being. Og and Mog see a rustling in the reeds and immediately think, "Sabre-toothed tiger! Run for your life!"

Change always threatens the status quo, with which most of us have grown comfortable and where we feel safe. It's a comfort zone where we comfortably and complacently go about our business. Even a minor change can send us reeling. IMC's CEO tells her people that the company will move from titanium micro machines to plastic, and most employees get nervous, duck for cover, or even flee to a safer environment. The Governor of Name-the-State tells his people that the state will drastically overhaul the way it conducts its business, and that message doesn't just make government workers nervous — it also scares them: "Oh My God, our work is so complex, we can no more change it than we could make an elephant do cartwheels!"

Experts who understand the natural human reaction to change suggest avoiding huge, radical changes that ignite all-out resistance. Instead, make steady, incremental changes that deliberately lead people from the perceived safety of the status quo to what, in time, can become a whole new way of doing business.

When you begin by emphasizing the need for better *results,* you keep people's eyes on the prize and away from the little changes that can make them feel uncomfortable. If they can see the ladder, they can climb to get away from the snarling tiger, and they stand a better chance of surviving the attack. Everyone likes the idea of better results in everything from micro machine performance to the line at the Department of Human Services. Better results are most obvious when they're measured: a micro machine that takes one rather than seven minutes to install, a ten-minute rather than one-hour wait in the DHS line. Results and measures give government workers a focus that reduces their fear of change, since they want to make a positive difference in the lives of those they serve.

A business like IMC can pull certain levers to improve profitability:

- Attracting and more fully satisfying customers
- Developing new markets
- Designing more effective marketing strategies
- Closing more sales
- Speeding up channels of distribution
- Offering more innovative products and services
- Seeking creative financing
- Reengineering the organizational structure
- Hiring and training more skilled employees
- Streamlining operations

A business leader selects the levers that will get results (i.e., increased profitability). In my book *Business at the Speed of Now* (2012), I showed how businesses around the globe have used the customer and employee levers to achieve the Lean Revolution. Essentially, the Lean philosophy insists that *cus-*

tomers define value (everything else is waste) and *employees create value* (they remove the waste and add only what the customer values). This strategic shift in focus automatically forces the organization to tweak ALL of the other levers, from sales and marketing to organizational structure.

Most traditional organizations like to pull the organizational structure lever (i.e., the organization chart with department heads and staff arranged by function). They emphasize budgets, staffing, annual objectives, and periodic reporting by each and every function. This creates and maintains "silos," where the functions sit alongside each other with little interplay and communication among them.

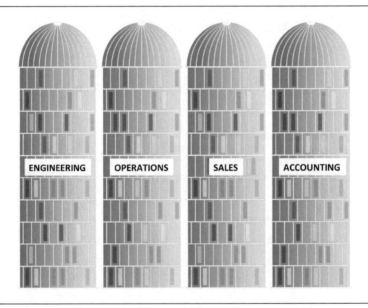

FIGURE 3.1: Traditional organizations focus on functions while results-driven organizations focus on processes.

When organizations use the customer and employee levers to implement a Lean approach, they get their people thinking less about organizational structure and more about efficiently and effectively satisfying customer needs. This shift creates a very different picture of how the organization operates:

FIGURE 3.2: The results wheel defines the core elements of a results-focused system of management.

With this approach, people think less about their functions and reporting up the silo to the top boss and more about what they can do to improve the processes they use to deliver goods and services to the customer. Reordering the importance of the elements within the organization completely changes the game.

Can government do that? Can government workers teach the elephant to do cartwheels? The answer is an emphatic, "Yes!" Amazingly, a single shift in perspective and emphasis to the *achievement of important societal results* can dramatically improve the success of any government. But, as with business, it will require the utmost commitment and creativity — something not easily accomplished when you're dealing with elephantine complexity.

According to the theory of Systematic Inventive Thinking (SIT), a creative approach to complex change developed in Israel in the mid-1990s, innovative solutions share certain common characteristics. One of them involves eliminating conflicts in the ways people do things (Wikipedia, 2014).

Let's say that Newton the accountant examines the cost to build micro machines using a sophisticated process that accounts for all related and supporting activities. In a conventionally organized company, he'd report his costs up the silo until it landed on the Bob the big boss's desk. Bob would send it down the operations silo for feedback. Operations disagrees with Newton's method for calculating costs, believing he is dramatically inflating the actual costs with his assumptions. The disagreement continues traveling up and down the silos until, months later, the people who actually do the work finally get involved in settling what the real costs will be.

By contrast, in a Lean organization, Newton would see the concern and then walk over to Mike in manufacturing and have a conversation. When he learns that design changes have increased sales by 20 percent and reduced the return of faulty micro machines to zero, Newton realizes the assumptions and calculations he had been working on were off the mark. Once Newton and Mike are communicating directly, they can have productive conversations. With Lean, the doors fly open and stay open. People talk to people across departmental boundaries. Functions don't matter; processes do. With the Lean management philosophy, the company solves its problems faster because when they pop up, people ask, "Why is this problem happening? How can we solve it quickly and effectively?"

When everyone stays on the *Results* page, conversations about problems begin with "Why?" and end with "Problem solved!"

Most people assume that the best solutions arise from creative brainstorming outside the so-called "box" of conventional thinking. But such *out-of-the-box thinking* seldom comes up with the best solutions. It often makes more sense to keep your thinking *inside the box*, because unfamiliar territory, like change, creates discomfort and instant resistance. Systemic Inventive Thinking further argues that the way to change a system from *inside the box* is to change the relative importance of the existing elements. As an example, if an overseas factory is threatened with closure because it has too many employees suffering serious, on-the-job injuries, making safety the top priority will have a profound impact on all aspects of factory operations.

Consider some typical problems that spark reaction by the executive branch of government:

- A lawsuit challenges a regulation or action
- The legislature passes a new law that requires tweaking
- A number of constituents lodge a complaint with legislators
- The media publishes an embarrassing story
- An audit surfaces an alarming problem
- A major project, such as a costly new website, fails
- Interest groups build pressure

Government officials cannot ignore such problems forever. They must sooner or later react, and many government agencies spend much of their time in reactionary mode. But when people in government prevent problems from arising (i.e., aim for a measurable *result*), it lessens the need to operate in reactionary mode.

Note that while reactionary government systems do measure many things, they rarely even talk about results. Instead, they address problems after they've arisen and try to come up with defensible solutions (the symbolic firing of the "guilty party" is a common defensive move). However, if they had concentrated on results and ways to measure progress toward them, the problems might not have arisen.

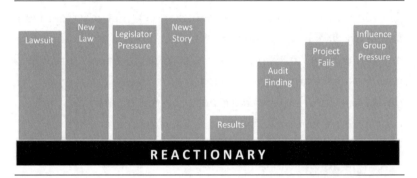

FIGURE 3.3: A reactionary system of government relies on events to organize its priorities rather than goals.

Besides, measures put problems in perspective. For example, if an agency tracks customer satisfaction, and one customer's horrific service experience ends up in the newspaper, the agency can say, "Yes, this one got away from us. But in the past three years, the percent of our customers who rate our service as outstanding has risen from 86 percent to 94 percent. We obviously have more work to do, but we are making progress."

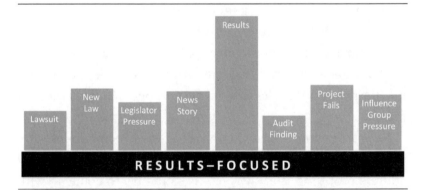

FIGURE 3.4: A results-focused system of government uses its goals and measures to organize its priorities. Events are viewed in the context of desired results and help identify gaps in current processes.

Stressing the importance of results shifts the center of attention and not only reduces the likelihood of problems occurring, but also provides a constructive framework for dealing with the inevitable problems that do crop up. Note how a results-based system both changes outcomes and shifts the public's attention.

The simple switch from a reaction-based system for decision making and problem solving to a results-based system will ensure the better outcomes the public wants and deserves, and far more efficiently than any other changes could. As water follows the path of least resistance, government will naturally begin the long and critical process of reorganizing itself around desired societal outcomes.

Capturing Data

You cannot successfully deal with government complexity if you base your decisions and solutions on hunches rather than on cold, hard data. To reach the best solutions, the state of Maryland developed a scorecard for measuring results based on the CompStat model we discussed in Chapter One. Beth Blauer, executive director of Maryland's StateStat program, wrote in a special report for The Center for Digital Government titled *The Government Dashboard*, "StateStat allows us to attack problems and make decisions very quickly. It has given government a level of agility that I never thought was possible before" (Center for Digital Government, 2012).

In today's hyper-connected world, where data keeps multiplying at exponential rates, we cannot bemoan the lack of available data. "Big Data" abounds. Used wisely, Big Data offers an unprecedented potential to drive waste out of government processes and to make what government does visible to the general public. For that to happen, however, you need a good filter for separating crucial data from all the rest. As data keeps piling up as though in a huge funnel, you need to make sure the "good stuff," the stuff you really need to make sound decisions and solve problems, gets through the hole at the bottom.

As a special report written in cooperation with the magazine *Public CIO* points out, "If data is indeed the common currency of the global economy, government is rich" (Center for Digital Government, 2012). The report proposes using "dashboards" to present the most valuable data. This device works much like the dashboard in a car, providing a glimpse at the data you need to drive safely. Car dashboards display key indicators, such as speed or distance traveled or an open door or engine failure. The examples below show the kind of key indicators government dashboards display, and how these offer quick and easy access to important data. As the report points out, "Because dashboards are designed to be intuitive and simple, they expand data access from highly trained data analysts to casual users."

Consider these examples:

- The Texas Education Agency has installed personalized dashboards on the desks of hundreds of thousands of educators. To help schools achieve better student outcomes, the dashboards include research-based performance metrics that create a profile of each student and help identify those who are struggling with their studies (Young et al., 2011).
- The City of Seattle developed a dashboard open to all citizens called Data.Seattle.Gov. The portal offers data on such topics as budgets, real-time 911 calls, and permits. It lets citizens see what's going on in their government each and every day (City of Seattle, 2014).
- The Maryland Department of Public Safety and Correc-

tional Services has achieved the lowest crime rates since 1975, due, in part, to dashboards that provide Maryland law enforcement agencies with access to details about a criminal subject. This enhances data-sharing and cross-agency cooperation.

With such devices, data becomes useful information. Now users understand what the data *means*. Another type of device called a "Heat Map" visually displays the frequency of incidences on maps so viewers can easily see any hotspots (areas with high number of incidences). *More on this in Chapter 10.*

Brian Rawson, Director of Statewide Data Initiatives for the Texas Education Agency, believes passionately in getting the right information to the right people in the right context: "The fact that this data is all in one place," he explains, "you could finally see the correlation between grades, attendance and assessments" (Center for Digital Government, 2012).

The same applied to the State of Maryland's public safety dashboard. As Director of the Department of Public Safety and Correctional Services Gary D. Maynard said, "The StateStat model called attention not just to the data but to the drivers of the data" (Center for Digital Government, 2012).

Understanding the data and its drivers helped decision-makers to pinpoint the causes of costly overtime in the agency. But the Government Dashboard Special Report cautions against making faulty assumptions about cause and effect, such as:

- Confusing correlation and causation (just because the groundhog saw its shadow does not mean it caused a longer winter)
- The infrequent or inconsistent use of statistical tools (using different average temperatures to mark the beginning of spring)

- The application of results from small groups to larger cohorts (if Punxsutawney Phil can predict the weather, all groundhogs can predict the weather)
- Misleading results produced by inference-based analysis (if the groundhog dies, spring will arrive earlier)
- Unintentional manipulation of results by the researcher (the groundhog's handler uses a spotlight to create a shadow)

With effective scorecards and dashboards in place, you must revisit the questions, "What will we measure? And why?"

Defining Outcomes

An old adage holds that "What gets measured gets done." Management consultant and professor Peter Drucker insists, "What gets measured gets managed."

Since government officials and workers must contend with so many varied and often-conflicting demands for their attention, and operate in a basically reactive mode, they sorely need a set of measures that supports a focus on results. The best measures gauge the degree to which government, from the governor's office on down, delivers results to individual citizens and to the general public. They reveal the degree to which state agencies achieve the goals of the governor and how well agency leaders and their teams perform their work. Priorities should be perfectly clear and measures ensure they are. That makes selecting and defining measures extremely important because *everything*, from initial planning to communication to execution, depends on those measures. Once they're in place, those measures make the work of government less bafflingly complex. They fire up the engine of *government that works*. With results securely installed in the center of everyone's concern, and with measures firmly in everyone's mind, a strong, interconnected web emerges, one that connects each and every government worker to the mission: delivering results.

How do you determine the best measures? As always, engage the people who actually do the work. They know best what works and doesn't work. Not only must they live with the measures, they must also own them with all their hearts. Otherwise, they will go through the motions, grow cynical about their leaders, develop a disregard for their customers, and go back to government as usual. As a postal worker once said, "This job would be great if it wasn't for my dumb boss, all this stupid mail, and the dummies who come to the counter with their idiotic questions."

Oregon offers a prime example of a well-intended but failed effort to use data to transform government. In 1994, the state received national recognition from Harvard's Kennedy School of Government for its Oregon Benchmarks (Harvard, 2014). The honor reflected unusual foresight.

Michael Jordan, now Oregon's Chief Operating Officer, looks back rather ruefully on that crucial point in his state's history because the benchmarks did *not* get the results everyone expected: "In those days, we did not know how to manage with data. We did not understand how to make policy with data, and then how to use it in our day-to-day operations."

Twenty-one years after the Harvard award, and despite deserving full credit as the state with the longest-standing set of measures in the nation, the state had not properly connected the measures to the people who most needed to understand and apply them. Leaders mistakenly thought that only people outside the system could create credible measures. The outsiders who created the measures would routinely look at them and hope they were driving improvement. But hope does not bake the cake. You might as well stand on the island in the middle of the freeway and hope that your radar gun measurements will automatically slow down all the cars.

Chalk Oregon's disappointing experience up to failed hopes. Chalk it up also to "politics as usual." Given the natural vagaries of a democracy in which periodic elections routinely rotate leaders in and out of office, the effectiveness of Oregon Benchmarks suffered under a series of administration changes that made it little more than a political football.

Measures show progress, but they do not *cause* progress. Just because you adopt excellent measures does not mean people will use them to guide their journey toward results. In 2012, Oregon's State Legislature eliminated funding for what had won admiration as the "world's best set of measures" — without fanfare and without any media coverage. As the famous benchmarks were dying a death of neglect, Oregon's state agencies on their own initiative went on to develop and use measurements in ways that effectively engage the public servants who can and do actually improve them. Today Oregon is once again demonstrating best-practice leadership, but this time it's moved from theory to results.

The best measures of government performance gauge improvements from the perspective of each stakeholder, from the bottom up, from the smallest process performed by a behind-the-scenes or frontline worker to the individual and collective recipients of that work. Both the person designing a driver's license application and the elderly woman renewing her license must see the results. And you cannot see results without a scorecard. Given the complexity of government, all this does not come easily. But it will never come if the folks who do the work do not get fully engaged in the program.

As our consulting group has worked to install measurement protocols with agencies in Oregon, Washington, Wyoming,

Tennessee, Michigan, and others, we have discovered that two types of measures can help connect all stakeholders. One set, which we call Outcome Measures, gauges results. The second set, called Process Measures, gauges the effectiveness and efficiency of the work that leads to those outcomes. This table includes both types of measures:

Measure Types Defined

TYPE	DEFINITION	EXAMPLES
OUTCOME MEASURES	Indicate societal health and vitality	
SOCIETAL	*Macro results over which government has some influence*	GDP, unemployment, net exports, inflation, poverty level, average wages, obesity
GOVERNOR	*Macro results over which state government has significant influence*	Recidivism, high school graduation rates, air polution index, new business startups
AGENCY	*Results over which an agency of state government has significant if not complete control*	Lottery dollars earned, access to affordable housing, bridge safety, crimes solved, meth labs shut down, licenses suspended
PROCESS MEASURES	Indicate performance of routine processes that are intended to support improvement of the Outcome Measures	
COST	*The cost to deliver a product or service*	Cost per permit, cost to issue a license, cost per vehicle mile driven, cost per employee
QUANTITY	*The number of outputs*	Permits issued, cases managed, inmates on parole, citations issued, DUI arrests made, audit findings, regulations eliminated
QUALITY	*The degree to which the output met the needs of those who received it*	Customer satisfaction, error rate, rework, complaints filed, grievances filed
TIME	*The time it took to get the work done*	Days to issue permit, minutes to get driver's license, on-time delivery, wait time, process time

FIGURE 3.5: These recommended definitions come from a combination of best practices in business and government.

While many people inside and outside government believe that not even Superman could wrangle better results from a government that operates like a herd of rampaging elephants, a number of states have begun to do it quite well. Take for example:

1. California has racked up an above 80 percent high school graduation rate for the first time in its history (Casear, 2014).
2. Maryland has achieved a 26.3 percent decrease in violent crime since 2006 (Maryland StateStat, 2013).
3. New York cut nearly 20 percent of its carbon emissions, a whopping 41 million metric tons, between 1990 and 2011 (EPA, 2014).
4. Wyoming's debt to Gross Domestic Product ratio fell 41 percent from 2003 to 2013 (usgovernmentspending. com, 2014).
5. Nevada has slashed its population of tobacco smokers by 30.4 percent since 2003 (americashealthrankings. org, 2014).
6. Median Household Income in Washington increased 37.6 percent between 2002 and 2012 (US Census Bureau, 2013).

While each of these states used its own unique set of measures to get results, all of their measures reveal progress toward clearly defined targets. To see how all of the 50 states stack up with respect to improvements in many crucial areas, you can visit this website to view and download some enlightening data: www.resultsamerica.org.

With respect to the list of goals cited earlier, from our research, these are the 48 measures we feel are the foundation of good measurement for the states. We call them our Essential 48 Outcome Measures (OM).

GOAL ONE: The best-educated people
  OM-1.1: K-8 Testing
  OM-1.2: High School Graduation Rates
  OM-1.3: College Preparatory Testing (SAT & ACT)
  OM-1.4: Associate's Degrees
  OM-1.5: Bachelor's Degrees
  OM-1.6: Graduate and Professional Degrees

GOAL TWO: The most innovative and prosperous economy
  OM-2.1: Gross Domestic Product
  OM-2.2: Economic Diversity
  OM-2.3: Business Competitiveness
  OM-2.4: Median Household Income
  OM-2.5: Unemployment Rate
  OM-2.6: Net Job Growth
  OM-2.7: Income Inequality
  OM-2.8: New Firms
  OM-2.9: Venture Capital Investment
  OM-2.10: Poverty

GOAL THREE: The safest place to live, work, and raise a family
  OM-3.1: Violent Crimes
  OM-3.2: Property Crimes
  OM-3.3: Rate of Recidivism
  OM-3.4: Rate of Incarceration
  OM-3.5: Cost of Corrections
  OM-3.6: Traffic Fatalities
  OM-3.7: Child Maltreatment

GOAL FOUR: The most responsible sustainability practices
  OM-4.1: Renewable Energy
  OM-4.2: Carbon Dioxide Emissions

OM-4.3: Water Quality

OM-4.4: Air Quality

GOAL FIVE: The healthiest and fittest people

OM-5.1: Cost of Healthcare

OM-5.2: Rate of Obesity

OM-5.3: Quality of Health

OM-5.4: Infant Mortality Rate

OM-5.5: Rate of Uninsured

OM-5.6: Smoking

OM-5.7: Workplace Injury

OM-5.8: Quality of Life and Happiness

OM-5.9: Food Insecurity

GOAL SIX: A second-to-none infrastructure

OM-6.1: Infrastructure Index

GOAL SEVEN: A government respected for its efficiency and effectiveness

OM-7.1: Government Debt

OM-7.2: Citizen Tax Burden

OM-7.3: Unfunded Pension Liabilities

OM-7.4: Federal Dependency

OM-7.5: Credit Rating

OM-7.6: State Employees

OM-7.7: Financial Transparency

OM-7.8: Government Use of Technology

OM-7.9: Results Champions

OM-7.10: Open Data Access

OM-7.11: Government Spending

While business focuses on a single measure, this list exemplifies how complex government is and how critical its influence is on our society.

"It's a jungle out there."

Yes, and it takes a reliable compass and an accurate map to guide your path through the thickets of brush and across the many rivers that block you from reaching your goal. But if you keep your goal firmly in mind, and if you constantly consult your compass and your map to see where you were, where you are now, and where you're heading, you'll get where you're going, albeit a little weary and bruised from the journey. It's worth the effort. After all, getting there *is* half the fun.

CHAPTER FOUR

The Missing Link

Redesigning the Management System

"We don't see things as they are,
we see them as we are."

~ ANAÏS NIN

In 2009, Brian Calley (R), then a member of the Michigan House of Representatives, received a call from one of his constituents saying she had received an order to "cease and desist" from allowing neighbor children to wait in her home for the school bus. This kindly woman, not wanting to see children standing in the cold until the bus picked them up, invited the kids into her home after their parents dropped them off on their way to work. An anonymous neighbor had lodged a complaint with the Michigan Department of Human Services, alleging that the woman was operating an illegal day care center. If convicted of that charge, she faced a $1,000 fine or up to 93 days in jail.

Calley, who later became Michigan's Lieutenant Governor and took over Governor Rick Snyder's (R) Reinventing Performance in Michigan initiative, began digging into the situation. To his surprise, he learned that Michigan's rules and regulations actually did make this Good Samaritan a day care operator because she sheltered the children on a routine basis in the absence of their parents.

Calley took issue with the technicality, arguing, "No, it's not a daycare — nobody pays anybody. It's just the neighbor kids waiting for the bus. Neighbors being good neighbors."

When the story leaked to the press, it went viral and eventually attracted the interest of NBC's *Today Show* host Matt Lauer, who showed up in town to perform a live feed from the "scene of the crime." Michigan moved swiftly to pass a new law introduced by Calley.

Calley went on to become the youngest Lieutenant Governor in the nation. He recalled his feelings after the incident: "I thought the original law was fine, if it had been reasonably interpreted. But over time administrative rules had been added and added and added to where somebody could really believe a bus stop needs to be a licensed daycare."

A law becomes a law with the governor's signature, but it does not go into effect until the executive branch has created the rules and regulations needed to implement it. In Calley's opinion, that's where the trouble starts. Well-intended rules piled on top of other well-intended rules can result in the sort of absurdity that turned a Good Samaritan neighbor into a potential criminal. To address that problem, Michigan launched its Reinventing Performance in Michigan (RPM) effort.

"When we started out, we knew we needed a very formal and deliberate process for evaluating the rules and practices that exist today," Calley explains.

Working with Steve Arwood, Director of Michigan's Department of Licensing and Regulatory Affairs, the program targeted several areas in which accumulating regulations were spawning a lot of complaints.

Arwood singled out one in particular: "My favorite example is our motor carrier licensing process that, for some reason, had not been looked at in 40 years. Every piece of freight that moves in the state has to have permission to move from this department to move their freight. The team that does this work did a self-assessment, and said, 'This is an old process we have never really looked at.' So we sent a group of folks over who have been through Lean training. In the end they took 64 steps out of the process; superfluous, unnecessary steps."

The overall RPM effort set some aggressive goals for streamlining the state's management systems:

- A 50 percent improvement in customer response time
- An overall 50 percent reduction in forms
- A 25 percent improvement in satisfaction with the regulatory process

Targeting areas of government regulation ranging from issuing liquor licenses to collecting taxes from employers, the program achieved impressive results: an average 78 percent reduction in processing time, and a 52 percent reduction in the number of forms required from customers. Overall, the people involved in the program evaluated a total of 2,198 documents for their utility. The bottom line: elimination of 1,577 sets of rules (State of Michigan, 2014).

Despite these accomplishments, Calley said Michigan had a lot of work ahead before it could declare itself a truly results-driven state: "That was a pretty good process to get started with, but it was never going to create the type of across-the-board changes that we needed. The first phase didn't get to the systemic issues, such as what things should or shouldn't be regulated. The initial work focused mostly on policy discussions as opposed to the hardcore regulatory environment that we have within the bureaucracy. Then it grew into something that I found more useful and substantial. Employees themselves are identifying the hindrances and roadblocks and delays and the things that are obsolete and not useful anymore."

Imagine that! Ideas for improvement began coming from the people who actually do the work. Calley and Arwood knew that the best ideas for streamlining the system would come from the bottom-up, not the top-down. That meant creating far greater employee engagement — a fundamental change in Michigan's management system. As Calley said, "This is where the real power of regulatory reform lies."

The opportunity goes far beyond getting rid of obsolete bureaucratic entanglements; it includes rethinking the rules, but it also extends to the way agencies implement the rules.

"I think what we have learned with this work has blown the doors off the potential here," Calley said. "Here's a regulation that's on the books and in statutes. How can we do it in a way that provides the highest degree of satisfaction and service to the customer?"

Despite the program's many successes, Arwood points out that only a fraction of his agency's employees and the state are engaged in these efforts. That indicates a tremendous opportunity for true transformation in the years ahead.

Managing on the Edge of Change

In the previous chapter we talked about the importance of setting goals and measuring results. However, those represent only the first two first steps on the long road to true transformation. Leaders who commit to a major overhaul of the way government does its business must dedicate themselves to streamlining management systems in deeply fundamental ways. Otherwise the United States will continue to lose ground in the global arena.

America Falling in Global Rankings

	2000	2012	Change
Math Score	20th	30th	⬇ 10
Science Score	15th	23rd	⬇ 8
Reading Scores	16th	20th	⬇ 4
Economic Freedom	8th	10th	⬇ 2
Press Freedom	17th (2002)	47th	⬇ 30
Democracy Index	17th (2006)	21st	⬇ 4

FIGURE 4.1: US world rankings are declining in dozens of categories.
Sources: Program for International Student Assessment, Heritage Foundation, Reporters Without Borders, The Economist, and The World Bank.

How have we come to this sorry state of affairs? You might point to the cultural and political and economic causes of the decline, or you can focus on something more tangible and fixable: *the current system of managing government.* Clearly, the management system itself needs repair.

Before you can set about streamlining that system to get the measurable results you seek, you must understand the concept of a *management system.*

According to Peter Senge in his breakthrough book *The Fifth Discipline* (Currency/Doubleday 1994) and its companion, *The Fifth Discipline Fieldbook*, a management system is a collection of people, processes and technologies that enable an organization to achieve its mission and deliver on its goals. It organizes and orchestrates all of an organization's resources:

FIGURE 4.2: In Peter Senge's book, *The Fifth Discipline,* he described business systems as consisting of three elements: people, process, and technology.

Think of a management system as a living, breathing organism. In a healthy one, all of the limbs and organs function smoothly and efficiently. In a sick one, a vital part has broken down and needs fixing (Senge, 2006). But if the whole collection of organs and body parts has stopped functioning properly, fixing just one sick piece of the organism will not likely restore its overall vitality. If the gangrene has spread throughout the body, amputating the infected leg will not save the patient.

You don't need to look far to find a guru or author who will happily prescribe the miracle cure that will "fix" your organization. You can see my recommended reading list in Appendix F. All of these are solid, useful books.

While all of the recommended books from *Good to Great* to *The Toyota Way* and *The Rule of Nobody* and many more models, methods, tools, and processes provide part of the cure; they do not materially cure the root cause of the current state of governmental breakdown. They do not address the underlying logic and capability of the management system itself. No matter how many of the techniques you apply, they no more transform an organization into a streamlined machine than a new fuselage or seatbelts turn a Piper Cub into a Boeing 767.

FIGURE 4.3: When beginning a transformation effort, most organizations fail to see the shift as a change in management system, but instead see it as a set of independent programs. The result is the various programs overwhelm the organization because of the sheer quantity of work the programs generate.

Each technique can work wonders, but applied in a helter-skelter fashion they amount to no more than random acts of improvement. As they accumulate, they can even work at cross-purposes and actually block the path to the true transformation of state government, lulling you into a false sense of accomplishment and complacency. You feel quite healthy and happy until the infection springs back up and knocks you flat on your back.

This brings us to the fairly technical subject of *process theory*, which offers the best cure for what ails any poorly performing management system. The theory holds that true transformation requires a close examination and overhaul of *process capability* (more about this in a moment).

All systems and all work organizations, both public and private, consist of a collection of processes. These processes receive input, and then work with that input to create output. Take a simple system like assembling a bicycle. You take the input (the parts and the instruction booklet), fasten all the parts together until, voila, you're cruising down the street on your brand new bike. The work you do to turn input into output involves people (the people who do the work), processes (the steps people follow) and technologies (the tools and techniques people use to get their work done).

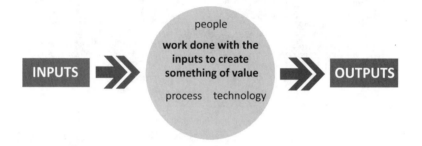

FIGURE 4.4: Every system has inputs, the resources it is given to work with; and it has outputs, the products or services that result from the work of the people, process, and technology.

Now, let's take a look at how this plays out in the legislative branch of state government. The State Legislature of Name-the-State receives a variety of inputs, including citizens' expectations, societal needs, and political necessities. The people who work in and for the legislature use certain prescribed processes and technologies to produce outputs in the form of laws, mandates, budgets, and controls.

FIGURE 4.5: The legislative branch transforms customer, societal, and political needs into laws, mandates, budgets, and controls (over the executive branch).

The executive branch receives the output from the legislative branch. The legislative output becomes executive branch input, and the executive branch applies its own set of people, processes, and technologies to deliver outputs in the form of programs, services, and products intended to meet the citizen, societal, and political needs.

FIGURE 4.6: The executive branch takes the needs of its citizens, the forces of politics, the laws and mandates, budgets, and controls given to it by the legislative branch, and transforms those into programs, services, and products to serve the citizens of the state.

Since the nation has been steadily falling in rank among the other nations of the world, we can reasonably deduce that the current system for managing the processes of government has become increasingly incapable of meeting the needs of our society. Otherwise, we would not be suffering such poor results.

Since governmental management systems involve people, processes, and technologies, one or more of those elements must have gone off track. This raises some good questions — questions that require tough-minded answers:

PEOPLE – Has the way government views the people who do the work become outdated?

PROCESSES – Has the series of activities used to get the work done grown cumbersome and wasteful?

TECHNOLOGY – Has government failed to obtain and use the best tools for doing its work efficiently and effectively?

Problems probably exist with all three. Experts schooled in the science of process theory would argue that performance and productivity problems arise when an organization's management systems grow up rather willy-nilly over time and do not reflect a deliberate and conscious attempt to design the best possible system. Decades of accumulating laws and rules and regulations and red tape and bureaucracy have created a sort of Frankenstein monster assembled from a lot of parts that do not work properly but go lumbering through the countryside scaring the villagers out of their wits. The experts would propose fixing the monster by going back to the drawing board and creating a system designed to get results as efficiently and effectively as possible. Of course, that's easier said than done. Even the most talented designer must cope with the complexity of our government.

With respect to PEOPLE, government, like most organizations, holds a set of unspoken assumptions about the role human nature plays in the work of the organization. The traditional view sees people as hands and feet, mere tools to get the work done. That view ignores the fact that human beings are complicated, unpredictable creatures filled with ideas and hopes and fears and sometimes hard-to-manage feelings. But they are also the source of all innovation, and the people closest to the work are the ones who can best design how that work gets done.

When it comes to PROCESSES, government, again like most organizations, began with a set of activities, such as assessing constituent needs, case planning, scheduling, and providing services but over time has tacked on an abundance of modifications and so-called "improvements" that have gummed up the works. The processes no longer focus fully on getting desired results.

Like any organization that uses TECHNOLOGY, government has bought and installed a lot of the latest tools, often without sufficiently understanding what the tools can and cannot do.

Even the best tools can end up wasting time and energy rather than helping users do their work more effortlessly and with less variation.

In the case of a particular government agency, the fault may be 10 percent with the people (90 percent possess the desire and capability to do a good job), 70 percent with the processes (30 percent run efficiently), and 20 percent with technology (80 percent do what they're supposed to do). Or it may be 1-89-10-percent, or 50-25-25 percent. Whatever the percentages, something somewhere has clearly gotten way out of whack.

This brings us to *process capability*, a topic replete with a lot of mind-stretching mathematics. Here, however, we will dispense with the math and look at the subject conceptually.

When considering process capability, you study two parts of the process under consideration: the variability of the output (its consistency), and how it compares to the original specification (the desired result). At the beginning of any process improvement effort, you want to reduce variation and make sure the process runs well enough to produce reliable and predictable results. If a stable process cannot consistently perform to specifications, you define that process as *not capable* of delivering what you need it to deliver. Think about that bicycle you need to assemble. If parts are missing or the instructions are unclear and confusing, you probably won't get the job done. Even with all the right parts and instructions, you still won't get the job done unless you have the right tools. Similarly, a state's high school students won't raise their scores on standardized tests unless the right people, processes, and technologies are put in place. In other words, *enhanced performance depends on improving process capability*.

While this all may sound terribly theoretical, you can see these concepts in action if you look closely at New York City's success with CompStat. The city's old system for managing public safety had become incapable of quelling the rampant street crime for which the city had become infamous. Residents and visitors alike feared walking the streets at night. But CompStat changed all that. It represented a total rethinking of the crime management system.

Any government agency can learn a lot from studying the CompStat approach. Not only did the new management system get desired results, it helped fashion a vastly more capable NYPD. As the whole department became more disciplined, accountable, and transparent, it achieved results far beyond the expectations of even the most optimistic New Yorkers. The moral of the story: if you improve the processes and change the culture, you *will* get better results.

As our management-consulting group has conducted its research into state government, visiting with and advising both leaders and workers in results-driven state agencies across America, we have seen amazing pockets of performance improvement. But we have seldom witnessed the sort of fundamental process redesign it takes to achieve lasting and permanent improvement. However, three states we came to know quite well — Maryland, Oregon, and Washington — have made impressive efforts. They created a model other states could adapt to achieve the broad-based improvement our country needs in order to restore its ranking on the world stage.

All three states have, to some extent, rethought and redesigned their overall management systems. Oregon has deployed our Now Management System across all agencies, Washington has begun to grow a similar system, and Maryland's long-running StateStat has produced truly impressive results (more on all three in Chapter Five).

These states have joined the ranks of the results revolutionaries who are working hard to deliver better services. Doing that requires a tight focus on people: both the employees who deliver services and the customers who receive them.

Putting People Front and Center

In the early 1980s, some American businesspeople began to take the threat from Japanese competitors seriously. One company in particular, Portland, Oregon-based Omark Industries, sent representatives to Japan long before that country's Quality Revolution (now known as Lean/Six Sigma) became front-page news.

In 1980, Omark Chief Operating Officer Jack Warne joined one of the first fact-gathering missions organized by Norman Bodek to help US business leaders explore what was happening in their upstart rivals overseas. Later, Bodek would publish for American businesses nearly 100 books by Japanese business leaders. Omark's Jack Warne employed 4,400 people in 20 plants around the world, and had always championed excellent quality. A well-managed and highly respected firm, Omark produced chains for chain saws, gun sports products, heavy equipment for logging, and other industrial and consumer products. When Warne returned from his tour overseas, he organized a seven-person in-house group called the "Japanese Management Systems Study Team." As a member of that team, I ended up touring many Japanese companies as well as some of the most forward-thinking firms in the United States.

As we studied these companies' best practices, three themes emerged:

- The management system actively engaged frontline workers in improvement initiatives

- Everyone concentrated on eliminating waste
- Quality was built-in, not inspected-out

Bringing those principles back to Omark produced across-the-board improvement in key results. In 1983, the success of our early initiatives landed Omark on the cover of *INC. Magazine*, which declared Omark (today known as Blount International) as one of two leading implementers of what would eventually evolve into Lean. The other company was Hewlett-Packard.

As with any rather complex subject like the design of management systems, it took many years for me to appreciate the deeper roots of what we had witnessed in Japan and later in our own company. On the surface, we could see the tangible results of applying the Japanese approach to process improvement, but the depth of the successes grew out of something deeper, a strong foundation of beliefs about people. Processes alone don't get results; people do.

What we learned in those early years delivered impressive results, but over time I came to understand the true depth of what the Japanese had accomplished. The best Japanese companies were not just striving for quality; they were applying process concepts to the work of management itself. This involved a set of beliefs about the roles of the two primary players who drive an organization's success: customers and employees. In a nutshell:

- *Customers* Define Value
- *Employees* Create Value

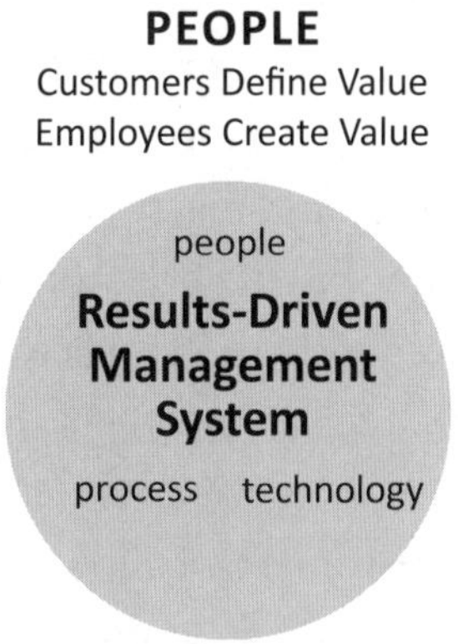

PEOPLE
Customers Define Value
Employees Create Value

people
**Results-Driven
Management
System**
process   technology

FIGURE 4.7: In a results-driven system of management the primary shapers of value are the customers (citizens), who define what they value, and the employees, the people who develop and use their processes and technologies to create that value.

This looks perfectly simple. Customers define value; employees create value. Everyone's happy with the results. But hold on a minute. Simple as it seems on the surface, this view of people residing at the heart of the system completely changes the nature of the system.

As much as leaders may claim that they keep customers at the very center of everything their employees do to get results, that proclamation seldom stands up to rigorous scrutiny. Folks who work in manufacturing at Perfecto Enterprises never see the customer, the accountants never meet the suppliers and distributors they call Accounts Payable and Accounts Receivable, customer service representatives in Bombay barely speak English, and the top executives consider the "Always Right" customer a pain in the posterior.

Customers: can't live with 'em, can't live without 'em.

That was then; this is NOW. The age of mass customization, in which each unique customer knows what she wants and wants it NOW, has replaced the age of mass production, in which customers could only buy a standardized product that conformed to the notion that "one size fits all." In the NOW era, employees will not sit still for a management system that treats them as robots. They are messy, emotional creatures composed of flesh and blood and sweat and tears. No longer content to work as mere hands securing nuts to bolts on a long assembly line, they desire meaningful work and respect and a chance to innovate in ways that will delight customers. Ignore these new realities at your peril.

In the NOW era, customers occupy the center of a web of dynamic relationships formed among all the employees who work in manufacturing, accounting, customer care, and the corner office of the executive suite. Without strong relationships among the people, you can forget about making any management system more efficient and effective.

The basic belief that *Customers define value* leads to an emphasis on continual improvement and a never-ending commitment to listening to and learning from customers each and every day. The basic belief that *Employees create value* causes every individual and team in an organization to view those who receive the product of their labor in the organization as *their* customers. That means that they, too, listen and learn all the time. Listening makes the organizational heart beat faster; a passion for continuous improvement inflames the organizational mind with innovative ideas. Whatever an organization does that fails to respect the customer (in the broadest sense of the term) is *waste*, pure and simple. The same should apply to government at all levels.

As we discussed in Chapter One, public servants come to their work with a built-in desire to serve others. When government leaders and managers respect that fact and encourage decision making and process improvement and innovation at the lowest levels, they can unleash their people's pent-up, heartfelt passion to serve their customers more efficiently and effectively, in big ways and in one micro innovation after another.

This simple yet powerful shift in beliefs stimulates a new way of thinking about management. Managers in the previous era thought about people in a paternalistic way and treated them like children who required constant prodding, supervision, and discipline. New era thinking, which puts people at the center of the drive for better results, insists that managers pay workers and customers the respect they deserve. It encourages managers to view people as responsible and trustworthy adults capable of making good decisions.

I started the shift to the new way of thinking back in the early 1990s, when I began to fully comprehend the Japanese model. As an executive running a supercomputer manufacturing plant, I had been working hard to apply what I had learned on my fact-finding journeys around the world. I found process improvement quite easy to implement. If we adopted a structured, fact-based problem-solving approach to our work, we would automatically push the performance needle forward. But I soon ran into the stark reality that process improvement to the routine work processes only scratched the surface of organizational performance. To push the needle all the way forward and to keep it there, we needed to grasp something more fundamental about the Japanese experience.

We had chalked up a lot of their success to hard work and cultural differences, but as I gradually came to see, they had built their success on a radically different management engine that not only emphasized the value a company created for customers; it treated people in ways that fully tapped their inherent talents and desire to solve problems.

Those who manage and work in government can learn a lot about improving results by incorporating the new era beliefs into their thinking about management. The old post-World War II top-down, military-style paternalistic approach may have built the great American middle class, but it no longer works in business, or in the state capital.

Interestingly, government leaders may find it easier to make the shift than American businesspeople did. For one thing, they can shorten the learning curve by studying what has worked and not worked in business. For another, they already enjoy a workforce motivated to serve the customer, people who would leap at the opportunity to perform the public service that drew them to their jobs in the first place. After nearly five years of working side-by-side with many public servants, how they feel about their work is quite clear:

> **We Care** – *We came to work in government because we wanted to make a difference but found ourselves struggling with a system that totally resists change. Unless it changes dramatically, we cannot possibly help create the best possible place for everyone to live, work, play, and raise a family.*

> **Our Work Matters** – *The work we do matters to us and to the people we serve. The product of our labor significantly affects the quality of life in our state. If only we could focus more fully on delivering the best possible programs, services, and products.*

> **We Respect People** – *Everywhere we look in government agencies, we see talented, gifted, passionate, and experienced people. Sadly, our approach to managing them stifles rather than releases their talent. We long for an environment that honors innovation and stimulates creativity.*

We Must Do Better – *We hate the fact that as a nation we have lost our dominant position in the world and are falling further and further behind in areas that really count, such as education and economic prosperity. We want to regain our pride.*

We Feel a Moral Imperative to Do the Right Thing – *We must do the best we can with the limited resources at our disposal. We must earn and keep the trust of those we serve by never wasting those resources.*

We Believe in the American Way – *We love our country and all that it stands for. We honor diversity and believe in the power of the people to uphold our sacred freedom. We have always served as a model for people around the world who desire happier, more affluent, and more secure lives. We want to regain the world's respect.*

This list comes from six years of working side-by-side with many people in state government and was reinforced through the people interviewed for this book.

One word leaps out of this list: CHANGE. But change will not come about until we find a better way to manage for results. Alan Mulally found a way. When he took over as CEO of Ford Motor Company in 2006, he noted that virtually all measures of performance reviewed by the executive leadership team during weekly business reviews appeared in one of three colors: green (for on track, in good shape), yellow (for a warning about problems), and red (serious problems, major shortfalls) (Hoffman, 2012).

How then, wondered Mulally, could a company with so much green on its scorecards be hemorrhaging a river of red ink? In 2006, Ford posted a whopping $12.7 billion loss (Hoffman,

2012). Mulally challenged his team to explain this disconnect from reality. "Just tell me about the real problems," he told them.

He made it clear that no one would receive a reprimand for telling the truth. That opened the floodgates. In the weeks that followed, Ford's executives, no longer living in a state of fear, began reporting a lot of measures in red. The team immediately went to work on those problems. Mulally's dedication to transparency and candor, which played no small role in Ford's subsequent turnaround, earned him recognition as one of the most capable CEOs in the world.

Dr. Peter Drucker would have applauded Mulally's approach to management. Drucker, often called the father of modern management, proposed that good managers know the value of:

- Making people's strengths effective and their weaknesses irrelevant.
- Enhancing people's ability to contribute.
- Integrating people in a common venture by thinking through, setting, and exemplifying the organizational objectives, values, and goals.
- Enabling the enterprise and its members to grow and develop through training, development, and teaching.
- Ensuring that people know what they need to accomplish, what they can expect from management, and what management expects from them.

Applying this definition and Deming's advice, we might construct this purpose statement for results-driven management in government:

PURPOSE STATEMENT: *Results-Driven Management System*

TO: *Prioritize, connect, enable, and drive the execution of all work*

IN A WAY THAT: *Ensures every resource drives toward the goals and every public servant receives the maximum authority to act*

SO THAT: *Government can enable society to achieve the goals most important to its citizens*

Note the emphasis on *people* doing the work more effectively and efficiently. To fulfill that purpose, they will need the best possible processes for doing their work.

Seeing the Organization as a Set of Processes

For a results-driven management system to work, it must adopt processes that create order, align efforts, define lines of authority, and clarify expected behaviors.

The four management processes of a results-driven system are:

- Improve fundamentals *(remove the waste from the routine work of the organization)*
- Achieve breakthroughs (effectively plan and execute the initiatives of the organization)
- Monitor performance *(build a healthy culture of accountability and transparency)*
- Solve problems *(remove the constraints that block results)*

Let's look at each of these processes more closely.

Improve Fundamentals

Before you can embark on any improvement program, you must define the routine work the organization does, pinpoint who owns each piece of the work, and put in place performance measures that show whether or not the results meet the customer's definition of value. This allows you to determine any gaps between what you deliver and what the customer expects.

Rather than viewing the organization as a set of departments, think of it as a collection of interconnected work processes. This *process orientation* draws your attention to the sort of overall improvement initiatives that go far beyond the *random acts of improvement* we discussed earlier.

Most organizations rely on strategic planning to help them set their short- and long-term goals. Before planning any new initiatives, leaders of results-driven organizations connect every employee to the organization's goals with process measures that mark progress toward the goals. This helps everyone get on board with the campaign for continuous improvement. There's *always* room for improvement. Since most every organization, in our experience, devotes 85 to 90 percent of its resources to doing the normal, day-to-day work, that's where you'll find the greatest opportunities to reduce waste and better satisfy your customers.

It all starts with writing a management process purpose statement:

MANAGEMENT PROCESS PURPOSE STATEMENT: *Improving Fundamentals*

TO: *Get the routine work done well and on time*

IN A WAY THAT: *Connects every employee to the goals and enables the people who do the work to continuously reduce waste*

SO THAT: *The results exceed customer expectations with the deployment of as few resources as possible*

Achieve Breakthroughs

Change initiatives usually emerge from an organization's strategic planning efforts, which aim to improve progress toward an organization's goals through the most efficient allocation of resources. Success hinges on selecting the right targets, coming up with sound plans for hitting them, and managing execution in a thoughtful and disciplined way.

Once you have selected the right initiatives, you must take great pains in planning their execution. Results-driven organizations develop detailed plans with the input of the people who must execute the projects. Experienced project managers know that success depends not only on solid planning, but also on remaining flexible when you need to adapt your plan to changing circumstances. No matter how carefully a coach crafts a game plan, he knows from experience that it must accommodate what actually happens on the field.

In our experience, 50 percent of initiatives undertaken by old era organizations fail. Their Information Technology projects usually take twice as long and cost three times as much as planned. So you can see why you must use new era, results-driven planning. Otherwise, you will more likely break *down* before you break *through* on your road to improved performance.

Consider the purpose of achieving breakthroughs:

MANAGEMENT PROCESS PURPOSE STATEMENT: *Achieving Breakthroughs*

TO: *Plan and manage initiatives*

IN A WAY THAT: *Leverages best practice planning and project-management disciplines*

SO THAT: *The organization achieves desired results with minimal resources*

Monitor Performance

What gets measured gets done. Old era managers liked to measure performance, but they did it in a controlling fashion, collecting data and keeping it to themselves, then dishing it out in dribs and drabs or in individual performance appraisals. New era managers make sure everyone involved in implementing initiatives sees and shares all relevant data. That's what transparency means: nothing hidden, everything out in the open. Smart coaches know that you can't win the game unless everyone knows the score. Can you see our target? Where do we stand with respect to hitting the bull's eye? What must we do to strike it dead center? With simple scorecards like the red, yellow, and green ones Ford used, everyone involved with the initiative can see at a glance the degree to which they are improving fundamentals and achieving breakthroughs.

The word "count" appears in the middle of the word "accountability." You can't expect players to take accountability for winning the game unless you make sure they know how their particular position fits into the whole team effort. They also need to look at the scoreboard from time to time as the game progresses. Once every team and every individual knows the part they play in the success of the organization, then they can more easily monitor what *is* and *isn't* working. You can conduct periodical appraisals of progress during formal Quarterly Target Reviews (QTRs), but you must also make them a daily part of everyone's job with Scorecards: "We're seven points behind where we need to be this morning. We've got to bump up the needle today."

Performance shortfalls will always occur no matter how well you have crafted and executed the plan. The real world is as messy and unpredictable as the people who live in it. Results-driven organizations accept that fact and add worst-case scenarios to their best-case planning. That way, when something bad happens people will not freeze in fear or run for cover. Instead, they'll ask themselves, "What more can I do to overcome this setback?"

In a truly accountable organization, people don't get slapped on the wrist for mistakes; they reap the rewards of figuring out ways to move past those mistakes.

That leads to the next purpose statement:

MANAGEMENT PROCESS PURPOSE STATEMENT: *Monitoring Performance*

TO: *Routinely review progress toward targets*

IN A WAY THAT: *Reinforces positive accountability and transparency*

SO THAT: *People see shortfalls immediately and take swift corrective action*

Solve Problems

Even the best-run organization can occasionally fall short of expectations in both fundamentals and breakthroughs, but results-driven organizations get back on track quickly because they have engaged *every* employee in improvement. Improvement is Job One, especially when it comes to the fundamentals.

When problems pop up, problem solvers get cracking. Structured, customer-centric, fact-based problem solving should pre-occupy every public servant in the quest to get results and eliminate waste. That's no small commitment, given the thousands, tens of thousands, hundreds of thousands, even millions of problems, both large and small, that agencies need to fix. Every employee must develop his or her problem-solving skills by becoming adept at gathering and analyzing data, mapping processes, drawing accurate cause-and-effect diagrams, and ultimately finding and eliminating the root causes once and for all.

In a mature, results-driven organization, employees routinely make improvements both as individuals and in teams *without* the involvement of their supervisors. They can do that because management has helped them build the necessary problem-solving skills and take the initiative to apply them to fulfilling their customer's needs. They listen carefully to customer feedback, test out any new ideas with the customer, and never assume, "*We* know what's good for you." This way, the customer becomes an ally in the work of waste elimination.

The final purpose statement:

MANAGEMENT PROCESS PURPOSE STATEMENT: *Solving Problems*

TO: *Engage each employee in improving the way she or he does the work*

IN A WAY THAT: *Stresses the need to take initiative at the lowest level*

SO THAT: *The agency can remove all obstacles to achieving desired results*

A results-driven set of management processes creates a whole new organizational culture. Think of an organization's culture as "the way we do things around here." Those "things" include all the unspoken rules about the organization's people, processes, and technologies. They dictate behavior; behavior shapes culture. Old era managers thought they could alter culture by training people in new behaviors and enforcing the new ways. New era managers know that the right behaviors come about when the system of management provides a healthy environment in which people naturally develop the right behaviors.

Change the system and you change the culture.

Ford CEO Alan Mulally understood this. By altering people's belief in the purpose of the company's weekly reviews from status reports to problem-solving agendas, he changed his executives' thinking and thus their behavior. Then, they took action to get the company driving toward much better performance.

Dr. Deming popularized a four-step management method, originally developed by Walter A. Shewart, known as Plan-Do-Check-Act, or sometimes Plan-Do-Check-Adjust (PDCA). A results-driven system uses some variation of this method:

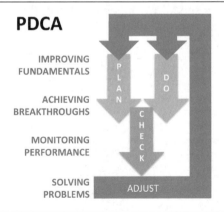

FIGURE 4.8: This is an adaptation of the PDCA cycle, plan/do/check/adjust (or act), which was invented by Walter A. Shewart and popularized by Dr. W. Edwards Deming.

PLAN – Defines the objectives, translates those objectives into measurable results, and then defines what the processes and initiatives must deliver in order to achieve the desired results.

DO – Gets the processes working and gathers data for the check and adjust steps.

CHECK – Compares the actual results to the targeted results. Determines any deviation from the plan in order to identify obstacles and redefine them as opportunities for improvement.

ADJUST – Drills down to the root cause of any deviation from the plan, then strives to eliminate the root cause as quickly as possible (balancedscorecard.org, 2014).

Lessons learned from one PDCA cycle fuel the next cycle. Progress never sleeps. An effective management system aligns all activities, all people, and all resources with the desired results. It then moves the work forward, monitoring and making adjustments to increase the likelihood of success.

Assembling that with the pieces discussed and defined in this chapter, we can see all of the elements of a results-driven management system:

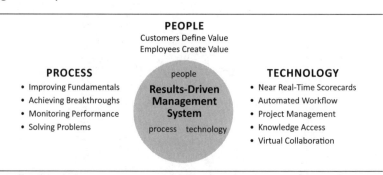

FIGURE 4.9: A systems view of results-driven management includes all of the elements that have to work together to transform the needs of citizens into programs, products, and services to meet those needs.

We'll look at the critical role technology plays in a results-driven management system in Chapter 10.

With a comprehensive, results-driven system of management in place, the organization, be it a Mom and Pop convenience store or the Department of Human Services, can set about dramatically improving performance and delivering results that delight the customer.

CHAPTER FIVE

The Fundamentals

Connecting the Work to the Result

"We cannot solve our problems with the same
level of thinking that created them."

~ ALBERT EINSTEIN

An order from the US Environmental Protection Agency put the Chesapeake Bay on a strict pollution diet. It established the Chesapeake Bay "total maximum daily load" for nitrogen, phosphorous, and sediment across Maryland and several other states. The largest inland estuary in the US, the Chesapeake includes more than 150 rivers and streams, with a drainage area spanning 64,299 square miles (USGS, 1998).

Maryland governor Martin O'Malley took the order seriously. Under his leadership, the state had developed the StateStat management system, which implemented the concepts behind New York City's CompStat crime fighting system and leaned heavily on his own experience implementing CitiStat in Baltimore, Maryland. To fulfill the Chesapeake Bay restoration order, Maryland relied on these precedents to devise BayStat. During

O'Malley's term in office, BayStat (2014) achieved remarkable results:

- Expanded the number of certified cover crops planted annually in the watershed from 52,305 to 410,530, a 685 percent increase
- Installed storm water retrofits that increased the removal of nitrogen from 42,391 to 198,527 pounds, a 371 percent increase
- Boosted the number of natural filters on private land from 69,973 to 108,012, a 54 percent increase
- Removed substantially more nutrients by raising the number of retrofitted wastewater treatment plants from 2 to 26, a 1,200 percent increase

These numbers symbolize Maryland's commitment to results-oriented government. That commitment to connecting the work of government to results demands tremendous drive, creativity, collaboration, and a relentless commitment to action.

O'Malley set a sweeping agenda of improvement in all areas of state government by setting 16 strategic goals for the state overall and countless less critical ones for every single agency.

The Maryland website's home page describes StateStat as "The O'Malley-Brown Administration's performance measurement and management tool. StateStat is how the administration manages our state."

All of this came in the wake of Governor O'Malley's experience setting up and running CitiStat when he served as mayor of Baltimore. That training ground gave him the skills, knowledge, and confidence to apply the same methodology to the state and all of its agencies when he rose to the governorship.

His 16 goals and their associated SMART Goals (Specific,

Measurable, Actionable, Realistic, and Time-Bound) create the context for monthly general and agency meetings, each focused on a specific goal.

No other state can match the system's results:

Maryland's SMART Goals

	GOAL AREA	SMART GOAL	STATUS
		OPPORTUNITY	
1	Jobs	Recover 100% of jobs lost due to the Great Recession by the end of FY 14.	100% Recovered
2	Education	Improve Student Achievement and school, college, and career readiness by 25% by the end of 2015.	34.8% improvement since 2006
3	Skills	Increase the number of Marylanders who receive skills training by 20% by the end of 2018.	15.3% increase since 2009
4	Veterans	Full employment for Maryland veterans by the end of 2015.	5.9% Veteran Unemployment Rate *(Declared Insufficient Progress)*
		SECURITY	
5	Violent Crime	Reduce violent crime in Maryland by 20% by the end of 2018.	26.3% decrease since 2006
6	Violence Against Women and Children	Reduce violent crimes against women and children by 25% by the end of 2018.	23% decrease since 2006
7	Homeland Security	Delivering and maintaining Maryland's 12 core goals for homeland security preparedness by 2016.	On Track in all 12 core goals
		SUSTAINABILITY	
8	Bay Restoration	Reaching the healthier tipping point by 2025.	On Track to reach tipping point by 2025
9	Transit Ridership	Double transit ridership in Maryland by the end of 2020.	14.3% Increase since 2006 *(Declared Insufficient Progress)*
10	Energy Efficiency	Reduce both per capita peak demand and per capita electricity consumption in Maryland by 15% by 2015.	14.6% decrease in peak demand since 2007
11	Renewable Energy	Increase Maryland's in-state renewable energy generation to 20% by 2022.	8.2% increase in renewable energy since 2007
12	Greenhouse Gases	Reduce Maryland's greenhouse gas emissions by 25% by 2020.	8% decrease in greenhouse gas emissions since 2006 *(Declared Insufficient Progress)*

Chart Continues ⟫

HEALTH			
13	Childhood Hunger	End childhood hunger in Maryland by 2015.	Progressing toward 2015 goal
14	Infant Mortality	Reduce infant mortality in Maryland by 10% by 2017.	21.3% decrease in infant mortality since 2007
15	Substance Abuse	Reduce overdose deaths by 20% by the end of 2015.	*New Focus*
16	Preventable Hospitalizations	Reduce preventable hospitalization by 10% by the end of 2015.	11.9% decrease since 2011

FIGURE 5.1: Maryland's results demonstrate the power of a strong focus on measurable results. Source: Maryland StateStat Office

As Matt Power, Director of Maryland's StateStat effort, said, "In state government it is hard to feel like one thing is connected to another without these overarching goals. The goals let everyone know they're in the same fight together and it keeps everyone's eyes on the same prize. This lets everyone be part of the same solution, something that hasn't happened before and doesn't happen without the collective consciousness of results-oriented government."

It did not happen overnight, Power said: "We brought in the agencies on a sort of sliding scale."

Power assigned a StateStat analyst to each agency's Leadership Team to help them develop their own measures: "We ask very basic questions. 'What do you do? How do you know you are successful? How do you hold your people accountable? How do you know that you are accomplishing your mission?'"

It takes time for people to work through these issues and to make sure that the work of the agency relates directly to the results citizens expect from their government. At times, this means starting almost from scratch. Power had six analysts and each one was assigned to several agencies and goal-related Stats. The analysts helped agency leadership create measures to get at the public policy the agency was created to address. The process takes time.

"A lot of times we don't really have the right metric to begin with," explained Power.

Experience taught him to allow for as much iteration as it might take to find just the right measure to gauge the desired result: "Sometimes we ask them to collect new data, and there is always a push-pull there. You have to make sure the data collected is worth the effort when looking at outcomes."

As businesspeople well know, you must always keep the customer in mind, making sure you look at your work from the customer's point of view and not just your own. Power does that all the time. He said: "As a citizen, if you want the keys to government, then tell me, what do you want to do? How will you measure it? How much do you want to improve it? And, please, would you tell me whether you are succeeding or failing?"

This helps ensure transparency. Citizens want the truth, the whole truth, and nothing but the truth. They will not sit still for hollow promises, hidden agendas, falsified data, cover-ups, and excuses for bad performance.

"We tell our citizens what percent of a goal has to be met by a deadline," Power explained. "And then we actually can see in real-time whether we are succeeding or failing."

That, believes Power, provides the true litmus test of results-driven government. A results-driven management system respects the need to connect every employee in a meaningful way to the work of the state and to the priorities of the governor, the state's chief executive. A good management system includes four management processes. The first of these, The Fundamentals, establishes the performance framework for the organization.

MANAGEMENT PROCESS PURPOSE STATEMENT: *Improving Fundamentals*

TO: *Get the routine work done well and on time*

IN A WAY THAT: *Connects every employee to the goals and enables the people who do the work to reduce waste continuously*

SO THAT: *The results exceed customer expectations with as few resources as possible*

Getting the Fundamentals Right: Michigan

In a fall meeting with one of his department directors in 2011, Michigan Governor Rick Snyder (R) drew a diagram that illustrated how the tyranny of the urgent can draw a leader's attention toward short-term, internally driven needs. This reactive approach to management, so prevalent in government, makes it almost impossible to sit back and ponder crucial long-term issues. So the fundamental shift is to learn to move energy, time, and resources from the urgent to the important.

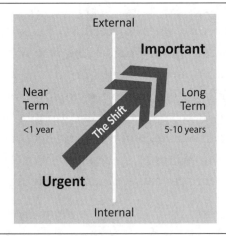

FIGURE 5.2: The challenge leaders face is to make the shift in time and resources from the urgent to the important. Without this shift in thinking, the urgent will consume all resources and building for the long term will be impossible.

Down at the worm's eye level, you can only see the dangers that keep popping up to threaten you, and you are unaware of the robin about to pounce. Obviously, you would stand a much better chance of survival if you could see your situation from a satellite's eye view, where you can detect danger before it strikes. In an ideal world, you maintain both perspectives.

Governor Snyder not only believes in striking a balance between the short- and long-term views as a critical management principle in his administration, but he also demonstrates a knack for it in his personal life.

His long-time colleague, friend and advisor Richard Baird, who is the Governor's right-hand aide, describes how Snyder developed a clear life-plan early in life. He would spend the first third of his career working in the business world, securing his financial position; the second third he would devote to public service; and the final third would find him teaching.

"In my entire career," said Baird, "I have never met anyone who has mapped out their life like Rick has. Most people are trying to figure out what they're going to be doing this weekend."

Snyder laid the groundwork for his life-plan by earning an MBA and a law degree by age 23. He then went on to gain credentials as a Certified Public Accountant. After putting all that education to work for 11 years at the firm that became PricewaterhouseCoopers, he joined Gateway computers, where he rose to the position of CEO and Board Chair. He later founded and co-founded several venture capital and investment companies before winning election as the Governor of Michigan in 2010. Having accomplished the first third of his mission in life, he launched into the second.

The transition into public service, beginning with a solid campaign strategy that won him the Governor's Office, proved fairly easy. He kept his focus on one simple principle: promise what you will do, then do it. His number one promise, reinventing state government, may have seemed far-fetched to some observers, but Snyder meant it with all his heart.

"We will," he promised, "implement billions in structural reforms, bring innovation to government and deliver a new level of transparency and accountability in Michigan."

All those years spent in the technical trenches of the rough-and-tumble business world had prepared him for the task. He became, as he likes to put it, "One Tough Nerd," who feels as comfortable reading and understanding Michigan's sometimes-convoluted statutes as he does wrestling with the details of the state budget. One of his first steps was to install the right measurements.

Set up the Right Dashboards

Immediately after his inauguration as Michigan's 48th governor, Snyder took his tie off (a sartorial embellishment he had only worn seven times in his life) and began constructing an accountability structure for his administration. This included the state's first set of scorecards, known as the Michigan Dashboard, which became a fixture in eight critical areas: education, health and wellness, infrastructure, talent, public safety, energy and environment, financial health, and seniors. The dashboards apply to key state departments guided by group executives. Each group executive takes leadership accountability in a particular area, and reports quarterly results with a target-specific dashboard.

Claire Allard, Director of the Governor's Office of Good Government, talked about the value of this business-like approach to connecting government's work to desired results: "The governor believes in what he calls 'Relentless Positive Action.' You have to move forward. He talks about and follows a cycle he calls vision/engage/adjust/attack; he believes you can't plan forever, you have to keep moving forward."

Michigan's Dashboard

Michigan	Economic Strength Health & Education Value for Money Government Quality of Life Public Safety
Education	Student Outcomes School Accountability Culture of Learning Value for Money Post-Secondary Education
Health & Wellness	Access to Health Care Health Indicators Healthy Communities Healthy Behaviors
Infrastructure	Economic Growth Safety Accountability Mobility Conditions
Talent	Attraction & Retention Employment Environment Innovation Global Connections
Public Safety	Crime Statistics Crime Prevention Law Enforcement & Criminal Justice Corrections
Energy & Environment	Energy Parks & Recreation Land & Air Water
Financial Health	State Governments Local Governments School Districts Aggregated Government
Seniors	Health & Well-Being Independence for Older Adults Reinventing Retirement Safety & Security

FIGURE 5.3: Michigan's Dashboard is a comprehensive view of nine critical policy areas each with its own complement of measures.
Source: State of Michigan

The scorecards track that progress. While people now see the value of this tool and rely on it to show them where they stand with respect to hitting their targets, they did not come to that appreciation right off the bat. It took time to get comfortable with the approach.

"At first, people were putting up output measures," Allard said.

In other words, they were measuring how many things were getting processed, not what really mattered: progress toward the results citizens expect from state government.

"The governor wants to know where the department leaders need help, where they are encountering challenges, where they

Infrastructure Dashboard

Economic Growth			
	Prior	Current	Progress
Commercial vehicle traffic in billions of miles	5.74 (2011)	5.81 (2012)	👍
Rail freight traffic in millions of tons	60.4 (2010)	58.6 (2011)	👎
Percentage of households with broadband	n/a	67% (2010)	n/a
Percentage of US trucking trade traffic through Michigan international borders	45.3% (2012)	43.1% (2013)	👎

Safety			
	Prior	Current	Progress
Individuals fatally or seriously injured in traffic accidents	6,612 (2012)	6234 (2013)	👍
Work zone injuries and fatalities	72 (2012)	117 (2013)	👎
Monitored beaches with no closures or unsafe advisories	76% (FY 2012)	80% (FY 2013)	👍

Accountability			
	Prior	Current	Progress
Percentage of road construction projects completed:			
- Percentage on time or ahead of schedule	99.6% (2010)	99.7% (2011)	👍
- Percentage within 5% of budget or less	77.8% (2010)	85% (2011)	👍

Chart Continues ⏩

are being successful," explained Allard, who loves her boss's approach to doing the work of government. "The measures are intended to tell a story instead of measuring just to measure. It's all about results."

Each dashboard encompasses a specific area of accountability and a specific set of measures for that area. For example, the Infrastructure Dashboard includes economic growth, safety, accountability, mobility, and conditions and measures for each category. Note how it compares current data to previous data, with a visual thumbs-up or thumbs-down to show the direction in which the measure is moving. Anyone can access this data and download it into a spreadsheet.

Mobility			
	Prior	Current	Progress
Percentage of traffic incidents cleared in less than 2 hours	88.8% (Jan 2013)	89.7% (Jan 2014)	👍
Passenger air service in and out of Michigan in millions of passengers	36.8 (2012)	37.1 (2013)	👍
Percentage change in passenger rail ridership	-1.8% (FY 2012)	2.2% (FY 2013)	👍
Percentage change in bus ridership	-1.5% (2012)	-2.1% (2013)	👎

Conditions			
	Prior	Current	Progress
Percentage of structurally deficient bridges	12.31% (2012)	11.78% (2013)	👍
Percentage of roads in good or fair condition in the paved federal aid system	66.4% (2012)	66.6% (2013)	👍
Number of dam failures	3 (2012)	4 (2013)	👎
Raw sewage discharge in billions of gallons	8 (2011)	1.21 (2012)	👍

FIGURE 5.4: Michigan's focus on measurable results demonstrates the power of a results focus. Source: State of Michigan

Because Michigan's 20 main departments include other functional areas, the system expanded to cover 661 functional departments, agencies, bureaus, units, etc. that display a grand total of some 3,761 measures.

The scorecards focus the Reinventing Michigan (State of Michigan, 2014) efforts and are used to drive accountability, transparency, and results. A special widely distributed pocket card communicates the governor's 10-point plan:

1. Create more and better jobs
2. Leverage our new tax system
3. Reinvent government
4. Keep our youth — our future — here
5. Restore our cities
6. Enhance our national and international image
7. Protect our environment
8. Revitalize our education system
9. Reinvent our health care system
10. Winning in Michigan through Relentless Positive Action

The back of the card summarizes Governor Snyder's desired Team Culture:

LEADERSHIP
- Enthusiasm – "Can do" and "will do" attitude
- Courage – Expressing viewpoints constructively
- Duty – Commitment to Michigan in word and deed
- Focus – Addressing and solving critical issues

EXCELLENCE
- Vision – Believing in our vision, goals and culture
- Integrity – Always do the right thing
- Measures – Results through measures that matter

- Accountability – Acting decisively, delivering on commitments

TEAMWORK
- Results – Valuing team results and sharing credit
- Collaboration – Respecting and engaging colleagues
- Loyalty – Supporting decisions and those who make them
- Camaraderie – Having fun together, reinventing our State

Put this all together, and you get a good idea of Rick Snyder's definition of good government.

Define Good Government

Claire Allard brings high energy and devoted passion to her job as Director of Michigan's Office of Good Government. Prior to accepting that appointment, she served on the staff of the Michigan Legislature.

As a first step in her role with the governor, she undertook the task of defining exactly what "Good Government" means. The initial definition combined performance management, service/process optimization (continuous improvement), employee engagement, and change management.

FIGURE 5.5: Michigan's Good Government efforts contain four core elements: performance management, service/process optimization, employee engagement, and change management.
Source: State of Michigan Office of the Governor

Realizing the importance of the two pillars of people and process, Allard recruited the right people for her Good Government team. The team began its work by posing some questions no one had really asked before:

- Who is our customer? Who are we trying to serve?
- What are we trying to do for them?
- What results must we achieve?
- How can government provide a positive and seamless experience for our customers?

In the spring following the governor's election, each department appointed a "good government champion" to serve as the primary liaison between the department and the Good Government project. These champions have contributed greatly to the transformation effort, spreading Lean training in their departments, conducting the employee engagement survey, and applying change management methods. Most importantly, their work has done a lot to shift the way public servants in Michigan view their jobs.

That represented a big turnaround. "There was a very negative connotation around being state employees," Allard explained. "Our people felt beat up."

Governor Snyder knew that customer service would not improve without "lifting employees up" to a higher level of pride in their work.

He and Lt. Governor Calley put into practice the use of "recognition coins," a simple device commonly used in the military. The minted coins reward government workers for general excellence, leadership, and teamwork.

Allard found them quite valuable as motivational tools: "It used to be you came to work and you do your job, then you go home," she said. "We want it to be that you come to work and do your job, and you make it better. And I think that is starting to catch on."

This and other tools got Michigan off on the right foot.

Launching Results Washington

Washington's incoming Governor Jay Inslee admired Maryland Governor O'Malley's efforts to connect the work of the state to results. But when he recruited Dr. Mary Alice Heuschel to serve on his transition team, she was prepared for the task of launching what came to be known as Results Washington.

Inslee knew that Dr. Heuschel had won national recognition for excellent leadership as a school district superintendent. That reputation stemmed from her work in a 15,000-student district in a Seattle suburb, where she used data and built collaborative teamwork with impressive results (Rosenthal, 2012). She effectively instilled a sense of urgency to make decisions and drive change.

On the very first weekend of his new administration, Inslee, his wife Trudi, Dr. Heuschel, and the newly named executive team went to work on a bold new agenda for the state's government.

"We did a full-day retreat to try and identify and communicate the governor's priorities," recalls Heuschel. "I was hired to take a strategic approach to the governor's priorities, to develop the right system to measure and communicate progress, and to ensure we hired the right people to do this work."

I met Dr. Heuschel when I served on Governor Inslee's Government Performance and Regulatory Processes Transition Advisory Group, which was aware of our company's work with the state of Oregon. They invited me and Mass Ingenuity President and CEO Aaron Howard to help formulate and draft the group's final recommendations to the new governor.

In the advisory group's recommendations to Governor Inslee, we acknowledged the strong Lean foundation of initiatives undertaken by previous Governor Christine Gregoire (D). During the previous year, the state's agencies had completed some 100 Lean projects that launched from an executive order from Governor Gregoire. The annual Washington State Lean Conference, convened in Tacoma every October, was attracting nearly 2,700 attendees interested in the subject and the approach to the work (State of Washington, 2013).

Heuschel believes strongly in an inclusive approach to achieving improvement goals. To build ownership in the process, every member of the governor's cabinet was required to attend all Results Washington meetings. Their leadership was an essential component to ensuring success, she says: "If they could not attend, they were to contact me and tell me why. This was the work and the meetings needed to be a priority. Setting and supporting this expectation was key."

It took all hands on deck to move the agenda forward, according to Heuschel. "When you look at the original system compared to where Results Washington is now, it's very different because people brought better ideas, developed ownership and contributed their expertise in so many ways. The governor's priorities remained constant, the strategies to achieve the goals were developed by the team."

The project's steering team consisted of: Dr. Heuschel; DRS Director Marcie Frost, who served as lead director for the effort; Results Washington Director Wendy Korthuis-Smith; and Results Washington team members Jessica Dang, KayLyne Newell, Pam Pannkuk, Chris Ramirez, Hollie Jensen, Tammy Firkins, Tristan Wise, and Heidi Loveall. I was also on the team as an external advisor.

While this overview depicts our work as a series of sequential activities, items 1, 2, and 3 in the list that follows sometimes occurred simultaneously:

FIGURE 5.6: Early on its efforts, Washington branded its efforts as Results Washington. Source: State of Washington

- Define a Strategic Framework
- Establish Goal Teams
- Build Goal Maps, including:
  - Outcome Measures and Targets
  - Supporting Measures and Targets
- Schedule Periodic Review Meetings with the Governor to Update Progress

Let's take a closer look at how these steps unfolded.

Define a strategic framework

The governor's executive team established the following (**bold-face** words actually appear in bold in official documents):

VISION:

A **Working Washington** built on education and innovation ... where all Washingtonians thrive.

MISSION:

Foster the spirit of **continuous improvement**

Enhance the conditions for **job creation**

Prepare students for the future

Value our **environment**, our **health** and our **people**

FOUNDATION:

Create a responsive, **innovative** and data-driven culture of continuous improvement

Recognize Washington's rich **natural resources**, diverse **people** and entrepreneurial **drive**, and build upon our legacy

Operate state government with the expectation that success is dependent on the success of **all**

Create effective communication and transparency on **goals, measures,** and **progress** in meeting expectations

Deepen our focus understanding and commit to our citizens: **Know our customers**

During his tenure, Governor Inslee wanted state government to concentrate on five sweeping yet simply articulated GOALS:

1. World Class Education
2. Prosperous Economy
3. Sustainable Energy and a Clean Environment
4. Healthy and Safe Communities
5. Efficient, Effective, and Accountable Government

Each goal consisted of several subgoals. For instance, the subgoals for Goal #3:

GOAL 3: Sustainable Energy and a Clean Environment

SUBGOALS: Healthy Fish and Wildlife

Clean and Restored Environment
Protected Working and Natural Lands

Establish Goal Teams

A number of cross-agency teams would examine each goal and work collaboratively to flesh out Goal Maps. Each team included a secretary or agency director and people from various agencies and departments with some interest and expertise in a particular goal area. Key partners were identified to serve on goal teams. In the case of *World Class Education*, the Office of the Superintendent of Public Instruction, a separately elected position in the state, was invited and served on the goal team. In the case of *Sustainable Energy and a Clean Environment* (Results Washington, 2014), the team included members from:

- Department of Agriculture
- Department of Commerce
- Department of Ecology
- Office of Financial Management
- Department of Fish and Wildlife
- Department of Health
- Department of Natural Resources
- Parks and Recreation Commission
- Pollution Liability Insurance Agency
- Puget Sound Partnership
- State Conservation Commission
- Utilities and Transportation Commission

Build Goal Maps

Once the Goal Teams broke the overall goal into a series of subgoals, they set primary outcome measures and submeasures for gauging improvement.

To help shape their maps, the Goal Teams reached out to their constituents by conducting public meetings and presentations and offering information and soliciting input online. Teams also met with various professional organizations and groups such as the Washington Business Alliance in order to share their work and gather suggestions for improvement.

David Giuliani, co-founder and board chair of the Business Alliance, appreciated the outreach. He said, "We are very pleased that Governor Inslee and his team are taking such a strategic, goal-driven approach. The governor's work is refreshing, winning, and fits well with the business community."

Giuliani built such well-known brands as Sonicare® and Clarisonic® and appeared as a featured speaker at the White House Conference on Corporate Social Responsibility. The Washington Business Alliance has created its own long-term plan for the state called Plan Washington, which we will discuss in Chapter Ten.

Eventually the team refined and finalized its map. For example:

The Results Washington Goal Map for
Sustainable and Clean Energy

GOAL 3: Sustainable Energy and a Clean Environment		
SUSTAINABLE AND CLEAN ENERGY		
Reduce our greenhouse gas emissions		
CLEAN TRANSPORTATION	CLEAN ELECTRICITY	EFFICIENT BUILDINGS & INDUSTRIAL PROCESSES
1.1 Reduce transportation related greenhouse gas emissions from 44.9 mmt/year (projected 2020) to 37.5 mmt/year(1990) by 2020	1.2 Reduce greenhouse gas emissions from electrical energy consumption from 18.4 mmt/year (projected 2020) to 16.9 mmt/year (1990) by 2020	1.3 Improve non-electrical energy efficiency of buildings and industrial processes to reduce greenhouse gas emissions from 21.7 mmt/year (projected 2020) per year to 18.6 mmt/year (1990) by 2020

Chart Continues ⟫

1.1.a. Reduce the average emissions of greenhouse gases for each vehicle mile traveled in Washington by 25% from 1.15 pounds (lbs.) in 2010 to 0.85 pounds (lbs.) by 2020	1.2.a. Increase electric load served by renewable energy from 3% to 9% by 2016 and 15% by 2020	1.3.a. Decrease non-electric fossil fuel consumption associated with residential and commercial end users from the 2010 three year average of 165.9 trillion Btu to 140 trillion Btu in 2020
1.1.b. Increase the average miles traveled per gallon of fuel for Washington's overall passenger and light duty truck fleet (private and public) from 19.2 MPG in 2010 to 23 MPG in 2020	1.2.b. Increase electrical load growth replaced by conservation from 112.5 average megawatts per year to 155 average megawatts per year by 2020	1.3.b. Maintain non-electric fossil fuel consumption associated with industrial buildings and industrial processes at or below the 2010 three year average level of 163.7 trillion Btu
1.1.c. Increase the number of plug-in electric vehicles registered in Washington from approximately 8,000 in		

FIGURE 5.7: Washington breaks its goals down into details and sets targets for improvements in a wide range of categories.
Source: State of Washington

Schedule Periodic Review Meetings with the Governor to Update Progress

Every other month, Goal Teams would schedule two-hour reviews with the governor and his executive team. The meetings focused on challenges and opportunities for advancing the Governor's agenda. The meetings followed specific protocol and presented a balanced overall view, with no single issue dominating or hijacking the discussion.

"It is easy to get caught up in the crisis du jour," said Dr. Heuschel. "The most challenging thing is balancing the day-to-day responsibility with these goals. This was very difficult to do."

Dr. Heuschel invested a lot of time and effort in building a strong team. She launched every session with a quick, engaging team-building exercise in which agency secretaries and directors would engage in sharing something fun regarding a personal preference on the topic. This made the work personal and allowed connections to be made among and between members of the team. She knew that while you need a strong and flexible management system, the system itself does not solve problems; people working with people solve problems. Recruit good people, forge strong working relationships, support and empower individuals and then let your people make the system work.

"In order to make real change, you need a structure people can count on," she explained. "And to build that system into something people can own, you have to keep it a priority. It is clear that successful companies, successful schools, successful school districts, and successful states have a clear framework that keeps everyone focused."

She also believes in balance: "You have to focus on systemic leadership. It's a total focus on the system, not on a single area. No one's goals are more important than another's."

If that's the case, how can you possibly set priorities? Surely some issues outrank others. That requires skillful judgment. At times, she needed to wean someone from a fondness for a pet project or curb someone's enthusiasm for an issue that struck a personal nerve. It took some deft leadership to keep everyone's eyes on many prizes and to get them to accept the fact that some prizes are bigger than others. A good leader knows that you must figure out not only what to do but also what *not* to do.

Ten months into the work, Dr. Heuschel spoke to a small group of business leaders from the Seattle Chamber of Commerce. She found the feedback tremendously gratifying and affirming.

"The feedback I got was that the system design was exceptional," she says. "That meant a lot coming from this particular team of professionals with expertise in this area."

Still, she knows that the jury will remain out until the results come in.

Adopting a Bottom-Up Strategy: Oregon

Michael Jordan, Oregon's first-ever Chief Operating Officer, offers an interesting observation: "Everyone thinks that elected officials are the bosses of government. They are not elected to be boss, but they are elected to imprint the values of the people that elected them onto the priorities for government. The real stewards of government are the people who work as the employees of government."

In other words, you find the true bosses of government at the bottom, not the top, of the organization.

As Oregon's COO, Jordan's job sits at the intersection of policy and the practical world of delivering results, between the Governor's office and all of the people who actually do the daily work of government. Governor John Kitzhaber, who served two consecutive terms between 1995 and 2003, regained the office in 2011. That's when he hired Jordan to take on the task of managing the business of government. Jordan worked collaboratively with the Governor's Chief of Staff, Mike Bonetto, who owned the policy side of state government. Kitzhaber, known for bold policy leadership, most notably in healthcare and education, separated the role of managing the state from the role of designing and driving a policy agenda.

Jordan liked that idea: "The Governor is quite open to and good at listening to the management implications to policy," he said. "I pay attention to how policy he wants to implement will play in the real world. We need the Governor's gravitas focused on the weighty policy issues. On the management side, the Governor plays light, leaving that responsibility to me. But on the occasion that I need him, I *really* need him."

In a sense, Jordan came aboard to apply business principles to government, and in some cases, he needed to overcome government workers' distrust of certain business techniques.

Repair Measurement's Bad Reputation

Jordan's extensive experience with Oregon Benchmarks (discussed in Chapter Three) convinced him that unless the people who do the work create the measures on their scorecards, they won't own them. In the absence of ownership, results simply do not improve. Just as a system itself does not solve problems, measurement alone does not guarantee improvement.

"Performance measurement has a really bad rep in the eyes of people who are being measured in that measuring devices are often used punitively," says Jordan. "Most people are thinking, 'We're going to get the hell kicked out of us' as soon as they hear the words."

It happened in Michigan, when the state was using the standard red, yellow, and green status indicators. People referred to a red condition as "the red scare."

Earlier, we talked about the need to replace people's perception of accountability as a hammer with a more positive view of accountability as a motivator. The same applies to performance measures. Jordan strives to make Oregon's measures inspire rather than frighten people.

"As a leader you have to be very diligent about correcting explicitly those that misuse the measure to embarrass and punish people," he said. "And the biggest challenge is many of these people are politicians."

To change the way people use and react to measures, Jordan makes sure they come from the bottom-up rather than the top-down. If you seed an agency with good practices such as Lean and Six Sigma techniques, people will welcome and even invent ways to gauge progress toward results success. But they don't do it to please themselves; they do it to serve their customers and the citizens of the state.

As Jordan points out, "Over time, citizens' expectation of their government rise driven by many factors, which are mostly represented by the increasing complexity of life. While we get more money over time, it is never enough to do all the things citizens want done."

You can only solve that discrepancy with higher efficiency and greater productivity. If that doesn't happen, citizens will see state government as a hopeless bureaucracy populated by lazy, incompetent workers. Or worse.

"This demands that government become more productive to be seen by citizens as effective," he says with caution in his voice. "If the gap gets too wide, government becomes unstable and things happen. The system is entirely dependent upon confidence of the citizens. If this grows too wide things get crazy. Initiative petitions, recalls, radicals being elected, huge swings — all in an attempt to get it to work."

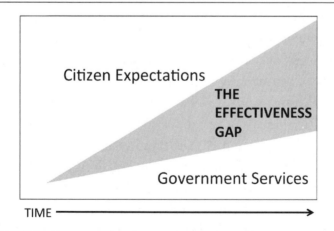

FIGURE 5.8: Government has to pay close attention to the gap between the services it provides and citizen expectations because the wider the gap the less stable the government.

In Chapter Two, you saw how the Oregon Youth Authority implemented The Now Management System, the results-driven solution we at Mass Ingenuity have created to close effectiveness gaps. That project's success inspired a dozen other Oregon agencies to implement the system, which contributed greatly to their ability to deliver demonstrable results. These included:

- Public Employees Retirement System
- Department of Environmental Quality
- Lottery
- Department of Human Services
- Health Authority
- State Hospital
- State Treasury
- Department of Education
- Department of Administrative Services
- Corrections
- Oregon Correctional Enterprises
- Commission for the Blind

Early in his stint as Oregon's COO, Jordan formed an Enterprise Leadership Team (ELT) that brought together the heads of the largest agencies. He charged them with the rather daunting task of tearing down silos that would stall progress toward achieving Governor Kitzhaber's groundbreaking 10-year plan. The ELT facilitated conversations on many levels. The governor's plan has the intention to withstand changes in the executive branch and even party swings in the legislature (read the plan at: www.oregon.gov/COO/Ten/Pages/index.aspx).

As The Now Management System took hold and the transformation toward results-driven government gathered steam in numerous agencies, Jordan and the ELT decided to implement this system across all state agencies. In every case, the transformation began at the agency level with a Fundamentals Map.

Creating a Fundamentals Map

As we saw in the case of Oregon Youth Authority (Chapter Two), each agency must create a comprehensive Fundamentals Map, which uses a common language for describing how the state manages the routine work done within its $30 billion annual budget.

The Maps point the way to better results. You can't get better results if you do not improve the way people do their day-to-day work.

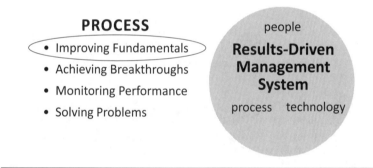

FIGURE 5.9: The first process to focus on in a results-driven management system is improving the fundamentals, the routine work that consumes the vast majority of the state's resources. This is where all the opportunity to eliminate waste resides.

An agency/department Leadership Team and other key stakeholders who must accept accountability for implementing an improvement initiative play key roles in creating the map. The very act of creating a clear and understandable map aligns everyone on the team with the transformation's goals as they answer the essential questions about their work:

- Why do we exist? (Mission)
- What beliefs do we hold? (Values)
- What reputation do we wish to develop? (Vision)
- What do we want to accomplish? (Key Goals)
- How will we recognize success? (Outcome Measures)
- What must we do well in order to accomplish our goals? (Core Processes)
- Can we identify those who benefit from our work? (Customers)
- How do we know that we are meeting customer needs? (Process Measures)
- Who takes accountability for what? (Outcome and Process Measure Owners)

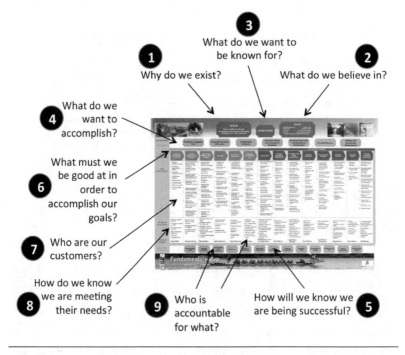

FIGURE 5.10: A Fundamentals Map is a single-page view of the organization's (agency or even the entire state government) routine work. It is a powerful tool not only for understanding the complexity, but also for communicating it to stakeholders.

As the team creates the Fundamentals Map, they systematically pull together many best-practice management methods and tools that will figure into the comprehensive management system. Gradually, people begin to shift their thinking toward a results-driven philosophy by:

- Removing ambiguity around **direction**
- Aligning with meaningful measures of **results** tracked on **scorecards**
- Thinking **process** rather than function
- Defining the organization's **customers**
- Establishing the foundation for **accountability**
- Creating the context for **employee engagement**
- Defining a **common vocabulary** for managing the organization

Outcome and process measures fuel the drive toward better results. Using a series of well-planned and focused workshops on the new approach, the team makes sure that the measures cascade into every nook and cranny of the agency, where they can guide the everyday work that delivers benefits and solutions to the customer. Once people see and engage with the goals, they can then align their daily activities with those goals. Finally, the people who do the work can make the decisions and take the actions that deliver better results.

As the Leadership Team moves through its examination of the agency's processes (the activities people must do well in order to improve the agency's outcome measures and achieve its key goals), they identify two different types of core processes:

- **Operating Processes.** *The routine work the organization must do well in order to meet the needs of the organization's primary customers.*

An organization's operating processes fit its specific mission. For instance, the routine work of an agency that administers retirement plans will differ from that of an agency responsible for protecting the environment. This picture shows the differences between a handful of state agencies:

Typical Core Operating Processes By Agency

Environment	Retirement	Corrections	Lottery
1. Assessing environmental conditions	1. Developing and implementing policies	1. Ensuring safe environments	1. Developing and marketing products
2. Defining pollution control strategies	2. Maintaining member and employer information	2. Assessing offenders	2. Conducting drawings
3. Implementing pollution control strategies	3. Accounting for retirement funds	3. Providing basic needs	3. Processing payments to winners
4. Permitting	4. Promoting retirement readiness	4. Providing opportunities for improvement	4. Warehousing and distribution
5. Determining compliance	5. Paying benefits	5. Managing emergencies	
6. Enforcing environmental law		6. Transitioning offenders into the community	
		7. Managing offenders in the community	

FIGURE 5.11: These typical core operating processes are drawn from maps of various state agencies.

- **Supporting Processes.** *The routine work the organization must do well in order to support the Operating Processes.* These activities enable the smooth operation of the operating processes. They seldom vary much from one organization to the next because every organization must perform certain basic supporting functions. In most cases, they include:

Typical Core Supporting Processes

1. Optimizing organizational performance

2. Developing talent

3. Engaging stakeholders

4. Managing finances

5. Procuring goods and services

6. Leveraging technology

7. Mitigating risks

FIGURE 5.12: Core operating processes from one department to the next are quite similar because the "back office" types of processes are common.

Take special note of the simplicity of the language used to describe both types of Core Processes. Simple language enables understanding by all stakeholders, from state workers in any agency to elected officials and citizens. Government can get mighty complex, but a Fundamentals Map can simplify it for all concerned.

A shared language everyone understands not only helps leaders and workers improve organizational performance, but it also supports cross-agency collaboration and shared learning. The folks who handle retirement might learn a few tricks from those who deal with the environment, and vice versa.

We at Mass Ingenuity have built Fundamentals Maps in some 100 organizations over the years. In every case, we have seen that the very act of performing this exercise gets people thinking and talking about their work in an orderly fashion, turning mind-numbing complexity into something everyone can understand.

Surprisingly few management teams engage their people in

deep conversations about their work. They just coast along unconsciously with all of the processes the organization has developed over the years. However, when they start viewing management as a system, they must *consciously* consider how they can construct and refine a better one. Any improvement, they know, will depend on getting their people thinking and talking about the fundamental work they do. If you don't talk about it, you can't fix it.

As the Leadership Team develops its Fundamentals Map, team members lay the groundwork for a comprehensive transformation to a results-driven approach to the work of state government.

Going Bottom-Up and Top-Down

Creating a Fundamentals Map for a Governor shows the entire state on a single page, making the complexity of the executive branch understandable.

The Governor's Map looks at the state not through the traditional lens of agency organizational structure, but through the lens of *process*. Looking at government as an assembly of organization charts does nothing to reduce its enormous complexity. Oregon's collection of organizations, for example, numbers a breathtaking 180 agencies, boards, and commissions. Think of it as a 180-piece jigsaw puzzle. Putting them all together to create a picture of how state government functions would test the genius of an Einstein and the patience of a Job. But when you cut the puzzle along process lines, it's simple and clear.

Example Governor's Map

MISSION:

Making X (STATE) a better place to live, work, and play

VALUES:

How We Operate

- Transparency and Accountability
- Operating as a Single Enterprise
- Shared Leadership through Demonstrated Collaboration

What We Ensure

- Fiscal Stability and Sustainability
- Equity to All Citizens
- Opportunity for Prosperity

KEY GOALS:

- World Class Education
- Growing Economy
- Sustainable Environment
- Healthy Citizens
- Safe Place to Live
- Efficient & Effective Government

CORE PROCESSES:

Operating Processes

- Educating Citizens
- Growing the Economy
- Sustaining a Healthy Environment
- Enabling Healthy People
- Ensuring Safety

Supporting Processes

- Leading State Government
- Managing Performance
- Managing Finances

- Attracting & Developing Staff
- Leveraging Technology
- Procuring Goods & Services
- Managing Assets

You can see an example of a Governor's Map in Appendix B, and online at: www.resultsamerica.org/govmap.

Through our experience helping agencies build Fundamentals Maps in several states including Oregon, Washington, and Tennessee, we have come to appreciate the value of a bottom-up, top-down rollout strategy:

STEP ONE: Initiate management system deployments that model success, starting with a Fundamentals Map, in two or three agencies in which the leaders enjoy the respect of their peers in state government. Use these early successes to validate the approach, build understanding, and develop internal advocacy.

STEP TWO: Build the Governor's Map to create a picture of the enterprise system and process structure.

STEP THREE: Extend the system to all agencies, forging direct connections between the Governor's Map and the agency/department maps.

The job of creating a management system that delivers results never ends. You build it, you tweak it, you rebuild it, and you repair it, ad infinitum. It's like Zeno's paradox: you walk halfway to the wall, then halfway again, and again, and again . . . You never reach the wall, but you get pretty darned close. That's the way you move toward "government that works."

By 2014, Maryland had gotten pretty close to the wall. At that point, the state enjoyed the most mature system of direction and measures in the US due in no small part to the initiatives launched by Governor O'Malley when he took office in 2007. While skeptics offer criticism ranging from accusations of fudging the numbers (How can we trust internally generated numbers?) to doubts about causality (Did a state program or a larger social trend reduce the crime rate?), Maryland's results told a singular story of broad-based societal improvements.

Governor O'Malley had been walking toward the wall ever since he installed CitiStat when he served as Mayor of Baltimore between 1999 and 2007 (Office of the Governor of Maryland, 2014). He has moved steadily forward ever since then, learning every step of the way. There's a reason we call it a learning *process.*

CHAPTER SIX

Big Breakthroughs

Planning and Managing the Game Changers

"You have brains in your head. You have feet in your shoes.
You can steer yourself any direction you choose."

~ DR. SEUSS

Unintended pregnancies can carry a huge personal and social cost, especially for teenagers. Colorado's Department of Public Health and Environment took bold steps to reduce those costs, as one 16-year old girl can attest. "My mom and all my sisters have been pregnant as teenagers," she said. "That's not what I want for me. I want to be the first to graduate high school. I want to go to college, and if I have a baby that's not going to happen." She had visited a clinic in Colorado where she received counseling and a three-year birth control implant.

Three years later the teenager returned to the clinic, a proud high school graduate now taking college courses to become a physician's assistant. "Without this," she acknowledged as she went through the counseling program again and chose yet another implant, "I would never be where I am today."

Between 2009 and 2013, Colorado reduced unintended pregnancies among 15- to 19-year-old residents by 40 percent, a remarkable accomplishment for a state where 70 percent of teenage pregnancies were unintended (Sullivan, 2014). The game-changing program began with a $23 million annual donation from a private foundation. It helped fund free long-acting reversible contraceptives (LARC) to low-income women in state-operated family planning clinics across Colorado (Sullivan, 2014). The contraceptives include intrauterine devices (IUDs) or implants recommended as the most effective form of birth control by the American College of Obstetricians and Gynecologists, the American Academy of Pediatrics, the Centers for Disease Control and Prevention, and the World Health Organization.

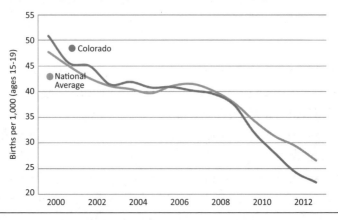

Teen Pregnancy Results in Colorado (Ages 15-19)

FIGURE 6.1: Colorado and National Teen Pregnancy Rates.
Source: US Department of Health and Human Services, Colorado Department of Public Health & Environment

Skeptics might argue that such programs could inadvertently encourage promiscuity and thus a costly increase in sexually transmitted diseases. That did not happen in Colorado.

According to Dr. Larry Wolk, a pediatrician who served as executive director and chief medical officer for the Colorado Department of Public Health and Environment, "We did not see an increase in the number of sexually transmitted diseases. Actually we have seen a bit of a decrease in a number of them and no change in others."

The sharp decline in teen pregnancies also decreased the incidence of high-risk births and abortions.

Teen Pregnancy Results in Colorado (2008-2011)

	2008	2011	Change
Percentage of Clinic Clients Using LARC's	4.50%	19.40%	431%
Number of Clinical LARC Insertions (Annual)	620	3,159	509%
Number of Clinical LARC Insertions (Cumulative)	620	8,435	13,605%
Ratio of LARC's to Low-Income Women	1:170	1:15	NA
Number of High-Risk Births (2009-2011)	4,052	2,940	-24%
Abortions per 1,000 (Ages 15-19)	10.9	7.2	-34%
Fertility Rate per 1,000 for Low-Income women (Age 15-19)	91	67	-36%

FIGURE 6.2: Teen Pregnancy Program Results in Colorado.
Source: Colorado Department of Public Health & Environment

All of these results increased the quality of life for the state's young women. The state won, too, with big savings in social and medical costs. Dr. Wolk underscored the victory when he said, "There are a lot of untold health risks as a result of unintended pregnancy, especially amongst younger women. There's the medical side, there is the social side, and there is the economic side of them as well."

Dr. Wolk knows what he's talking about. Before taking on his post with the state, he had worked as a frontline practicing physician and founded the Rocky Mountain Youth Clinics in 1996. These clinics provided a large safety net for Colorado's young residents and became a national model for providing healthcare to the uninsured.

Greta Klingler, the Family Planning Supervisor in Colorado's Department of Health, shared Dr. Wolk's passion for helping young people whose lives could be shattered by unintended and unwanted pregnancies. "Women experiencing an unintended pregnancy have a much higher risk of domestic abuse, of relationship instability, of not finishing their education whether it be high school or college, depending on the age. This in turn leads to higher rates of poverty and higher rates of lower economic self-sufficiency. They're less likely to receive prenatal care and as a result they are more likely to give birth pre-term or to a low-birth weight baby."

The mothers, the fathers, the babies themselves can face a dark future. Klingler expressed deep concern about those kids who often suffer from developmental delays and mental disabilities. They can so easily follow in their parents' footsteps, creating an ever-expanding circle of abuse, poverty, and neglect. It takes a real game-changing effort to break that cycle.

Achieving Breakthroughs: Colorado

Game changers like Colorado's LARC initiative demonstrate the full power of results-driven government. Of course, states embark on major initiatives all the time, but far too many either stall or fail to achieve desired results. Once an agency has set its sights on a major breakthrough, it must follow through on its good intentions. As with all major projects, success will depend on well-planned and carefully managed implementation.

Results-driven organizations strive for two types of breakthroughs. A **performance** breakthrough involves doing something more efficiently and effectively, not in an incremental fashion but in a truly significant way. Suppose you have always run three miles a day but want to step up your performance. Adding a few hundred yards to your routine would not provide much of a stretch. But setting your sights on finishing the Boston Marathon would pose a huge challenge and could lead to a major performance breakthrough. The second type of breakthrough, a **Capability** breakthrough, adds a whole new set of skills to your repertoire. Conditions change, and you must change with them. If conditions prevent you from keeping fit on the track, you may need to learn new workout routines at the gym. Results-driven management systems seek both types. They not only need to do a lot of what they have always done more effectively and efficiently (collecting taxes, for instance), but they also need to adopt whole new capabilities (such as providing universal healthcare).

Breakthrough Type	Definition	Example
Performance	The step-function improvement in the performance of an existing process	Reducing the wait time to register your car from 80 minutes to <8 minutes
Capability	Development of a new process or service offering	Enabling a business to use its basic business information across a broad range of services from business registration through payroll taxes to environmental permitting

FIGURE 6.3: Breakthroughs, which are significant improvement efforts, fall into two categories, performance and capability. The methods to implement the two types are different.

Each type of breakthrough requires a different methodology. You cannot plan and manage a performance breakthrough the same way you would plan and manage a capability breakthrough because the former addresses changes in established processes, while the latter sets up new processes. Performance breakthroughs employ such tools as Lean techniques and other methods for re-engineering processes. A runner designs a training program that will get her running faster and longer.

Capability breakthroughs also rely on process improvement tools, but they apply them to a brand-new process. When our runner moves her training program to the gym, she will embark on a whole new set of exercises, but she will want to do it as effectively and efficiently as possible. In this chapter we will concentrate on capability breakthroughs, the major new game-changers that deliver huge benefits to government's customers.

The undertaking begins with a clear statement of purpose:

PURPOSE STATEMENT: *Achieving Breakthroughs*

TO: *Plan and manage initiatives*

IN A WAY THAT: *Leverages best practice planning, change, and project-management disciplines*

SO THAT: *The organization achieves desired results with minimal resources*

With that overriding purpose in mind, leaders can begin the arduous and time-consuming process of creating the game changer. Whatever the specific project, the capability breakthrough should progress through seven distinct phases:

1. **Define** the business problem or opportunity and the scope of the project

2. **Analyze** the current situation and develop future scenarios
3. **Design** the future model in detail
4. **Build** the detailed workplans that will implement the future model
5. **Implement** the workplans to create the future model
6. **Evaluate** the project's results and the efficiency and effectiveness of the new model
7. **Sustain** the new capability by making it a routine core process

Before every great success a lot of detailed work takes place. Colorado's unintended pregnancy initiative paid strict attention to the details. The state defined the opportunity when a private donor provided funds for the relatively expensive long-acting reversible contraceptives. A single device could cost as much as $300 to $1,000, a steep fee for the typical teenager or for women living in poverty.

The Department of Health had already analyzed the need to tackle the problem, but it could not move forward and actually design a new program without funds to implement it. Before long, with the commitment of the donor, the Department had built and begun implementing workplans to provide the new care. Within a few years the evaluation of the program revealed impressive results, as we saw earlier. That convinced state officials of the importance of sustaining the initiative to the benefit of everyone who lives in the state of Colorado, from teens and their families to taxpayers and state workers who deliver healthcare services.

The results in Colorado have inspired other states to embark on their own breakthrough initiatives to solve the problem. For more information visit: www.thenationalcampaign.org.

Colorado's Family Planning Supervisor Klingler marveled at

the accomplishment. "I don't think anyone expected the numbers to drop like we've seen them do. Public health doesn't see numbers like this very often, if at all. And I really give credit to the clinics and to the providers who have done all this amazing work to service the clients in their communities."

Note her emphasis on the *people* side of the equation. When it comes to breakthroughs, it's the people who count; they make it happen.

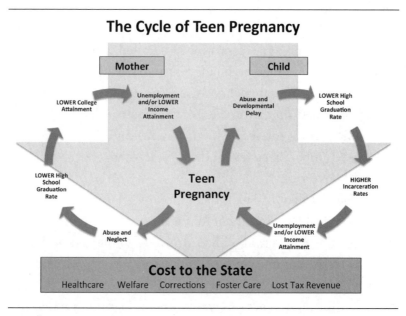

FIGURE 6.4: Teen pregnancy in many ways can be seen as a root cause of many social issues for both the mother and the child.

Investing in People: Lead Tennessee

In an in-depth interview for this book, Trish Holliday, Chief Learning Officer for the State of Tennessee at the time, observed that when it comes to developing talented people, government often falls short. "The first thing that is always cut in government is the development of people. It's been that way forever. Wait a minute. As leaders we talk about people being our greatest asset, but we don't put our money where our mouth is?"

The enthusiastic and outspoken public servant never hesitated to express her views about government's all-too-frequent failure to develop its leaders, the workers she called "the forgotten population." In her view, past training efforts had not focused on the development of this population and it contributed to a mindset of indifference and knowledge hoarding.

An aging government workforce exacerbated the problem. "We are looking at a significant percent of our workforce being eligible to retire in the next 10 years," she said. Clearly, government needs to prepare for this inevitable talent drain.

In 2009, Holliday presented a compelling business case for more heavily investing in Tennessee's next crop of government leaders. Some observers questioned her timing because the proposal came with one scant year left in the current administration's term in office. After demonstrating that this investment was right for the business of state government, she gained approval for her initiative.

"Even during the end of an administration, the state's leaders stepped up and supported launching Lead Tennessee," Holliday told us. That got the ball rolling. Finally, the state would be putting resources into its claim that it views its people as a valuable asset. A year later, the program continued and grew during Governor Bill Haslam's administration. In 2012, the governor signed the TEAM (Tennessee Excellence, Accountability and Management) Act, which redefined the employment practices in Tennessee (For more about the TEAM Act, see Chapter Ten).

Rebecca Hunter, then Commissioner of Human Resources for the state of Tennessee, described one key result of the Act. For the state's commissioners (their term for what other states call Directors or Secretaries), she said, "It's really the start of changing our state government from one based on seniority to one based on performance. We're approaching leadership and development with the same mindset. And all our learning and development is aligned with the governor's vision and priorities."

By 2014 LEAD Tennessee had gained national and international attention for its approach to leadership development. Any government organization in the world can do it. You start by understanding and defining the need, ensuring the full support of the chief executive, turning important stakeholders into champions of the effort, and then designing a system that will implement the initiative. In Tennessee, the LEAD Tennessee Executive Leadership Council oversaw the crucial implementation step.

At the outset, the Council listed desired competencies for three categories of leadership: "Lead an Organization, Lead People and Lead Self." Each category contains specific qualities and their associated behaviors. You can find more details about the behaviors in Appendix C. In addition, you can see the Leadership Competencies for the NOW Management System in Appendix D.

Holliday shared her thoughts about the initial hurdles the program needed to overcome. "It started out as being more of an emerging leader program, so we were getting a lot of the lower-level managers who didn't have enough context to think strategically about the system, about government as an enterprise. We realized very quickly that we had to shift the audience to 70 percent current strategic leaders, 30 percent emerging leaders. With emerging leaders sitting with current leaders, the growth potential was going to be astounding."

Another major hurdle arose when she realized some viewed the program as an old-fashioned reward system. She didn't want anyone to assume that admission to the program came simply because they had clocked a certain number of years on the job.

"It has taken us a good three hard years to get the message out that this is performance based."

Summary of Lead Tennessee Competencies

COMPETENCY	DEFINITION
Lead an Organization: Guides overall strategic and operational direction	
Customer Focused	Places the customer at the center of strategic and operational planning
Innovative	Demonstrates flexible thinking while producing creative thought process; open to suggestions of others
Mission-Driven	Demonstrates through actions, absolute clarity as to the purpose of the organization
Lead People: Enables others to achieve high performance and full potential	
Courageous	Demonstrates understanding of concerns; takes responsibility and addresses them with fortitude and composure
Talent Focused	Demonstrates the ability to create an environment that encourages outstanding individual performance from each employee
Lead Self: Expands depth and breadth of capability	
Self-Management	Actively works to continuously improve, deploy strengths and compensate for weaknesses and limits
Integrity	Takes responsibility for personal actions, follows through on commitments, and instills confidence that all words and actions are the truth
High Performance	Sets a high standard that represents the organization in the best light to both internal and external customers and produces results that exceed expectations

FIGURE 6.5: LEAD Tennessee Competencies were developed so that the leadership development program could serve defined skills needed to support the state's focus.
Source: Tennessee Department of Human Resources

By its fifth year the selection process had reached a healthy balance of veteran and emerging leaders. Each year the resultant "alliance" included 120 people, with the number of each agency's selections based on its overall number of employees. Candidates filled out detailed applications, which agency leadership then sorted and prioritized. In the end, Commissioner Hunter and Chief Learning Officer Holliday made the final choice.

Those selected for each year's alliance entered a comprehensive training program that included:

- Pre- and post-program competency-based 360-degree performance assessments
- A professional development plan
- A professional, external executive coach
- Six day-long leadership summits
- Twice-a-year coaching labs
- Assigned books on relevant topics

An every-other month Leadership Summit allowed for immediate application of growing competencies and behaviors in the real world. During these sessions, the participants received training in specific processes and frameworks that would allow them to transfer their learning to the workplace.

A member of the Council that oversaw LEAD Tennessee sponsors each Leadership Summit. As Holliday explained it, "They have time to talk about their personal experience with the competency they are sponsoring." This sharing of personal experience made each topic highly relevant to the leaders-in-training. Commissioner Hunter also hosted an executive panel discussion that added depth and differing perspectives to the participants' understanding of the topic. In addition, Holliday said, "We select a business leader we think represents the competency to come in and talk." The program brought in people with vastly different expertise, ranging from university presidents to prominent business leaders and even the governor.

During each session participants rolled up their sleeves and applied their learning for 2-3 hours. Holliday loved that part of the program. "This is what I call 'getting messy', people applying these competencies, working side-by-side with their coaches."

Holliday quoted one key state official's thoughts about the reading list: "Our state's Chief Operating Officer Greg Adams has been very influential and coined the phrase, 'leaders are readers'." He strongly supported the inclusion of the best books on management and leadership as a vital element of the professional development.

Although Commissioner Hunter came on board after the state had already adopted the LEAD Tennessee program, she fully committed herself to making it even better. She took great pride in the effort's accomplishments. "When we talk to folks in the private sector, they tell us this is as good or better than anything they've seen. I am a life-long learner and when I first heard that the State of Tennessee already had a dynamic leadership development program in place, it was beyond my wildest dreams."

Holliday added that the program's customers, the leaders of Tennessee's many agencies, loved the fact that they got a big return on their $2,800 per participant investment in developing their people. "We've not received any pushback on the cost because of the value."

The state could actually measure that value. Pre- and post-360-degree assessments of the competencies, skills, and behaviors exhibited by LEAD Tennessee participants generally showed an improvement in every single category measured.

Like most human enterprises, a person who performs admirably on the job does not necessarily do as well as a manager. Employees may display incredible skill designing information systems but fail miserably when assigned management responsibility, mostly because they lack sufficient training for the new position. Why should it be any different in government? Management is a profession and requires the development of skills, just like any other profession.

When Hunter took over as Commissioner of Human Resources, she quickly promoted Chief Learning Officer Holliday so that the CLO would report directly to the Commissioner. Soon thereafter, the TEAM Act gave Human Resources centralized control over all of the state's leadership development efforts.

The annual Tennessee Government Leadership Conference supports the ongoing development of people in the LEAD Tennessee initiative and two other allied programs. The project includes a leadership Black Belt program whereby participants perform community service both inside and outside of state government in addition to continually developing their strategic leadership knowledge and skills.

The state's Learning and Development Council, which included the number one person in charge of learning for each agency, also gave a big boost to the program. Since many agencies must design specific types of training for their own unique needs, the council offered an opportunity for sharing across areas of functional responsibility. Agency B discovered that it could borrow and adapt something that got great results for Agency A. This benefited everyone at every level of state government.

Ironically, LEAD Tennessee generated much more demand than the program could supply. The state turned that bad news into good news when the gap motivated agencies to develop feeder programs for LEAD Tennessee. Even the Department of Human Resources developed its own internal leadership program known as the Next Level Leadership Academy.

Hunter appreciated these innovative steps but still championed the need for centralized coordination of the state's learning efforts to align with the Governor's priorities. To prove her point, she cited her agency's partnership with Governor Haslam's Customer Focused Government Office. Her agency's involvement made it possible for customer service training to migrate into every corner of state government. "Every employee in state government has been trained in customer service, customized to the agency, reminding each and every one of them that we are here to serve the taxpayers. That's been a huge initiative."

Tennessee backed its commitment to developing its people with financial and personnel resources, and it won a big return on that investment: a highly skilled pool from which the state could draw its next generation of leaders.

Setting Bold Targets: Washington's Target Zero

During an important planning session in 2000, Washington State's Traffic Safety Commission struggled to set a target for reduced traffic fatalities. Darrin Grondel, who later became Washington's Traffic Safety Commission Director, recalled the debate. "The numbers (of traffic fatalities) represent people who were planning to have dinner with their families that night and were making plans for their lives." At the dawn of the new century, more than 600 people were losing their lives annually on Washington's roadways. Somehow, coldly debating a target goal for the deaths of hundreds of people seemed wrong. So the commission made a surprising decision. It would set its goal at zero by the year 2030. The resulting program became known as Target Zero.

"Some people thought it was insane to set such a goal," Grondel told us. However, as a former captain for the Washington State Patrol, he liked the idea, which eventually led to other states taking a similarly bold approach to the problem. Between 2005 and 2012, Washington cut traffic fatalities by 31.4 percent, and in 2013 reduced them from 658 in 2002 to 439. In 2012 Washington ranked 5th nationally at 7.82 deaths per million miles driven. The District of Columbia boasted the fewest deaths at 4.20, while West Virginia scored the most at 17.63 (Washington State Department of Transportation, 2013).

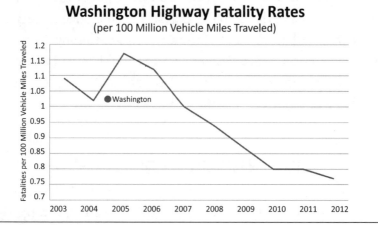

FIGURE 6.6: Washington highway fatality rates, in no small part because of its Target Zero efforts, have declined at a rate far faster than most states.
Source: Washington Highway Traffic Safety Commission

"We elected to call our Strategic Highway Plan Target Zero with the mindset that the loss of one life is too many," said State Patrol Chief John Batiste. Still, he knew that any major reduction would require a close examination of relevant data. "We look at the data to tell us where our incidents are occurring and what behaviors are causing them." By using reliable incident data, the State Patrol and partner law enforcement agencies could determine exactly where they should tackle the problem.

As Chief Batiste explained, "We were experiencing a large number of fatality collisions in Snohomish County in 2006. We looked at the data to tell us the leading causes of collisions, where they were occurring, and at what hours of day and night they were occurring."

An examination of such facts enabled the State Patrol to assign experienced and deeply motivated troopers to certain locations, where they could effectively remove from the roads any drivers who were operating their vehicles under the influence of alcohol and/or drugs. The decision to base the solution on cold, hard facts not only clarified the problem, it also helped convince the State's Legislature to support and fund the initiative. According to Batiste, "Within a year's time we were able to reduce highway fatalities, specifically those related to alcohol and driving effects, by 40 percent."

As a key component of the Target Zero Drive, Washington's State Patrol holds two-day Strategic Advancement Forums every other month, formally reviewing all new data in great detail.

Eventually, Target Zero became part of the Results Washington effort under Goal Council 4, Healthy and Safe Communities. This added clout to the program. It raised awareness and support for efforts both internally and externally to address the relatively high rate of fatalities and serious injuries among young drivers 16-25 years old. As Pat Kohler, Director of Washington's Department of Licensing, explained, "Our key focus is public safety and customer service."

In 2012 the agency moved driver testing from its own licensing offices to the private driver training schools that were already doing the training. This was a convenience to students and their parents since they were already taking the required training. Testing transactions were one of the most time-consuming services at the licensing offices so another outcome was a reduction in wait times due to decreased workload. The agency closely monitors and audits Driver Training Schools to ensure public safety standards are being met.

The agency implemented a successful practice used with 16- to 17-year-old drivers who hold an intermediate driver's license and by sending early warning letters to drivers aged 18-21 who commit their first moving violations. The letter cautions them that such risky behavior dramatically increases the odds that they will get involved in a collision that could cause serious injury or even death. The state had already been sending warning letters to 16- to 17-year-olds with an intermediate driver's license.

Do the warnings work? Kohler's team extensively studied the impact of the letters during the first 16 months of the program, when the agency mailed an average of 2,100 letters per month. Comparing the later driving problems experienced by those who received the letters with a comparison group that did not, Washington's Department of Licensing calculated that the correspondence approach may have resulted in over 11,000 fewer violations, 42 fewer injuries, and 14 fewer fatalities.

Facts don't lie. But what you do with the facts makes all the difference between lackluster performance and terrific results. In Washington, the way the state structured its Traffic Safety Commission (TSC) played a major role in its ability to move ever closer to its Target Zero goal. All of the important stakeholders work and communicate with each other effectively. As Grondel told us, "I've worked with my counterparts across the country, and they say, 'I can't even get my department of transportation in the room'."

Governor Jay Inslee chaired the TSC, which included State Patrol Chief Batiste and Licensing Director Kohler, as well as these important stakeholders:

Kevin Quigley, Secretary of Social and Health Services
Lynn Peterson, Secretary of the Department of Transportation
John Wiesman, Director of the Department of Health
James P. Swanger, Clark County District Judge
Randy Dorn, Superintendent of Public Instruction
Sharon Dillon, Washington State Association of Counties
Jon Snyder, Association of Washington Cities

But the collaboration only begins with this inclusive council of stakeholders. When Grondel became Director of the Traffic Safety Commission in 2012, he launched a new three-year Strategic Highway Safety Plan. Stressing his commitment to broad and deep communication across agencies, he teased the new program manager he had hired that if she did not attract at least 100 people to the initial partners' meeting he would fire her. They needed to hit that number in order to multiply the influence of the small 22-person department.

The new manager made it happen and 185 people showed up, including representatives from state, county and city entities, multiple American Indian tribes, behavioral science groups, the insurance industry, and many more. That pleased Grondel to no end. "We had a 360-degree perspective on what the problems are and how to address them."

That approach sparked some interesting results. For instance, the inclusion of State Farm Insurance in Target Zero prompted the company to offer $500 grants to high school groups such as dance or football teams that joined the campaign to ensure greater highway safety for youth. The effort involved peer-to-peer, rather than cop-to-student communication, because, as Grondel observed, "Research shows that peer-to-peer communication has a better effect than having a uniformed officer come in and talk."

State Farm required that participating students take on at least 5 of 15 proposed topics addressing common teen driving risks, such as impaired driving, distracted driving, and speeding. "The schools have done an amazing job and have come up with some creative ways to deliver the message."

There's that word again: "creative." Innovation, more than anything else, helps results-driven government hit its targets.

Designing Innovative Solutions: New Mexico Healthcare

Toward the end of its 2013 fiscal year, New Mexico was heading toward a $70 million deficit in its employee healthcare insurance fund. The state insured itself, and four recent 13 percent annual increases in cost, with no boosts in the premiums employees paid for their insurance, found the fund teetering on the brink of a very deep hole. The program had 82,000 beneficiaries at the time.

The options did not look good. On the one hand, the state could decrease benefits, which would surely ignite outrage among employees, or it could raise premiums, an equally unappealing option for a workforce typically earning only $38,000 and $44,000 a year.

To solve the problem New Mexico's leadership needed to put on its creative thinking cap and hammer out an innovative solution.

Ed Burckle, Cabinet Secretary for New Mexico's General Services Department, described the state's first step in that direction. "So we've undertaken a transformational approach," he explained in an interview. But before New Mexico could pursue that approach, it needed to get the fiscal ship sailing in the right direction with a $10 million contribution from the state legislature and a significant one-time premium increase. Only then could the state put some innovative wind in its sails and move closer to long-term stability.

"We want to keep our healthcare premiums in the single digits moving forward," explained Burckle. "We hope that will be a 3-5 percent range increase, and so long as we can stay behind the national cost trends in healthcare, we're going to be satisfied."

A. J. Forte, Risk Management Director for General Services, described the next step toward an innovative solution. "We want our employees to get the healthcare they deserve. So, when we found out we're going to be fiscally sound in the short term, having solved the (immediate) fund problem, we took a three-phase approach to keep it that way." First, the state would totally redesign its health insurance plan; second, it would aggressively emphasize wellness as a way to reduce long-term costs; and third, it would open its own healthcare clinics.

Working with the state's claims administrators, BlueCross BlueShield and Presbyterian Healthcare, New Mexico added new plans and cut employee deductibles from $700 to $500 or $325, depending on the specific plan. No insured employee would ever suffer out-of-pocket expenses beyond $3,500.

Forte pointed out, "That makes us one of the richest plans in the state, having such a minimum out of pocket max. It's truly a benefit to our employees." Even better, the monthly cost per employee for the newly designed plan amounted to about $1.50 increase per pay period.

That was the first phase. A good wellness program must *actually* improve subscribers' health, no easy goal to achieve. Forte knew that. "So we have been paying for wellness to the carriers, but the problem was we were never seeing a return. Our members were never actually seeing a wellness benefit." Why did that happen? Because people simply did not participate in the fully volunteer program. It would only work if the insured fully bought into the idea. To turn that around, the state shifted its wellness dollars to Catapult Health, which provided a mobile service that delivered on-site health screenings.

Burckle credits Forte with the initial success of these innovations. "So far, for every 50 people we screen we find 2 who have 911 blood pressure levels when they came in for detection of strokes." "911" refers to blood pressure readings that indicated the patient should go straight to an emergency room because he or she might suffer a stroke at any minute. "We arranged for a provider, so they could see them immediately, who put them on medication, and prescribed lifestyle changes."

That's good news, but here's the really good news. "This program is cost neutral," said Forte, meaning it cost not one penny more than the previous wellness program. However, because it reduced the chance of stroke and other life-threatening medical problems, and expensive emergency room visits, the program returned a huge human and financial return on the neutral investment.

Phase three, opening state-operated clinics, took more time. "The provider network in Albuquerque and in Santa Fe is horrible," said Forte, referring to the difficulty of getting a prompt appointment in the state's two largest population centers. "There's a 30-day wait to get in to see a general practitioner. Once you get in to see that GP, it's a sit and wait mentality in Albuquerque."

The state needed to fix that, said Burckle. "Probably the most transformational change we are making is to actually locate a health clinic on state property, run by a third party healthcare provider. We are going to waive all the co-pays for anyone who wants to come to the facility."

By putting a third-party operated clinic on state property in Santa Fe (and eventually in Albuquerque) the state hoped to make healthcare more convenient for the insured. That could add up to major savings. "We have almost 9,000 state employees in the Santa Fe area," explained Forte.

When people cannot easily access their healthcare provider, they often wind up in the emergency room, a much costlier option at $800 and $1,200 per visit. The new clinics gave state employees easy access. They could make an appointment via the Internet, and walk down the hall or across the street to the on-site care suite, with little or no waiting on weekdays and even the weekend.

"The idea is our employees will have access totally free of cost," explained Forte. "And for us it's a fixed cost. On a monthly basis we pay a set amount whether the clinic sees 1 or 500 people." Once the clinic logs 200 patients in a given month, the state starts saving money. It also benefits from purchasing pharmaceuticals wholesale. Forte sees a bright future for the program. "So right now, and it's a wide projection, but it looks like the clinic will deliver a $3.5 to $5.5 million savings on an annual basis to the fund."

Who could ask for more? With healthier employees and controlled costs, everyone wins. Of course, it takes more than imagination to effect such a large-scale change.

Sponsoring Large-Scale Change

Imagine repairing a jet engine while the plane zooms through the stratosphere. No easy task, right? But that's exactly what you must do when you make any large-scale change. Take major Information Technology (IT) overhauls, for example. Research by the Boston-based Standish Group reveals that a scant 32 percent of IT projects succeed as well as expected, 24 percent fail miserably, and the remainder cause their share of headaches (Standish Group, 2009). The same applies to any big change initiative in business or government. It takes skillful leadership to beat the odds.

In the case of state government, no undertaking poses a more complex challenge to executive branch leaders than overseeing a breakthrough solution to a big problem. Whether the solution involves a team of 10 people replacing a paper-based employee wage reporting system with an electronic one or moving the entire state workforce to a high-engagement, high-accountability management system, success always begins and ends with the sponsor of the breakthrough. Sponsorship of enterprise-level change requires deep involvement of the organization's top leadership team. Senior government executives need to be skilled sponsors for breakthroughs to be successful.

Think again about fixing a jet engine in mid-flight. You not only face a complex engineering problem as you switch out portions of a ten-thousand part contraption, you've got a team of worried technicians to worry about, you've got a cabin full of panicking passengers to keep in their seats. As every leader knows, it's not the technical details that doom so many major change efforts; it's all those sticky-gooey people issues.

No matter how well you've planned the change, if you do not fully engage your people, you will probably crash and burn. Effective results-driven management depends on achieving levels of employee engagement uncommon in state government. And full engagement depends on effective delegation.

Mass Ingenuity Senior Consultant Beth Doolittle summarized the role of the breakthrough sponsor. "It's delegation on steroids. If you're are not good at delegating, you will find sponsoring a breakthrough will require the development of a new group of management muscles."

Breakthrough sponsors should not actually serve as the project's leader. Those roles require different perspectives and skills. You need one person with a satellite's eye view of the initiative and one watching at ground level. As Doolittle advises, "If sponsors are too close to the project, they will lose their real value to the team. We count on sponsors to have the breadth and scope to see what the project leader won't see as their focus narrows to the breakthrough topic. We count on sponsors to use their network of peers and stakeholders for the good of the project. While the team leader and members will also network, their focus is largely on finding solutions that everyone agrees to."

Great sponsors possess two critical skills:

- The ability to define and guide the scope of the mission, provide needed resources, and remove major obstacles
- A knack for establishing, building, and nurturing organizational support

These skills apply to both performance and capability breakthrough initiatives because, when you get right down to it, change is change, no matter what the arena. All change efforts aim at solving a problem and to solve that problem you have to answer a set of questions:

1. Why do we need the change?
2. Who will need to be doing something differently?
3. What is it that they will need to do differently?
4. When will they need to be doing it?

In the case of breakthroughs, the answers to these simple questions will not come easily. Just think for a moment about applying them to the big problems state governments face today, ranging from widespread poverty to the treatment and rehabilitation of prison inmates to traffic deaths. Setting the direction that will lead to solving those problems takes great sponsorship skill.

Define and Guide the Scope of the Purpose

Before launching a breakthrough initiative, the sponsor plays the lead role in drafting the effort's charter. The charter states the compelling need for a change, the work required to get it done, who should do the work, when the work should conclude, and the resources available to do it. The sponsor also prepares mentally for the unexpected problems that will arise along the way.

"The sponsor's job is to think about where he or she wants the team to go," explained Doolittle, "Not the how, but the what. They need to define the end result."

Doolittle, a 25-plus year veteran of organizational consulting, worked with such large organizations as Levi Strauss, Nike and Sun Microsystems before beginning her involvement with state government.

She found that organizational politics exist in every organization. "From the outset sponsors have to be very clear they have the political will and support of their colleagues. And they need to recognize they are going to be responsible for maintaining their peer-level support throughout the effort."

After the sponsor has clearly defined the scope of the intended change, the hard work begins. And it spans the length of the initiative. "At a certain level sponsors know what they want when they launch the team. And the thing that I think is often unaccounted for, especially in long projects, is as the chartered team is doing work, the team begins to know more about the problem than the sponsor."

That knowledge gap can cause some thorny problems. "The sponsor needs to remain curious about what the team is learning and thinking, and the team needs to remain curious about what the sponsor is learning and thinking." Doolittle recommends that the sponsor keep a close eye on developments, not appearing to be looking over people's shoulders as they do the work, but making it clear that he or she cares deeply about progress and will jump at the chance to remove obstacles to success.

Sponsors and teams can remove obstacles in three ways: communicate, communicate, and communicate. That also helps keep the natural tension between those who set the course and those who must sail the boat at a healthy level. "I like the motto for teams to 'Update your sponsor until they don't want to hear any more.' Keep them really, really, really informed and involved, not just about the project plan, but about the issues the team is wrestling with."

Doolittle cautions sponsors that they cannot launch the team and then wait until they are readying their recommendations before they talk again. Instead, they need to be actively and routinely talking to build shared understanding and influence of each other's thinking.

Lack of communication can create an atmosphere of defensiveness, which can derail the effort. "When they start to sell each other, rather than inviting challenge by making the thinking and conclusions clear, the gap between the two can get pretty wide," Doolittle warns.

Too wide a gap courts disaster. When that happens, the implementers can lose heart and disengage, and the sponsor can end up without the information he or she needs to maintain the support of peers who will be affected by the change. Their support is crucial.

Establish, Build, and Nurture Organizational Support

Never underestimate the need for support. As Doolittle says, "The sponsor is responsible for keeping the members of the leadership team and key stakeholders up to date. Done right the sponsor is raising the issues and seeking peer guidance sufficiently to make sure the team does not run into opposition later."

As the team moves from the satellite's eye view of the change to the mountaintop view, and finally the boots-on-the-ground view, they must pass through a series of go/no-go decision gates. At these pivot points, the sponsor and often their peers must decide whether or not to keep the troops marching forward. Smart decisions require full disclosure, not just of the project's current status but also of any and all problems that endanger its success.

"The more complex the change and the more history there has been with the issues, the more you want to involve people early on," says Doolittle. "It's how you keep from going all the way down the wrong road."

Doolittle likes to think about this aspect of change leadership as "accordion activity", where the breakthrough team goes back and forth with those whose lives the change will affect just as the sponsor goes back and forth with the executives who oversee those people. This accordion activity not only informs people about what's coming down the road — it gets their ideas about additional creative solutions. The biggest changes require the highest engagement.

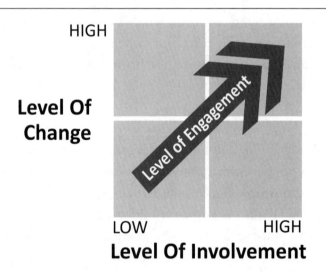

FIGURE 6.7: As a basic rule of thumb the more a desired change impacts a person or team, the more they need to be involved in its design.

Imagine a football stadium full of 50,000 cheering fans. If a small change occurs and one fan holds up a "Go Bears!" sign, only one person needs to get engaged in that action. But what if stadium officials want all 50,000 fans to hold up cards? Now

50,000 people need to get engaged in the project. Otherwise you will get spotty results. Whatever the size of a change effort, you need to get *all* stakeholders engaged in the effort, even if they are only slightly affected by it.

Doolittle compares a breakthrough sponsor to a coach who makes sure everyone remains dedicated to getting results with the new program. "As sponsor your role is to hold the line, don't let people go back," she says. "No, this door is closed. We are going *forward*."

You must also account for time. Small changes might take a long time to take hold; larger ones may happen swiftly. The longer the breakthrough project runs, the more effort it takes to hold all the fans together. People grow tired or bored and wander off, leaving their signs on their seats. The remaining fans resent the betrayal and worry that the final result will not materialize.

Breakthroughs, those big leaps forward, whether with a brand-new system or major process improvement, fuel the results engine. Whether you're looking to solve a relatively simple problem, such as reducing unintended pregnancies or something more complex, such as developing a new generation of leaders, eliminating highway fatalities, or controlling spiraling healthcare costs, you need more than a campaign slogan — you need a solution that will get results. That's how government leaders in Colorado, Tennessee, Washington, and New Mexico achieved the breakthroughs we have witnessed in this chapter.

These and other results revolutionaries across the nation see unlimited possibilities for achieving similar breakthroughs, both those significant process improvements that turn heads, and those bold leaps into the future that change lives.

CHAPTER SEVEN

True Accountability

Using Business Reviews to Drive Action

"There is nothing more difficult to execute, nor more dubious of success, nor more dangerous to administer than to introduce a new order of things."

~ NICCOLO MACHIAVELLI, THE PRINCE

If you want to clean up a badly polluted body of water, you must stem the flow of nitrogen and oil from the surrounding land. You use a "cover crop" strategy, which means farmers plant crops on otherwise un-farmed land to then naturally help with the scrubbing of pollutants. That is one part of the State of Maryland's persistent and effective effort to clean up the Chesapeake Bay.

Early on, the project got stuck. Matt Power, who ran StateStat for Maryland, told the story. One day Governor Martin O'Malley posed a key question to those accountable for the cover crop initiative during a monthly two-hour meeting: "Why didn't we spend all the cover crop money?" he asked.

Power remembers the answer: "The people from Agriculture said that 'we really saturated demand on this. That's about as much as you're going to get from people (the farming community).'"

"How do you know that?" asked the Governor. Silence. No one could cite clear facts about the supposition. In the absence of facts to prove otherwise, the governor concluded, "Well, you *don't* know."

To remedy that shortcoming, the state launched surveys to determine the potential interest in planting cover crops. Before long, Maryland managed to increase demand *beyond* the level of current funding. To deal with this dramatic turnaround, the state moved money over to support the program.

"Then, we did targeted mailing to anyone who had land zoned for agriculture," said Power. "And sure enough, demand increased again; because they were getting money for something that they otherwise would not. But had we *not* started measuring who had it (the land), where they had it, and graphed it, none of this would have ever happened."

Power believed that state agencies tend to get so close to the people they serve, they start to operate on assumptions that may or may not hold up to scrutiny. Couple that tendency with the inertia of long-standing policies and programs, and you end up perpetuating a status quo that resists change.

BayStat's measurements, presented during many two-hour, outcome-specific business reviews held by Maryland's State Government, did change the game. Certified cover crops planted annually in the Chesapeake Bay watershed grew from 52,305 acres at the beginning of Governor O'Malley's tenure to 410,530 acres by the end of 2013 — a whopping 685 percent increase (Maryland BayStat, 2014). Chalk up the improvement to a whole lot of government leaders and workers taking account-ability for those results. BayStat drew focus and resources from many agencies across state government.

Professor Robert D. Behn of the Ash Center for Democratic

Governance and Innovation at Harvard's John F. Kennedy School of Government has studied and advanced a practical model for getting results from government called "PerformanceStat." He drew foundational knowledge for this approach from New York City's CompStat program. A number of governmental organizations around the world have used variations on the model to support their transformation efforts, among them the State of Maryland, whose StateStat program represents the longest-standing state application of the approach in the US.

In his book *The PerformanceStat Potential: A Leadership Strategy for Producing Results* (2014), Professor Behn details the "several core leadership principles" common to all Stat-style strategies for getting better results. The leadership team:

- Focuses on achieving specific *public purposes*
- Seeks to eliminate or mitigate current *performance deficit(s)* by hitting specific *performance targets*
- Collects and analyzes up-to-the-minute *data* that measures any gaps between current performance and targets
- Establishes a series of *regular, frequent, integrated meetings* in which leaders and key workers analyze the data, follow up on previous agreements, provide feedback on progress, determine what is and isn't working, and decide on any changes they should make to their current efforts
- Persists in its effort to improve performance in ways that fulfill the specific public purposes

Leaders can follow these principles to guide the third of the three management processes we discussed in Chapter Four (Improve Fundamentals, Achieve Breakthroughs, Monitor Performance, and Solve Problems). Routine reviews of the organization's progress toward results provide the foundation for accountability and transparency.

MANAGEMENT PROCESS PURPOSE STATEMENT: *Monitoring Performance*

TO: *Routinely review progress toward targets*

IN A WAY THAT: *Reinforces positive accountability and transparency*

SO THAT: *People see shortfalls immediately and take swift corrective action*

Maryland's Stat program and related ones used by Oregon and Washington rely on business reviews to promote true accountability. True accountability is not a punishment for transgressions. "We will hold you accountable" does *not* mean, "We will punish you for making mistakes." It *does* mean, "We want you to figure out a way to get better results." It's positive, reinforcing, and, in the end, rewarding.

When a measure falls short of expectations or an unexpected problem arises in an old-school reactive management system, leaders organize a search party to hunt down and punish or even eliminate the perpetrator. In government, that usually means finding a scapegoat who can take the blame for the crime. Goodbye, true accountability; hello, blame game. The scapegoat exits stage left, the measure does not improve, and the problem does not get solved.

Think of measures not as report cards but as *sensors* — the canaries in the coal mine that warn of impending danger. Governor Rick Snyder of Michigan maintained a "no credit, no blame" management philosophy that removed finger pointing and scapegoating from the system. Yes, an official or worker can commit a crime such as falsifying information or bribe taking, but that's another story altogether. Then you really do need to punish the culprit. But in the day-to-day work of government, the lion's share of mistakes are made by well-intentioned, hard-working people who can and will correct any shortfalls, once you bring those results to their attention. Reviews bring them to their attention. When the canary sings, the miner asks, "What can I do to save lives?"

When a measure of government performance goes *red* in Maryland, those responsible for improving the situation ask, "What more can I do to get the results we want?"

Structuring Stat Reviews: Lessons from Maryland

An interesting slogan appeared on StateStat slides at every review meeting in Maryland: *A deadline is the difference between a dream and a goal.* The man responsible for administering the StateStat program for Maryland, Matt Power, oversaw a team of six analysts, each assigned to a specific area of interest: BayStat, VetStat, StudentStat, ClimateStat, ReEntryStat, etc. These analysts brought their expertise to relevant agency reviews as well as the Departments of Transportation, Labor, Licensing and Regulation, Health and Mental Hygiene, etc. Maryland posts Agency Reports, Charts/Maps and Meeting Summaries online at www.statestat.maryland.gov/reports.html.

Prior to an agency review session, the assigned analyst prepared a Meeting Memo that contained three crucial elements:

1. Follow-up on Commitments – an update on action items from previous meetings.

2. Analysis – fresh data to help advance understanding of the facts pertaining to a particular topic.
3. External perspectives – a summary of best practices from outside the state, such as emerging thinking and innovation in business and initiatives in other states and at the national level.

Meeting Memo
1. Follow-up on commitments
2. Analysis on relevant data
3. External perspective

FIGURE 7.1: Maryland's StateStat meetings are a combination of highly structured and free flowing.

The meeting would conclude with items that required follow-up at the next review meeting. "We will create 10 to 20 to 30 follow-ups in any given meeting," explained Power.

Systematic and thorough follow-up reinforced accountability. During each meeting, people would look closely at the measures, devise new ones if necessary, determine any gaps between current results and goals, identify problems, enumerate missing facts, debate solutions, brainstorm new ideas, and set a date for the next follow-up meeting.

For its reviews, Maryland set up a special StateStat room where monitors displayed tons of data. During meetings, the Governor, Power, Legal Counsel to Power, the Governor's Chief of Staff and Deputy Chief of Staff, and the heads of Budget Management and Information Technology sat at a table opposite relevant department leaders and other key officials involved with the topic at hand. Some 30 additional seats accommodated any other interested parties. The Memo guided the discussion.

As Power described it: "The memo is created for the Governor and myself and the people on our side of the table. This is the Governor's raw look at what's going on in state government."

Goal oriented Stat review meetings, such as BayStat, use a similar approach. In agency reviews, Power said, "In their routine communications each of the cabinet secretaries talk with the governor about the 10 percent of things that are going well and the 10 percent of things that might blow up so the governor has a heads-up. Stat meetings get at the *other* 80 percent of daily operations of state government."

"The governor reads every single memo written by my analysts, and I get feedback from him constantly," says Power: "I kid you not, there are times when he's read the StateStat memo before I have, and that's astounding. He cares tremendously about it, and it's his way of keeping a finger on the pulse of what is happening not just on the things that are going to blow up, not just the things that are going to be front-page news stories, but just the raw mechanics of governing and paying attention to what is important to constituents and citizens and taxpayers."

Governor O'Malley would circle worrisome items on the memos, scribble comments and questions in the margins, and make sure Power knew where he wanted people to concentrate their efforts. Even when he did not attend a meeting, everyone in the room felt his presence and his relentless interest in getting results. His virtual presence kept people working toward creative solutions that would deliver the highest value to the customer.

When it comes to analyzing relevant data, you need to make that data available in a clear and detailed presentation. Powers says, "So, all the charts, analysis and graphs, I throw up on a bunch of TV screens and we talk about what the trends are and what they aren't."

In Maryland, the meeting memo is issued *only* to the people at the governor's table, an unconventional practice. It works in Maryland, but it's not easy to replicate because of its controversial nature. At least one state attempted to replicate it, but eventually shifted to a different approach.

The unconventional approach caused people to come to the meeting with open minds and without a lot of prefabricated and rehearsed responses. Power believes that this approach enhances the quality of the conversation about an issue and has led to much more creative problem solving: "It starts a brainstorming discussion that would not have happened if we gave them all the information in advance," he said. "If we give them the information in advance, one of their staffers will read it and write the response." In Maryland, the Governor expected people, especially the agency heads, to come to the meeting prepared but unscripted to answer any questions about what's going on in their areas of accountability.

The best review meetings focus on facts, stimulate frank discussions, stress non-judgmental analysis, and emphasize imaginative solutions. In the meeting, people abandon adversarial stances and approach every problem in a collaborative posture. Prepackaged agendas do not accomplish those goals as well as a more open-ended, free-for-all engagement around important issues and of course, around facts. Power loved it when people just started throwing out ideas to spark a conversation. The resultant energy and enthusiasm often resulted in surprisingly innovative solutions. One example was Corrections getting inmates involved in planting trees as a part of helping protect the Chesapeake Bay.

The third item on the review agenda, gaining an external perspective, also stimulates creative thinking. Sometimes just hearing about the way someone outside the organization solved a particular problem can untangle even the thorniest issue.

Maryland's eight years perfecting its StateStat system offer some instructive lessons for anyone intent on getting better results:

Lesson One: The governor's enthusiasm drives everyone's enthusiasm.

Lesson Two: Relentless follow-up with deadlines propels the work forward.

Lesson Three: Facts reveal the truth about what works and does not work.

Lesson Four: Structured regular meetings maintain momentum.

Lesson Five: Accountability stimulates creative solutions.

Of course, these lessons apply to every results-driven management system. Improvement always hinges on enthusiastic leadership, frequent follow-up, constant pursuit of the truth, ongoing conversations, and accountability. Without them, even the best intentions will result in "all smoke and no fire."

Doing It the Washington Way

When Washington state's Governor Jay Inslee talked about the way his people conducted Results Washington Goal Council Reviews, he drew a comparison with the television series *Downton Abbey*. Which would you prefer: a stiff and excruciatingly polite discussion during a formal dinner under a crystal chandelier, or the real-world banter around a huge wooden chopping block back in the kitchen? Most people would prefer the kitchen. So would Governor Inslee.

Wendy Korthuis-Smith, Director of Results Washington, described Governor Inslee's approach to the task of getting better results: "The governor is really trying to embody the *leader as coach* model, and not be the one with all the answers. He's the one who asks a lot of questions versus making statements — and that is the kind of culture we want."

Rather than sitting at the head of the table in formal attire and having stuffy conversations, Inslee talks of being in the kitchen "peeling the potatoes and slicing the onions" and discussing what needs to be added to the stew on the stove to make it just right.

Korthuis-Smith added, "When we look at a Lean culture we look at, obviously, creating value for our customers. We're looking at constant improvement. And we're looking at employees as problem solvers because they have the knowledge to make things better. They work with the customers, they are the ones that have had to create the workarounds, and they work with constraints in the system. So they have the ideas of how to make it better."

That philosophy reflects Washington's deep commitment to and lengthy experience with a Lean approach to getting results. Results Washington aims to keep everyone in state government looking at their work in terms of getting better results for the customer. And everything they do demonstrates respect for the people who do the real work of government. It's a systemic approach to improve the quality of life for all Washingtonians.

Results Washington includes five Goal Councils, each of which meets on a monthly basis. In addition, a two-hour Results Review session is held each month with the governor for one of the five goal areas. The Councils match the goals the Governor has set for his administration:

Goal Council One: World Class Education

Goal Council Two: Prosperous Economy

Goal Council Three: Sustainable Energy and a Clean Environment

Goal Council Four: Healthy and Safe Communities

Goal Council Five: Efficient, Effective and Accountable Government

Every Goal Council includes members from multiple agencies and other groups who share some accountability for achieving the goal. For example, the Prosperous Economy Goal Council (Results Washington, 2014) includes the following agencies and groups:

- Washington State Commission on Asian Pacific American Affairs
- Department of Commerce
- Employment Security Department
- Department of Financial Institutions
- Office of Financial Management
- Governor's Office of Indian Affairs
- Office of Minority and Women's Business Enterprises
- Department of Labor and Industries
- Office of Regulatory Innovation and Assistance
- Department of Revenue
- Department of Services for the Blind
- State of Washington Arts Commission
- Department of Transportation

Consistent with the Lean philosophy, the Councils keep a sharp eye on continuous improvement and constant learning.

One particular Prosperous Economy Goal Council review focused its agenda for the two-hour meeting with the Governor on three topics, all directly tied to current or planned outcome measures or leading indicators for the Council: financial literacy, water infrastructure for agriculture, and the Genuine Progress Indicator (GPI), a recently adopted new measure.

The Council meetings allotted a certain amount of time for each major topic and in most cases involved a presentation by a state agency leader (often focused on an improvement plan) and comments by citizens interested in the topic. Throughout the meetings, the customer's best interests remained front and center. To underscore that theme, the state broadcast the meetings live and for later viewing on TVW (www.tvw.org). All Results Washington meetings are available online. "Getting the right perspectives at the table is part of the tone we're trying to create," says Korthuis-Smith.

Agency heads are busy people in that they have accountability for what is often a multi-billion dollar business. In the public sector, that's not just a full-time job; it's a job-and-a-half. How do you find time to do the work, much less interact with a dozen other CEOs? Korthuis-Smith cited the danger that arises when one agency leader fails to connect with another on a crucial topic: "It's easy for an important opportunity to end there."

Fortunately, the Goal Councils help avert that danger. "The fact they can have that discussion in a Goal Council session helps," she says.

That underscores the value of composing a Council of members from all relevant agencies. That facilitates cross-agency conversations not only between agency heads, but also among the various agencies' research teams and data folks. "That has not happened before and it's led to some great collaboration," says Korthuis-Smith.

At the Prosperous Economy Goal Council meeting, Brian Bonlender, Director of the Washington State Department of Commerce, presented a new measure called the Genuine Progress Indicator (GPI). Maryland, Vermont, and Oregon had already adopted this controversial measure intended to complement the traditional Gross Domestic Product (GDP) as a way to quantify the overall quality of life in the state.

Bonlender argued that while almost every state and country uses GDP as a leading economic indicator, the factors that contribute to that statistic do not provide a complete picture of quality of life. For example, after a hurricane strikes Florida, a subsequent increase in cash transactions might seem to indicate an economic windfall, when, in fact, many citizens are suffering a much poorer quality of life. In addition, GDP ignores the costs and consequences of pollution, the asset value of infrastructure, and the economic contribution of volunteerism and housework. GPI, on the other hand, takes those and many other variables into account.

GPI draws from measures with regards to quality of life, living conditions, economic well-being and economic growth. The illustration that follows shows the basic framework for its creation.

Factors in the General Progress Indicator

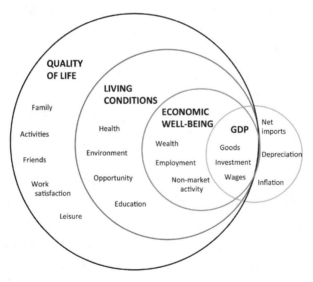

FIGURE 7.2: The General Progress Indicator utilizes a comprehensive set of 26 measures to guide the progress of society from a holistic point of view.

Source: Stefan Bergheim, Measures of Well-Being (Frankfurt, Germany: Deutsche Bank Research, 2006)

Jaime Rossman, a senior economic analyst for Washington's Department of Commerce, extended Bonlender's reasoning: "GPI is a way to begin to ask the question, 'What if we defined the quality of life not by the amount of money and goods and services we consume, but by the quality of life we create?'"

Korthuis-Smith, Director of Results Washington, agrees: "It's a great example of a measure that cuts across all five of our goal areas."

As an example, she described a Goal Council Three (Sustainable Energy and a Clean Environment) review where the conversation focused on forest preservation: "Showing the GPI, one of the 26 measures is for forest preservation, and another for water preservation." You could not see the full picture of environmental sustainability without those crucial factors, which the old GDP calculations would have excluded.

The growing interest in the GPI measure reflects the more systemic view favored by a results-driven approach to government. It helps ensure that all Councils and meetings include the widest possible constituency and allow for more complete conversations about an issue. The more inclusive Councils help officials maintain a satellite's eye view of the impact of government on flesh-and-blood human beings. Otherwise, they can get lost in all the ground-level minutiae that clutter the worm's eye view.

Korthuis-Smith said, "I think it is very important that we always connect the conversation to the broader picture. The question we have to ask about everything is, 'For the sake of what?' What's important when an agency head brings up a particular measure is the *context* for it. Where does it fit in with what we are trying to accomplish for our citizens?"

Results revolutionaries like Korthuis-Smith know that effective problem solving begins with a thorough excavation of *all* the facts surrounding the situation. Otherwise, you cannot hope to unearth a problem's root causes. "All of these conversations help move us from symptoms to root causes," she says.

Of course, the more inclusive conversation starts at the top, when the Governor sets the strategic goals for the administration. Only with the Governor's steadfast commitment to results-driven government can the other leaders down the line keep the ball rolling. The Governor's words drive the action.

"One of our mottos is *action not perfection*," said Korthuis-Smith. "That goes back to the Lean principle that 30 percent today is better than 50 percent tomorrow."

While she sees great progress toward better results throughout the state, she could also see the need for even more: "We have a ton of work to do."

That's the nature of Lean. No matter how much progress you make, government never reaches the point where officials can sit back and congratulate themselves on finishing the job. It's like home repair that way.

And like home repair, it can get pretty messy, as Korthuis-Smith discovered every day on the job. Still, she would do it no other way: "I'm pleased we have a top-down and bottom-up approach."

That approach connects the person at the top with every other member of the food chain. Everyone feels respected and connected and fully engaged. She smiled when she shared a story about a meeting with the Washington Federation of State Employees, the union that represents state workers: "They all had on buttons that said, 'We are Goal 5'."

Goal Five was Efficient, Effective, and Accountable Government. "I was shocked but thrilled," she said.

Even the most ardent fans of results-driven government need a little reinforcement from time to time.

"I was at a conference recently and someone said, 'How do

you know all the things you are doing are the right things?'"
Korthuis-Smith said. "Well, we don't. We are peeling back the
onion and trying to see how a particular area might be affecting
this outcome, but again we ask, 'For the sake of what?' So, we're
trying to keep that perspective and the broader perspective
both."

Peeling onions. Slicing carrots. Keeping the pot simmering. It
gets hot in the kitchen, but that's where the action takes place,
not in some sterile chamber of government or some once-smoke-
filled back room. Government that works, works.

Oregon's Retirement System: Thinking in Terms of Process

Government that works also requires teamwork, and effective
teamwork depends on everyone knowing how to look at and
talk about the work. According to Steve Rodeman, Chief Operating Officer for Oregon's Public Employees Retirement System (PERS), "When you're talking about government improvement, one thing that gets us to improve is when we are all
pulling on the same oar in the same direction."

This principle, he says, is maximized when it applies to every
agency and the state as a whole.

By mid-2014, Oregon had adopted the results-oriented NOW
Management System as its standard. This supported a "we are
all in this together" atmosphere in which everyone in state government shared a common language for doing and talking about
the work of improvement. As a result, learning flourished.

A centerpiece of this statewide team approach, the Quarterly
Target Review (QTR), established a structured agenda that
guided agencies as they examined the extent to which their
improvement efforts were getting results. At review meetings,
the owners of routine work processes and breakthrough initia-

tives reported on their progress toward performance targets and invited feedback on any efforts that had fallen below expectations (i.e., either a "red" or "yellow" status).

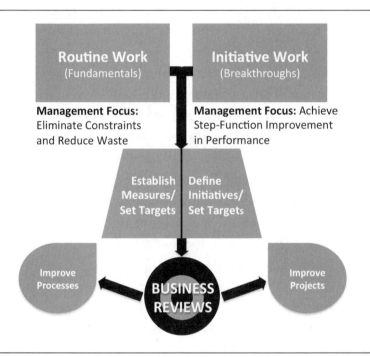

FIGURE 7.3: Effective Business Reviews routinely bring accountability and transparency to both the routine work as well as the initiatives.

Rodeman pointed out how this shared language facilitated cross-agency communication: "Our quarterly target reviews have improved because we have gone to other quarterly target reviews for other agencies, and we have seen other elements in theirs that we wanted to 'steal', and vice versa."

A common system enables shared learning; learning drives improvement; and improvement sustains a results-driven culture.

"These Quarterly Target Reviews have had several cultural benefits," acknowledged Rodeman. "The first foundation is that the QTRs create a structured conversation with a broad base of participation. Previously in manager meetings, a manager might bring something to a meeting that they think is pertinent, but we didn't have a structure for that conversation to occur. So results were haphazard, and sharing only happened when the issue was something a manager thought needed to be shared, or was directed to by an executive."

Oregon's Public Employees Retirement System (PERS) found the structured QTR a valuable tool because it kept everyone's eyes focused on closing any gap between performance and desired results. "It helps managers engage in a conversation about our success and barriers to success across the agency's structure so they have a consistent forum and framework to identify and execute improvements," says Rodeman.

Rodeman cites one specific example of the QTR in action. One of the agency's key outcome measures, the number of *manually produced checks*, serves as a "canary in the mine" because a check that isn't automatically issued through the payment system signals a failure in other processes.

"It turns out that when that number is high, there are a number of predicate processes that are not executing properly," explained Rodeman.

The canary tells everyone that they need to fix something. Note the emphasis on process. When you look at an organization's work from a process point of view, rather than an organization chart perspective, you can see exactly where you need to make corrections that will improve performance. Obviously, a standardized way of thinking and talking about work processes gets everyone on the same improvement track.

When the agency first began doing QTRs, Rodeman said, they focused on measures that were failing to reach their targets. Unfortunately, this emphasis on under-performance contributed to a "reluctance to own the results."

"So you have to be disciplined about and acknowledge the need for improvement, and also the process to improve. This is critical, so the conversation doesn't devolve into finger pointing," he says. "QTRs are where we discuss how to fix problems, not where we fix the blame."

You also need to acknowledge improvements, not just focus on the under-performing measures.

He added, "Over time I think the discipline that we have shown in focusing on improvement instead of focusing on blame has led to greater comfort in discussing where improvements need to be made. People want to be sharing their successes in turning around performance and outcomes, so we need to have space for that as well."

Rodeman took a number of other steps to leverage the benefits of having a structured, healthy process review. For instance, he opened up the QTR meetings to include staff as well as managers. Folding in the frontline workers expanded awareness of the processes the agency used to make important decisions. When frontline workers saw the agency's dedication to improvement in action, they became more fully engaged in the effort to improve results.

"That allows them to see how we make decisions," says Rodeman. "It shows them we make structured and objective decisions based on results rather than whatever they might imagine about how management makes decisions. The other thing that it has demonstrated is our openness in having them involved in the decision-making process so that they are part of the solution instead of victims of the solution."

After a particular session that included 15 non-management employees, Melanie Chandler, Legal Liaison, commented, "I was pleasantly surprised by the lively and honest discussion among the managers about past and present performance and their plans for how to improve the system going forward."

Vitaly Putintsev, a Support Specialist at PERS, added, "It was eye-opening to hear about the volume of calls and emails received daily/monthly, but also reassuring to know that the sections responsible for calls and emails were making great strides in minimizing wait time and in properly addressing various inquiries/questions."

Senior Retirement Data Analyst Matthew Rickard was asked to take charge of the QTR for PERS. About his role, he said, "In its purest sense, the old adage 'what gets measured gets managed' is at the heart of the measurement and review process. But it goes beyond that. If we're managing for outcomes and focusing on continuous improvement, which are key elements of outcome-based management, then there must be a method for tracking the progress. The use of process measures and scorecards has given us a balanced assessment of performance with a process-driven approach. But the scorecards without any focused review leaves an accountability and focus gap."

Note the shared vocabulary that promotes focus and accountability: "measures," "reviews," "results," and "process." That last word deserves special attention.

Best Practices for Business Reviews

There's a right way and a wrong way to conduct formal business reviews. Too many organizations use them as tribunals, where managers hold people's feet to the fire for their mistakes and shortcomings. Such public rebuke makes people dread the sessions. Worse, it sends exactly the wrong message about accountability. Fear causes people to duck, rather than accept responsibility for results. True accountability stresses taking action to get better results.

Tom Moore, Regional Vice President for Mass Ingenuity, quoted the one word a state agency official used to sum up his prior experience with performance reviews: "Brutal." The official recalled that some people actually shed tears during the ordeal. If someone came to the review unprepared or lacking a single piece of key information, the person conducting the review publicly chastised and humiliated them in front of their peers.

Moore likes to tell that story because it drives home the point that poorly conducted reviews can do more damage than good. "This is a perfect example for review leaders to bring up, because it immediately creates an anchor point for them to say what they do and don't want their people's experience to be. For business reviews where someone new to the meeting is being introduced and prepared, they can tell this story and share the new norms they will use."

When people know that the meetings will focus on accountability for results in a positive and nurturing way, they actually look forward to them.

Business reviews include Daily Management "huddles," periodic Stat reviews, and formal Quarterly Target Reviews. Results-driven organizations use regularly scheduled QTRs at all levels, cascading them upward from the team level to the group level, and finally to the agency or department level. This "cascading up" approach creates a thorough, bottom-to-top review of all outcome measures, process measures, and organizational initiatives (breakthroughs). Each review follows a set structure:

- Overall performance against target
- General trend (improving, holding steady, or declining)
- Any need for corrective action

Cascading Quarterly Target Reviews

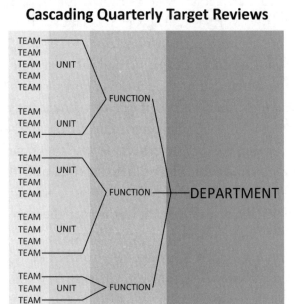

FIGURE 7.4: Business reviews cascade results up from teams to units to functions and eventually to the department. Departments then roll up to the state.

This approach to reviews incorporates the classic *plan, do, and check, adjust* cycle that acknowledges the fact that in the real world, even the best-laid plans can go awry. Remember, however, that the reviews do not pinpoint problems for which someone should receive a slap on the wrist but seek to identify opportunities to improve results.

All results-driven government efforts breathe focus and accountability into the organization. That helps ensure that people remain fully engaged in the mission and strive to perform to the best of their ability. Set the right expectations, communicate them clearly, work tirelessly to fulfill them, close any gaps along the way, and, as if by magic, people start to get better results.

Taking Seven Sure Steps to True Accountability

Mass Ingenuity's Tom Moore summarizes what he suggests results-oriented leaders use to drive true accountability:

1. **Establish Clear Roles and Responsibilities:** Disciplined QTRs reflect an organization's dedication to getting results. Since so much depends on effective QTRs, leaders must make sure everyone involved knows their areas of accountability and comes to the meeting with as much relevant data as possible.

2. **Create a Safe Environment:** Positive accountability creates a safe environment for people to speak freely about their work and any problems that have arisen since the last QTR. Leaders must carefully define the way people should behave in meetings. If the highest-level meetings adhere to the cultural norms leaders want everyone to adopt, meetings at every other level will follow the model. Over time, a positive, safe environment will make true accountability a daily habit throughout the organization.

3. **Elevate Importance:** Full engagement demands full attendance. Set the expectation that everyone on a given team must attend every QTR. The "no excuses" rule should apply. People should plan their schedules in such a way that they never need to make an excuse for an absence. When everyone knows that attending and actively participating in QTRs is Job #1, they will make it a top priority and come better prepared to wrestle with any problems that are keeping the organization from getting the results it seeks.

4. **Demonstrate Long-Term Commitment:** It takes time to get results; the work never ends. Leaders should lock down dates for at least 4-6 QTRs. This long-term approach tells

everyone in the organization that "we mean business" and "we're in this for the long haul."

5. **Create Consistency:** Predictability engenders trust. A structured and standard agenda is one way to build this, but it also applies to how the leaders behave and interact in the QTR. If, for example, the department leader always offers support to anyone reporting indicators in red, the organization will understand that if things are in red, you will be offered support rather than the criticism that would otherwise be anticipated.

6. **Support Measure Owners and Data Stewards:** Patience wins the day. Quality should overrule overly ambitious schedules. It can take months to get new measures up and running smoothly, especially if the organization is adding several at once. A lot of people must collect a lot of data. Everyone needs to see and discuss the data. Leaders must make sure they give the owners of each measure sufficient time to do it right. Those who lack experience with quantification may need the help and support of data professionals. As the program moves forward, leaders must couple patience with perseverance. It's easy in the rush toward improvement to go too quickly. Haste, however, can create the same waste the improvement initiative aims to eliminate.

7. **Reward and Challenge:** Rewards reinforce motivation and engagement; new challenges stretch the imagination. People need recognition for hitting their numbers, reaching their goals, and solving problems along the way. Smart leaders take time to celebrate major milestones, at the same time setting new milestones that will pull their people toward achieving even greater results.

In all three of the examples discussed in this chapter, business reviews fueled the performance engine. Maryland's BayStat, Washington's lean program, and Oregon's full-engagement initiative used various types of reviews to create a culture of true accountability and inspire action.

There's no surefire formula or set of ironclad rules for building a results-driven government. Each state and its agencies will adapt the basic principles we've been discussing in this book, with their own unique needs and goals in mind. But no matter how else they get to a results-driven government, they will all ride on the back of effective business reviews.

CHAPTER EIGHT

Creativity on the Frontline

Engaging Employees in Removing Waste

"I hear and I forget. I see and I remember.
I do and I understand."

~ CONFUCIUS

As Colette S. Peters, then Inspector General for the Oregon Department of Corrections, approached the entrance to the Oregon State Penitentiary one day in 2006, she noticed an elderly woman standing there crying.

Peters approached and asked, "What's wrong? Why are you so sad?"

The woman told Peters that a friend had driven her hundreds of miles from California to Salem, Oregon, to visit her incarcerated grandson, but because she could not produce a valid driver's license, the officer at the prison's entrance would not allow her inside.

Peters, who became Director of Oregon's Department of Corrections in 2012, says of the incident: "Of course the officer was doing exactly what his post orders said he should do. Even though the woman's driver's license had only expired a few days prior, it was not considered a valid piece of identification."

But because the license was valid in all other respects as identification, Peters intervened and saved the day. Ever since that chance encounter with someone in need of better service, Peters has championed the principle that the people who work for her should be able to exercise the authority to do the right thing.

Inside almost all government agencies, and perhaps even more so in a sensitive one like the Department of Corrections, policy does not permit deviation from prescribed rules, even when, in certain instances, a rule defies common sense. You can't decide on your own "to do the right thing." All too often, an official responds to a citizen's unusual need with the tried and true, "Just following the rules, Ma'am."

Peters understands why that happens: "That officer on duty did exactly what he was told to do because that is what the system expects of him," she explains. "In a system based on the fear of disobeying orders, people will follow the orders, even if it is clearly the wrong thing to do."

Doing the wrong thing, or, for that matter, a right thing that falls outside the boundary of a regulation, can get you into a lot of trouble. You might get "written up" for the infraction or find yourself out of a job.

Peters explains that in the case of correction facilities, officials must scrupulously follow protocols about dealing with major disturbances such as fights or forcibly removing an inmate from a cell. In those instances, an officer cannot waste time or risk injury by thinking creatively about the situation. The officer must follow predefined protocol. A life might depend on it. But what about the woman with the expired driver's license? Surely that situation called for some creative thinking that paid a little more attention to the spirit of the rules.

Back in Chapter Three, we discussed the 2008 "turnaround" of the Oregon Youth Authority overseen by then-Oregon Governor Ted Kulongoski. You might recall that Colette Peters (then OYA Director), along with her Deputy Director Fariborz Pakseresht, decided that turning around the agency depended on turning around the culture. To do that, they decided to change their management system, creating a level of accountability, transparency, and openness rarely seen in government. Core to that was setting in motion the management process of Solving Problems, which encourages the people who know the work best — the ones who do it — to use their skills and authority to improve it.

MANAGEMENT PROCESS PURPOSE STATEMENT: *Solving Problems*

TO: *Engage every employee in improving the way they do their work*

IN A WAY THAT: *Stresses the need to take initiative at the lowest level*

SO THAT: *The agency can remove all obstacles to achieving desired results*

Within a year, Oregon legislators proudly referred to OYA as the "poster child of good government," a testament to the success of the new culture created by Peters and Pakseresht. One powerful tool the two leaders had was the OYA Fundamentals Map that appeared in Chapter Two; it facilitated communication with legislators by making it easy to understand what the agency did and how it measured its success. Peters then set about doing the same for the Oregon Department of Corrections, a far larger and more complex organization with over 4,500 employees and 14,600 people in custody.

Creating a Safe Improvement Zone

Peters' strategy to activate results-driven government in the agencies she directed revolved around allowing public servants to take control of *how* they do their work. The shift from thoughtlessly obeying orders to making creative decisions on the frontline may, at first glance, seem like a slippery and perilous slope that could end in chaos. Well, it could, unless, as Peters did, you honor the three primary Force Fields that create a *Safe Improvement Zone*:

Force Field #1: *The Law*
The executive branch plays the lead in implementing the laws created by the legislative branch and refined by the judicial branch. Any improvements must adhere to the law. If the law does not permit desired changes, then the system provides a means for removing or changing the law. However, that's usually much easier said than done. On the other hand, the executive branch can fairly easily alter the rules and regulations and resulting procedures it has created to implement the law. If the issue surfaced by the elderly visitor to the Oregon State Penitentiary was in the law, that would be one thing, but like most problems, the ability to change the procedure is well within the scope of the executive branch.

Force Field #2: *The Management System*
The management system itself restricts what an employee can and cannot change. As we saw in Chapter Five, the outcome and process measures built into a results-driven management

system stimulate continuous improvement. The people on the frontline who do the work can see where they need to make modifications. When measures indicate that service has failed to deliver desired results, those delivering the service can and should make immediate adjustments to their work. In a results-driven system, an officer who confronts a visitor who cannot provide identification that adheres to protocol should feel free to question the rule and even to make an exception in certain exceptional cases, without setting aside the overarching law.

Force Field #3: *Structured Improvement Methods*
Well-designed improvement methodologies help ensure that employees do not waste time fixing what isn't broken. The proven methods and tools for process improvement, many of which we will discuss later in this chapter, guide people through the steps they must take to achieve well-informed, effective, and fact-driven improvements. These range from methods to reorganize the workspace to methodology for improving the most complex and critical high-volume processes. In a results-driven system, the Oregon Corrections officer would know exactly how to set in motion the steps that will allow for the right amount of flexibility in the visitor-identification process.

Safe improvement hinges on engaging the people who do the work in making needed changes to the way they do their work. Those who work on the frontlines see what needs fixing, what wastes time and money, what fails to get results, and what makes customers happy or unhappy. Every day they see many, many opportunities to improve their routine work. It takes too many steps to issue a new vehicle title? Remove a step or two. Retirement checks arrive three days late? Find and eliminate the bottleneck. A woman cannot get past the officer to visit her grandson in prison because her driver's license has expired? Permit another form of valid identification.

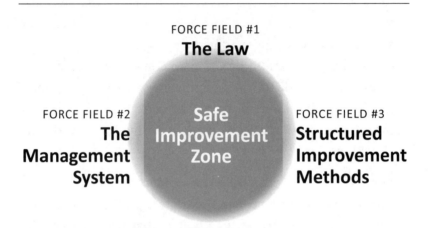

FORCE FIELD #1
The Law

FORCE FIELD #2
The Management System

Safe Improvement Zone

FORCE FIELD #3
Structured Improvement Methods

FIGURE 8.1: Clear boundaries create a Safe Improvement Zone in which employees can make improvements without the direct involvement of their supervisor.

This idea of safe improvements applies to everything government does, from conducting a workplace safety audit, testing water for toxicity, and training people on the subtleties of workplace sexual harassment to reducing the costs of printing tax forms, speeding the delivery of invoices, closing the loopholes that allow for abuse of Medicare, and ensuring that veterans get prompt and appropriate medical care.

Whatever the issue at hand, public servants who are motivated to make a positive difference in citizens' lives will always jump at the chance to help government deliver speedier and more cost-efficient service.

Oregon's Peters talks about a more recent chance encounter in 2014: "I'm in the foyer of the penitentiary and there's a family standing there and they said, 'Ma'am, we'd like to talk to the superintendent.'"

Peters offers to help them, saying, "I would be happy to get the superintendent, but I'm the director. Is there anything I can do for you?"

One of the family members offers a big smile and says: "We wanted to give him a compliment. We drove hundreds of miles to witness our brother getting married. My father, who has been disabled for years and hasn't driven for years, did not have a photo ID. We explained that to the woman at the front desk and she did not hesitate to make an exception to the rule. She let us know she was making an exception and told us we needed a valid ID the next time we came."

Peters loves the fact that the results-driven management system has begun to drive out fear of retribution for making exceptions when doing so causes no harm and improves service. It happens because she and her leadership team have engaged her staff in helping their customers.

"I travel around the state, and I can't turn a corner in one of our facilities without seeing an employee that is engaged. They're happy to be here and feel connected to our mission," she said.

Delivering better results makes everyone happy, especially customers. Before employees can deliver exceptional results, however, they must relentlessly detect and eliminate waste.

Ridding the System of Waste

If you want to get a feel for the amount of waste in government, ask Google, "How much waste is there in government?" You'll click onto a whopping 176 million links you could spend a lifetime exploring. Imagine ridding the system of all that waste. Before you launch such a campaign, however, you need to define precisely what you mean by "waste." Such dramatic examples as the $91 screw and the $500 hammer purchased by the federal government make shocking headlines, but they only represent the tip of a massive iceberg that includes all the inefficiencies, duplications, and red tape that bog down the routine work of government. To start wiping out waste, you must focus not on the hammer itself, but on the processes that made it such a terrible waste of taxpayer dollars.

The Lean approach used in the business world defines waste as *all activities that don't directly create value for the customer.* That simple definition does not include the many obligations a company must fulfill beyond just serving its customers, such as its responsibilities to shareholders, employees, auditors, and the government. The same applies to government, which must not only respect the needs of its employees but also the public interest and the law. Nevertheless, when an organization's leaders focus on the waste in everything the company or agency does to deliver results to customers, they can better serve all their stakeholders.

An effective "waste elimination" campaign begins with a careful evaluation of all of an organization's processes, with an eye toward spotting the **Seven Deadly Sins of Waste** (first mentioned in Chapter One): waiting, inspecting, re-entering, searching, moving, reworking, and over-processing.

In a manufacturing business, these sins typically consume 20-25 percent of operating costs. In a private sector service business, they can consume even more — up to 30-40 percent of operating costs. What percentage of the money it spends does government waste?

We've asked state employees this question countless times in group sessions. Some employees calculate the amount of waste in their functions as high as 90 percent. We often ask government workers to think about one simple process: the number of approvals needed to generate and handle a $50 invoice. Most of the people we ask will estimate that the work costs as much as three times as the value of the invoice itself. That's $150 spent to collect $50!

Seven Deadly Sins of Waste

1. **Waiting** – time lost re-handling and re-starting work as you wait for things needed to complete it

2. **Inspecting** – checking work to try and catch errors

3. **Re-entering** – putting information in one place that already exists in another

4. **Searching** – trying to find data, materials, reports or whatever else is missing

5. **Moving** – routing things or moving people from one place to another, staging work, etc.

6. **Reworking** – doing work over again because it was incomplete or incorrect

7. **Over-processing** – doing work that serves no identifiable customer or purpose

FIGURE 8.2: Creating a language for waste facilitates seeing it.

How does that happen? As we have noted in earlier chapters, government processes start out with all the good intentions in the world: "We need to buy a hammer. Let's buy a good one." But then over the years process has been piled on process and approvals piled on approvals to the point where the hammer that needs to be purchased becomes incidental to the whole process. We talk to people in government every day who attest to the 15 signatures needed on a document, and while it looks like it improves control, it becomes easy for each signer to assume, "With all these people signing it, why should I bother to review it?"

The more people who are accountable, the less accountability there really is. Most all government processes have evolved over the years as many well-intentioned people made well-intentioned decisions about getting the work done, and involved too many people in it. Of course, the path to the everlasting bonfire is *paved* with good intentions.

So, what's the alternative? How do we get back on the track to heaven? It starts with two truths about ridding a system of waste:

- Experienced "waste managers" have created a toolbox full of proven, highly reliable, readily available, and easily learned process-improvement methodologies.
- Motivated public servants possess an inherent motivation to improve the service they provide to their customers.

Because process-improvement methods do get results, and because the people who do the work want to do it more efficiently and effectively, ridding the system of waste is a perfectly achievable goal.

Learning the Vocabulary of Waste

"Muda, KATA, Kanban, Kaizen, Poka-Yoke, SMED."

No, those are not words spoken by the characters in *The Lord of the Rings*. They are terms that experts in the world of process improvement use every day when they talk about their work. If they sound vaguely Japanese, you can thank Dr. W. Edwards Deming, the Godfather of Quality, for that, because he taught the Japanese a different way to run an organization. Take a quick look at this list:

Lean Terminology At A Glance

TERMS & TOOLS	
Daily Management	Work teams spending a small portion of time each day to meet and work on process improvement
Gemba/Gemba Walk	Managing by walking around; going to where the work is being done
Hoshin Kanri	A set of tools that takes organizational strategy and aligns all activities of the organization to that strategy
Kanban	A physical location that controls production quantity; when it becomes empty it pulls more production
Lean (big "L")	A high-engagement philosophy and system of management driven by the beliefs that customers define value, employees create it, and that everyone's job is to eliminate waste
lean (small "l")	The use of the term "lean" when it refers to process improvement activities
Muda	Japanese word for waste
Poka-Yoke	Method built into a process that detects and prevents errors
Six Sigma	Set of techniques and tools used for process improvement developed by Motorola
Standard Work	Documented best practices for getting work done
The Five Whys	A method for seeking root cause
Visual Management	Using displays and other visual means to track performance and process improvement
5S	Method for organizing the workplace: Sort, Straighten, Shine, Standardize and Sustain
PROCESS IMPROVEMENT METHODOLOGIES	
A3	An improvement process developed by Toyota that ends up on an A3-sized sheet of paper
DMAIC	A five-step improvement method: Define, Measure, Analyze, Improve, Control
Kaizen	The daily practice of continuous process improvement using PDCA
Kaizen Blitz	A rapid improvement workshop designed to produce results in a few days
KATA Coaching	A 5-Step improvement coaching methodology
PDCA	The Shewhart cycle is a scientific approach to making improvement: Plan, Do, Check, Adjust
Six Sigma	Improving quality and efficiency of processes with a heavy reliance on statistical methods
7-Step Problem Solving	A seven-step process-improvement method that identifies and eliminates the root cause of a performance shortfall

FIGURE 8.3: The world of waste has its own vocabulary, and behind the words are a myriad of tools and methodologies.

For the purposes of our discussion here, let's create a simpler vocabulary for Lean process improvement. We'll begin with seven key terms (known as the Seven Basic Quality Tools) that **everyone** intent on reducing and eliminating waste must learn.

These terms and the tools they represent can enable leaders and employees to address 80-90 percent of the process-improvement opportunities in their organizations.

Seven Basic Tools

1. **Check Sheet** – gathers data about processes
2. **Cause and Effect Diagram** – organizes brainstorming about causes of a problem
3. **Process Map** – draws a picture of workflow
4. **Pareto Analysis** – pinpoints primary causes
5. **Histogram** – reveals variations and abnormalities
6. **Scatter Diagram** – shows the relationship between two variables
7. **Run Chart** – displays process stability over time

You can find out more about these and other Total Quality Management and Lean Six Sigma tools in *The Complete Idiot's Guide to Lean Six Sigma* by Breakthrough Management Group and Neil DeCarlo (2007).

The number and complexity of process improvement tools can boggle the beginner's mind. Organizations often hire consultants or trainers to help demystify them. However, you can start the learning curve on your own by adopting the 7-Step Problem Solving method. That protocol uses all of the Seven Basic Tools and progresses through predictable stages.

The Three Stages of a Lean Process Improvement

Low Level of Lean Maturity: *7-Step Problem Solving*
Identify and eliminate the root cause of a process performance problem.

Medium Level of Lean Maturity: *Kaizen/Lean Process Improvement*
Identify and eliminate unnecessary activities to improve process performance.

High Level of Lean Maturity: *Six Sigma/Statistical Methods*
Understand process characteristics and capability in order to improve process performance through the reduction of variation.

Process Improvement Maturity

FIGURE 8.4: A common mistake made is to use tools that are too difficult to learn and use successfully. Basic 7-Step-Problem Solving provides an important foundation for organizations before advancing to Lean and Six Sigma.

Going from lean to Lean

When "Sandra Elliott" takes over Name-the-State's Department of Employment, she finds the 1,200-person agency already immersed in the early stage of process improvement. The people there have made some noticeable progress toward the goal of pushing creativity to the frontlines of service, but they still face a long journey before that becomes an everyday reality. A master of the art herself, she knows that her people will need to traverse a much longer learning curve before they can reap the full benefits of Lean. While they have fallen in love with process improvement and have accomplished a lot, the department still suffers from an unacceptable number of glitches in its electronic filing system. Key people spend way too many hours each day fielding complaints from business owners and trying to solve their problems over the phone.

Just one week into her new job, Sandra sees what's wrong with the picture. Despite all the enthusiasm for Lean initiatives and a lot of training and reading and studying, the people at DOE have not achieved the measureable results the Governor and the previous head of the agency expected when they launched the program. That's why the Governor transferred the former head of DOE to another position in her administration and appointed Sandra to fix the situation.

Because Sandra has experienced the Lean learning curve first hand, she knows that the process improvers at DOE have become mired in little "l" lean thinking. They see lean as a set of tools to engage people in process improvement rather than as a management philosophy and system that focuses on results by putting the customer in the middle and engaging employees in the elimination of all forms of waste. That's what she means by big "L" Lean. Until she gets her people thinking big "L", they will accomplish little more than the *random acts of improvement* we discussed earlier in this book.

Jim Clark, an experienced CEO who serves on the Now Management System consulting team at Mass Ingenuity as a regional vice president, points out that random acts do not add up to overall improvement: "When we as leaders talk about improving performance, whether it is private or public sector, it all begins with defining what performance we want."

In other words, leaders must emphasize Big Lean, not a collection of little leans. You must solve the Big Problem, not just a series of little ones. And the Big Problem is true engagement at every level of the organization. As we said in Chapter Four, **Solving Problems** is the fourth of four management processes in an effective, results-driven management system.

Clark, after a long and successful career working in the outdoor industry in which he held executive positions at Coleman and, most recently, served as CEO of Yakima Products (bike racks, roof rack systems and trunks, etc.), decided he wanted to spend more time with his growing kids. In 2012, he joined our effort to implement results-driven government in state agencies.

"Once you have determined the context for improvement, problem solving becomes the key skill in results-driven management," Clark argues. "It greases the gears of improvement . . . As a CEO you are so focused on strategy, you're involved in the day-to-day issues that arise with projects and operations, and it's easy to overlook the central importance of basic problem solving."

So what would he urge Sandra Elliott to do over at DOE? He would tell her to remember what she already knows. She needs to:

- Install a results-driven management system that will drive the shift to a true Lean culture.
- Ensure every employee becomes an effective problem solver.

While some conventionally trained managers like the idea of letting lean tools and methods develop organically based on individual initiative, interests, and passions, too many different applications of lean can cause as many problems as they solve. Yes, they can plant the seeds of change, but in the end you can end up with a garden full of mismatched and competing plants, not to mention a few weeds. When you rely on a bunch of individually tailored methodologies, people speak different languages when they talk about process improvement, creating a modern day Tower of Babel where different teams do not fully understand one another. The vocabulary of improvement varies from team to team, but variation is the enemy of overall improvement and the philosophy of Big Lean. With Lean, you want to reduce, not increase, variation.

Reduction of variation, one of the most basic concepts of improvement, argues that before you can improve a process, you must stabilize it, and you stabilize it by removing whatever causes it to vary. Reducing variation automatically improves the output of any process. If you need to assemble a dozen smoothly operating, 100-component contraptions, you would not put them together a dozen different ways.

At the outset of her tenure, Sandra addressed the fact that the people at DOE had been using far too many *different* improvement methods based on individual preferences. In effect, they were solving problems a dozen different ways, which resulted in highly variable output. They introduced too much variation into the system. So they needed to learn and master **one methodology** that every DOE team can use to improve all of the processes that need to run more smoothly in order to achieve better overall results. The same holds true for a state: a single methodology broadly used will accelerate learning and improve collaboration.

Sandra redirected the Lean initiative by making sure everyone in her department was learning and gaining certification in the Seven Basic Tools, to get everyone back on the same page. The people who solve problems together, thrive together.

Living the Lean Life

At Washington State's Lean Conference in 2011, Washington Governor Christine Gregoire said, "The best solutions to our problems come from those on the line every day seeing what works and doesn't work and how to fix and how to solve it." The now-former-Governor had issued executive order 11-04 Lean Transformation in 2011, mandating that all cabinet agencies in the state learn Lean principles, concepts, and tools; complete a Lean project; begin building a Lean agency culture; and report results and lessons learned to the governor (State of Washington, 2011). The results of this program provided the foundation on which her successor, Governor Jay Inslee, built his Results Washington effort.

Hollie Jensen, Enterprise Lean Consultant for the State of Washington and a member of the Results Washington team, joined the effort in 2013 after a 17-year stint with Starbucks. During her years at Starbucks, she had moved up from a store manager to corporate Lean practice strategy manager. She wanted to offer her expertise to her home state. That proved an enormously satisfying but significant challenge.

"There're so many opportunities to improve in government that it is an overwhelming mission at times," she said.

Jensen knows the power of frontline results from a business perspective. One of her projects involved improving productivity and customer satisfaction with Starbucks' blended drinks. One organization-wide Lean initiative from 2008 to 2012 improved customer satisfaction for handcrafted beverages from 66 to 81 percent and increased productivity from 9.8 to 11.6 transactions per hour. Starbucks got those results, in part, because the leadership was committed to rethinking how Starbucks did business, rather than just applying process improvement tools to eliminate waste.

Jensen loves the way an overarching Lean strategy engages and values people who work on the frontlines and inspires them to innovate in ways that provide exceptional service to the customer.

"On a personal level I am really proud to be a part of this movement," she said. "Delivering more value for Washingtonians is huge. Sure, the results talk for themselves, but Lean did so much for the spirit of the Starbucks stores and it does so much for the spirit of the environment I'm in today."

Like DOE director Sandra Elliott, Jensen knows if you think of Lean merely as a way to improve processes, you will fail to tap its power to install creativity on the frontlines. Lean as process improvement provides only the first shot in The Results Revolution. If you stop there, you may win a lot of battles, but you will end up losing the war.

Jensen understands that winning the war requires committed leadership at the top of the organization. A lack of leadership ruins all too many Lean efforts.

"When that happens, it is because we do not yet have the support at the leadership level," she said. "Up and down, any employee, from the frontline to the expert to the leadership, all should be involved in improvement work everyday. It is very easy not to develop the management systems, the mindset, and the cultural components necessary for sustained success."

In the ideal environment, every worker leads, and every leader works on process improvement. Jensen knows that the appropriate leadership support is in place when she sees leaders actually walking the walk and modeling the sort of customer-focused thinking they expect from their people. They themselves speak the language of Lean and know how to use the tools the organization has adopted to improve its processes and get better results. In Washington, the heads of agencies and the Governor do not merely tell the troops what to do; they fight right alongside them to achieve The Results Revolution. The message? "We do it the Lean way."

In far too many instances, leaders want their people to live the Lean life, but they fail to build it into their organizations' DNA. You can't just tack it onto the existing system. Rather than stimulating creativity, add-on Lean becomes a burden for frontline workers who see it as just another management fad that will quickly fade when the next one comes along. In the worst-case scenario, workers wait for a supervisor or manager or Lean expert to tell them what to do. In the best-case scenario, they take initiative without waiting for someone to give them orders or approval.

As Jensen said, "When it is seen as extra work, when you hear people say, 'We're not doing Lean today,' it's clear Lean is still just about process improvement."

In other words, "We'll fire a few bullets when someone tells us to shoot, but we could care less about winning the war."

Effective Lean leaders don't tell people to shoot at a target; they pick up the rifle themselves. In one agency in Washington's Department of Licensing, Director Pat Kohler required all members of her senior management team to complete Lean Six Sigma/green belt training.

Her leaders model Lean behavior. Kohler says: "Asking all of my senior leadership team to take Lean training was an easy decision because until they understood it, getting their full support in developing a Lean culture from the ground up would have been hard. I knew once they understood Lean, they would become strong advocates and integrate it into the work being done at every level of our agency."

Washington's State Department of Corrections Correctional Industries division shines as one of the most advanced Lean agencies in Washington, if not the nation, and it has extended its Lean philosophy to the businesses it runs. If you travel into the rural countryside about 10 miles south of Washington's State Capitol Dome, you will see something rather remarkable: the agency's Correctional Industries (CI) division. CI operates 22 different businesses, ranging from tilapia farming to eyeglass and furniture manufacturing. It also provides three meals a day to 17,000 offenders in custody. The CI businesses employ 340 civilians and 1,600 offender workers. The operation has done exactly what Jensen advocates for all state agencies (Washington State Correctional Industries, 2014).

Founded in 2007 under the leadership of former CI Director Lyle Morse, an experienced private sector furniture manufacturer, CI has delivered impressive business results. It has, for example:

- Reduced processing steps from 22 to six in one operation
- Shrunk sales order processing time from 30 days to three days
- Collapsed purchasing lead time on raw materials from 26 days to three days
- Slashed inventory by $700,000
- Reduced food costs by $1.3 million
- Increased available production hours from 15.6 to 22 hours per week

- Eliminated 98 percent of cardboard waste
- Cut the lead time to process a commissary order by 86 percent
- Improved the pocket design on a clothing product to reduce waste of motion and increase output from 60 to 120 pieces per hour
- Reduced tilapia farming water consumption from 6,000 to 2,500 gallons per week
- Achieved a 35 percent reduction in the size of the tool room by getting rid of unnecessary items

Current CI Director Danielle Armbruster made an interesting point about living the Lean life: "What we say is once we stop calling it Lean, we have reached our goal. It's just part of our daily lives. Whether it's a five-minute KATA board conversation or a five-minute waste walk we are always looking at our pinch points, our processes, our equipment, our training."

Getting to that point took a lot of time and effort. Armbruster admitted that CI's people found the first 12-to-18 months especially challenging.

"When we talked about Lean and the philosophies of Lean, the first thing everyone thinks is we're downsizing, we're eliminating positions. We had to engage everyone in understanding it's not about less people, it's about how we utilize our time and our resources."

She makes an extremely important point. Lean brings change, and change can ignite fear. And fear, as we have seen, can make it impossible to succeed with any major new organizational initiatives. However, once people have experienced the benefits of Lean, their fear evaporates and they rely on the new philosophy to guide everything they do.

Building Internal Capacity

When you get Lean right, process improvement initiatives enhance important basic skills and increase the organization's overall capacity to get great results. For example, as people participate in high-engagement, team-oriented, results-driven efforts to improve various processes, they also learn how to:

1. Conduct better meetings
2. Unleash more frontline creativity
3. Communicate more clearly and concisely
4. Plan and manage projects more effectively

When a results-oriented team tackles a problem, team members automatically hone those skills. Rarely taught, especially in old school, top-down control structures, these skills enable employees to take action without a boss's permission and supervision. More freedom to solve problems plus sharper skills equals greater capacity.

In the 1940s, Professor Reginald Revans developed the concept of action learning while training to become a physicist at the University of Cambridge. It may seem perfectly obvious today, but this simple idea made a big impact on the field of learning theory. Basically, it held that the best way to learn something is to do it, provided you ask a lot of questions as you go along (Action Learning Associates, 2014). You need to solve the problem of putting together your new unicycle. Take all the parts out of the box, read the instructions, question anything you don't understand, and ask for advice and feedback as you fasten Part A to Part B and Part Y to Part Z. You do that a few times, and you'll become an expert unicycle assembler. You will even increase your capacity to assemble anything.

Call it "on-the-job-training" or "earning while you learn"; it happens as you work on solving everyday problems. The best learning doesn't take place in a formal setting. It doesn't happen in some classroom where people feel no keen motivation to do their work more efficiently and more effectively.

To reap the benefits of action learning, we encourage teams to engage in what we call the 12-Week Problem Solving Learning Burst. The diagram below gives you a feel for the sequence of events, from Agreeing on the Problem to Reflecting and Learning:

12-Week Problem Solving Learning Burst

WEEK	THE WORK	STEP NUMBER	TOOLS LEARNED/APPLIED
1	Team role assignments	1. Agree on the Problem	Systematic Problem Solving
	Team groundrules		Teamwork
	Decision-making process		Data Gathering
	Validate the problem statement		Meeting Effectiveness
2	Create a common understanding of how the work is currently done	2. Map the Current Process	Process Mapping
	Identify process breakdowns		
3	Identify potential causes	3. Uncover and Prove the Root Cause	Brainstorming
	Prioritize potential causes		Multivoting
	Assign data gathering		Cause and Effect Diagram
4	Gather data		Checksheets
	Analyze data		Histograms
5	Continue data gathering and analysis		Pareto Analysis
	Begin root cause analysis		
6	Identify small number of root causes		
	Select primary causes		
7	Brainstorm solutions	4. Develop Solutions	Basic Project Planning
	Use criteria to select best solution		Criteria-Weighted Voting
	Develop implementation plans down to the task level		Workplans/Gantt Charts
8	Plan needed implementation resources		Project Planning
	Gain input from those impacted by the change		
9	Incorporate feedback into implementation	5. Implement the Fix	Basic Project Management
	Finalize implementation plans		
10	Manage implementation		
	Monitor and adjust plan		
11	Plan follow-up and control methodology	6. Hold the Gains	Run or Control Charts
	Develop controls for all critical changes		
	Set performance levels		
	Establish escalation paths		
12	Capture lessons learned	7. Reflect and Learn	Project Post-Mortem
	Present Project for final approval		Presentation Skills

FIGURE 8.5: This 12-week schedule is an example of action learning where participants learn tools and immediately apply them in order to solve a real problem.

Well-designed and well-facilitated problem-solving experiences enhance learning, spark creativity, and increase capacity. When they have these skills and methods, individuals, teams, and the whole organization get better results in everything they do in service of the customer.

As a rule, leaders must think strategically about the connection between action learning and building capacity. In other words, you want to plant the seeds that will produce a bountiful crop of creative frontline problem-solvers. The leader responsible for building this strategic capacity:

1. Decides whether to build capacity or buy capacity
2. Selects the right facilitators
3. Stresses action learning on real projects
4. Ensures that facilitators coach the whole class

Let's put these four concepts to work.

Decide Whether to Build or Buy

As a rule of thumb, an agency needs about one skilled facilitator for every 100 employees. This ratio should support enough problem-solving learning bursts to spread the skills across the organization over a two-year period. Most employees will need to go through two or three projects under the guidance of a skilled facilitator before they can confidently apply their new skills on their own.

Where do you find good facilitators? You either create them in-house, or you bring them in from the outside. Before you choose one of those options, think about the pros and cons of each:

	BUILD	BUY
PRO		
	Know the culture	Bring immediate skills
	Understand the business	Have demonstrated successes
	Have existing relationships	Can accelerate learning
CON		
	Takes six months	Don't know the culture
	Low experience level	Don't know the business
	Will make mistakes	Don't have relationships

FIGURE 8.6: Determining whether to build or buy internal capability is a matter of how fast the organization wants to build problem-solving capacity.

Quite often, a blend of build and buy works best. Let's say that 1000 people work for the Department of Employment. You need 10 good facilitators. To start off on the right foot, you might hire a consulting firm to conduct a three-day workshop on effective facilitation for 20 of your best candidates, perhaps a mix of middle managers and frontline workers. At the end of the workshop you can select 10 people who will serve as your in-house facilitators. Now that they know how to facilitate, they have to learn about process improvement.

Select the Right Facilitators

The best facilitators bring a lot to the task: mastery of Lean techniques, proven problem-solving skills, a track record in process improvement, experience leading teams, and the ability to orchestrate action learning. You can find a lot of good books on each of these topics in the *For Further Reading* list at the back of this book.

Facilitating learning requires a deep understanding of the way a group functions. The Holden Leadership Center at the University of Oregon (2014) describes how good facilitators enhance group dynamics through:

- Observation – discerning patterns of communication
- Participation – monitoring and stimulating healthy interaction
- Decision Making – ensuring shared decision making
- Role Definition – putting each team member in the right position

Good facilitators also display a fair amount of Emotional Intelligence, a concept popularized by Daniel Goleman (2005) and skillfully applied in *The Emotionally Intelligent Team* by Marcia Hughes. In her book *Primal Teams,* Jackie Barretta shows the direct relationship between optimum emotions and creative problem solving.

Stress Action Learning on Real Projects

You can launch a lot of Lean initiatives, but if they do not achieve measureable results, you'll soon get fat again. Lean often fails in no small part because of the failure to deliver real results. As much work as a project takes, it must have a high return on investment in practical terms, because in absence of that the emotional cost will be too high. What that means is that the people involved in these projects put a lot of emotional energy into them, largely in terms of "hope" that this time things will be different and that the solutions will be used to make things better. Failure to deliver hard results runs up a huge soft cost in terms of doubt, fear, disappointment, and disengagement.

You want your people to acquire and sharpen what we call "sticky" skills — the ones they will use every day in their routine work, not just "once and out." If Fred needs algebra for his day-to-day work, teach him algebra. Schooling him in calculus will just go in one ear and out the other.

Real-time action learning that delivers tangible, meaningful results will cause the skills to stick. It will take more than a single cycle of improvement for this to happen, but rest assured, it will.

Ensure that Facilitators Coach the Whole Team

Make this your mantra: "Every worker is a problem solver." If you want to grow a big crop of problem solvers, don't restrict the opportunity to a select group of people. While you cannot expect every single employee to solve problems like an Einstein, you can get them all on board with your organization's problem-solving approach. The best teams include a broad range of people with a wide variety of skills: Evelyn the Expert, Chuck the Communicator, Ginny the Genius, Gerry the Grinder, Nora the Newbie, and Vic the Veteran. As each individual displays his or her special talent, the whole group benefits. Gerry gets smarter, Nora grows into her job, and Evelyn learns how to keep her expertise from irritating her less-experienced teammates.

A good facilitator knows how to tailor coaching to the needs of both the group and its individual members. Even the best team in the world will struggle from time to time. That's why a good facilitator practices the Three P's: patience, perseverance, and professionalism.

Making Magic on the Frontline

Oregon's Director of Corrections Peters will tell you that her agency's success rests in the hands of the people who do the work — the real down-and-dirty, day-to-day work of corrections. Moving from long-held traditions of command and control to an environment in which people eagerly take accountability for removing waste and feel free to make judgments that align to the mission, vision, values, and goals of the agency creates a magical, unending journey that gets amazing results no other management approach can deliver.

Why did Peters bother? Just to transform an organization and its culture? Not for a minute. She did it to benefit the "customer behind bars." Her heart swells over the youthful offenders at the Oregon Youth Authority who have gained a better shot at productive lives. Peters often tells a story about delivering a lecture to a room full of students working on their master's degrees in criminal justice.

As she reviewed the relationship between inmate education and recidivism, she talked of a positive correlation between the amount of education an inmate receives and the likelihood that he or she will sooner or later end up back in prison. An associate's degree drops the recidivism rate to 14 percent, a bachelor's degree to six percent, and a master's degree to zero percent.

"When I got down to the data on the master's level, the class roared with applause," she says.

It turned out that Peters had met one of the students in that classroom some years earlier when he was in the custody of the Oregon Youth Authority. When he came into the system, he lacked a high school diploma. Over the years, he progressed all the way up to the master's program, working hard to pay his own way through school. Oregon Youth Authority had done its job for this young customer.

Peters' eyes twinkled at the memory: "It was so good to see *him* again."

CHAPTER NINE

The Results Leader

Turning Resistance into Opportunity

"The most important thing in communication
is to hear what isn't being said."

~ PETER F. DRUCKER

F ew contemporary business leaders have engineered a more impressive results-driven transformation than Ford Motor Company's Alan Mulally. Rated by *Fortune Magazine* as #3 on its 2014 list of The World's 50 Greatest Leaders, Mulally was only outranked by Pope Francis and Germany's Chancellor Angela Merkel. He even beat out Warren Buffett. Nevertheless, not many people recognize his name, which is a testament to his humble and unprepossessing style of leadership.

When Mulally joined Ford in 2006 as president and CEO after a successful career at Boeing, he said about his new employer, "We have been going out of business for 40 years" (Hoffman, 2012).

That seems like a harsh statement coming from a man widely known as the "Cheerleader-in-Chief." Often described as a dead ringer for the fair-haired Richie Cunningham, played by Ron Howard on the television show *Happy Days*, Mulally quickly got Rambo-level results at Ford. Four months after he took the helm, the company reported a whopping $12.7 billion loss. That sad news couldn't have come at a worse possible time, as the world teetered on the brink of the 2007-2008 Global Financial Crisis. But that predicament makes the subsequent turnaround all that much more impressive. When the dust settled after Mulally's three-year shakeup of the moribund auto giant, Ford reported a total of $42.4 billion in earnings between 2009 and 2013, with an enviable reputation for quality and innovation (Ford Motor Company, 2014).

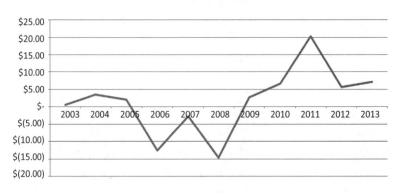

Ford Motor Company

Net Income (Billions)

FIGURE 9.1: Ford was the only company of the big three automakers that recovered without going into bankruptcy, a reality made possible by Alan Mulally's results-focused leadership. Source: Ford Motor Company

Why didn't the Great Recession drive the final nail into Ford's coffin? Because Mulally saw the financial crisis as an opportunity to unite his people. He smilingly told the company's chief economist, "You just have to deal with the realities and face it together" (Hoffman, 2012).

Face it they did. They suffered through painful but inevitable layoffs, difficult labor contract cutbacks, cash-demanding suppliers, massive pension costs, and a wide range of tough choices and tough-to-negotiate deals, but through it all, Mulally unwaveringly led the company to the turnaround he knew would come.

When you talk about uniting your people behind a cause, you're talking about energizing your organization's culture. At Ford, Mulally set his sights on building a corporate culture defined by a commitment to disciplined execution, top-quality processes, high employee engagement, accountability, transparency, and results. That meant demolishing the status quo culture that had flooded Ford with so much red ink. When you make such sweeping changes, you always run into stout resistance (Hoffman, 2012).

Shortly before Mulally took the helm, a fellow named Bennie Fowler had been named global head of quality. A member of the status quo led by Mulally's predecessor, Fowler assumed he would lose his job as Mulally brought in his own people to build the new culture. However, when Fowler ran into Mulally in the hall soon after the new CEO's arrival, he couldn't believe what his new boss said: "Hey! I'm your new quality guy" (Hoffman, 2012).

The two men talked for 15 minutes, after which Mulally assured Fowler that he need not worry about losing his job: "We're going to focus on quality and productivity at the company," he said. "We're going to make it a priority. You're the guy" (Hoffman, 2012).

Within weeks, Fowler was reporting directly to Mulally as Ford began the arduous work of establishing global standards, measures, and scorecards in the company's culture. The rest, as they say, is history.

Business and government cannot operate exactly the same

way. While a business can focus on a single do-or-die measure — profitability — a government, at any level, must grapple with many more variables. Ideally, government must not only manage its finances properly and not "lose money" (i.e., rack up huge deficits), but it must also deliver hard-to-quantify bottom-line social benefits. If a Mulally does not get results, the Board of Directors will probably fire him; if a government leader fails to get results, the voters will kick him out of office. In both cases, results matter. But reelection is in many ways the least of society's drivers for the results government produces. Think education, economy, environment, health, public safety.

Government leaders who want to get results and hold onto their jobs can learn a lot from Mulally's story. You can read that story in the book *American Icon: Alan Mulally and the Fight to Save Ford Motor Company*. It tells the stirring tale of a take-no-credit, pull-no-punches leader who displays the sort of behavior that can help every leader at every level of government deliver results that matter (and hang onto his or her job). Several tried-and-true principles guided Mulally as he led his people toward world-class results:

- Share the vision
- Describe the gap
- Teach the new thinking
- Model the new behavior
- Remove the resistance

That last principle could top the list. How do you overcome the natural human inclination to resist change? Change scares people. It makes them want to do what a rabbit does when it hops into the path of a hungry coyote: freeze, flee, or fight. That's when a great leader remains cheerful and positive. You can't tell people not to feel frightened by change any more than you can tell them not to get the flu, but you can behave in a way that inspires trust in a better future. Otherwise, fear can easily stifle the candor, innovation, and dedication necessary to getting great results. In short, you need to turn resistance into opportunity.

In this chapter, we look at the three levels of leadership that helped Mulally do that at Ford: leading oneself, leading others, and leading through situations. First, however, let's discuss the principles that guided the turnaround at Ford.

Sharing the Vision

According to James M. Kouzes and Barry C. Posner (2012) (authors of *The Leadership Challenge* and a series of related books), leaders like Alan Mulally stand out from their peers because they know how to enlist others to pursue exciting possibilities. Their research into the behavior of strong leaders suggests that while people look for honesty and other ethical behaviors in a leader, they will most eagerly follow someone who sees and describes a better future.

As Robert Kennedy famously said, "There are those who look at things the way they are, and ask why . . . I dream of things that never were, and ask why not?"

Kouzes and Posner argue that asking such questions engages and inspires others to create a better future.

The traditional one-sentence vision statement may serve as a rallying flag, but true inspiration depends on creating a shared vision that goes far beyond a rousing slogan like Hilton's "To fill the earth with the light and warmth of hospitality." The transformation of any organization, from the Ford Motor Company to a state's Department of Revenue, requires a leader who can paint a vivid picture of the safe harbor that lies across a sea of troubled waters. But first, he or she must connect with people in the present.

In a blog for *Harvard Business Review* (Kouzes & Posner, 2009) based on research involving nearly a million participants in their Leadership Practice Inventory, Kouzes and Posner write that, "Constituents want visions of the future that reflect their own aspirations. They want to hear how their dreams will come true and their hopes will be fulfilled. As counterintuitive as it might seem, then, the best way to lead people into the future is to connect with them deeply in the present. The only visions that take hold are shared visions — and you will create them only when you listen very, very closely to others, appreciate their hopes, and attend to their needs."

A compelling shared vision comes from a deep respect for people and their knowledge, passion, experience, and desire. That respect creates the foundation for the authentic engagement that motivates people to row hard toward the distant shore.

A shared vision often takes the form of a narrative — a story that *shows* rather than merely tells people about a brighter future, where, for example, "We score a solid 10 in terms of customer satisfaction." It can take a thousand words to create a complete picture of that ideal world.

Describing the Gap

Like Mulally, transformational leaders describe the reality of the distance between where the ship lies and where it needs to go. From the gap springs hope for change. As we said in Chapter One, most public servants want to make a real difference. That desire helps fuel the journey from today to tomorrow.

It takes a lot of hard work to push steadily toward the horizon, and the rowing feels much less taxing to those who feel the pull of a shared vision. Strong push/pull energy arises when the leader creates *awareness* of the gap between where we are now and where we want to go. You can measure the gap: "We now score 3 on a 1-to-10 scale for customer satisfaction and want to boost that score to at least 8.5 in 12 months."

Citizen expectations and the growing needs of society demand that higher score, but if getting there conflicts with the internal capability and capacity of the organization, the gap becomes painfully clear.

Seeing the gap is one thing; closing it is another. Reaching the desired shore will require a new way of thinking, and new thinking does not come easily. It hinges on the leader's ability to model the new behavior that will turn thoughts into action.

Teaching the New Thinking, Modeling the New Behavior

Michigan's Governor Rick Snyder offers an excellent example of a state leader who did a great job teaching new thinking and modeling new behavior. He did it because he consistently stayed on message and practiced what he preached. That explains why he could speak, at the drop of the hat, about his vision for Michigan without depending on notecards and canned presentations. When you remain true to your beliefs, you do not need to describe them from a prepared script. They flow naturally into everything you say and do.

Take his belief in accountability for results as the foundation for state government. Immediately after taking office, Governor Snyder asked the leaders of every department to build a scorecard that accurately reflected their department's mission and strategic objectives. At the same time, he oversaw construction of dashboards for statewide objectives.

Claire Allard, who led Governor Snyder's Office of Good

Government, said, "The governor likes to go at the pace of the fastest runner."

Nevertheless, he also knows that he must seek progress, not perfection.

The initial scorecards got mixed results. Some department heads offered well-conceived and powerful ones that included all the right measures, while others reported outputs that were not connected to citizen needs. Governor Snyder praised the good ones and suggested improvements for those that fell short of his expectations. Nobody's perfect, especially when it comes to new ways of thinking and behaving. But we can all learn from one another and make steady progress across the troubled waters. Row halfway to the shore and halfway again and again. You won't hit the beach of perfection, but you'll get pretty darned close.

As Allard put it, "In our office we believe you can't drive people to change, but you can drive change through people. We continue to build, continue to build, continue to build. You can't do it all at once."

If you want people to behave in a way that moves the organization closer to its objectives, you need to show them the goal line. That means providing measures that let them know the score. Allard admits that it takes time to do that right: "There's been tons of adjusting and learning."

Through it all, Governor's Snyder's commitment to government that works remained unflagging, as he encouraged people with memory jogger cards including content such as this:

- Use scorecards to measure results
- Focus on customers
- Use facts to make decisions
- Engage employees; they are the source of innovation

- Run at the pace of the fastest runner
- Lifting up employees
- The people who do the work know it best
- Real innovation
- Relentless positive action
- No credit, no blame

In the early days of a new administration, people sit on the sidelines, waiting to see if the Governor's actions will match his words. Allard pointed out that most people expect little to happen: "Here in Michigan in the past it has felt like the flavor of the month."

What made Snyder's arrival any different?

"Right out of the gate he made it clear how he wanted to manage," recalled Allard. "This is what he believed in, customer service, lifting up employees and giving them the tools and training to be successful. And he has stayed really positive about this, and we have just kept at it and drummed it as hard as we can."

Snyder pledged from Day One that he and his team would work in "dog years" (i.e., cramming in seven years' worth of work into one), while successes are celebrated in "mosquito years" (i.e., a few minutes). Good government isn't about patting yourself on the back. Rather, it's all about tackling one challenge and moving on to the next, thoughtfully but aggressively.

However, successful and innovative behavior does not accomplish much if people lack the tools they need to do their work well.

"You can't expect your people to be innovating if they don't have the right environment, the right tools, the right training and the right support for them to be centers of innovation," said Allard. "We're still running fast, we get faster every day and everyone knows we're serious about it."

Removing the Resistance

Any journey from the status quo to a far shore and a brighter future takes time and effort, not to mention the courage to conquer all the dangers and demons that get in your way. Ancient cartographers marked the unknown regions across the sea with a dire warning: "There be Dragons!" Just like sailors contemplating a confrontation with fire-breathing dragons, people often react to the idea of transformational change by hunkering down and resisting all movement forward, preferring their current plight, no matter how miserable, to the unknown threats that might lie ahead.

Positive action requires a bit of heroism. In his classic book, *The Hero with a Thousand Faces*, Dr. Joseph Campbell (2008) describes the heroic effort it takes to create a better future:

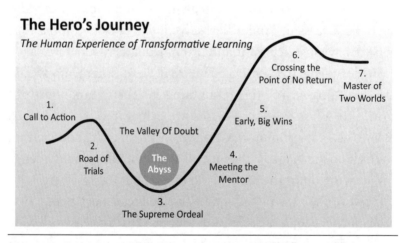

FIGURE 9.2: Transformation is an intensely personal journey, and Joseph Campbell's Hero's Journey model helps people understand what they are experiencing, all the while knowing it is very natural. Source: Adapted from Joseph Campbell's insights in *The Hero With a Thousand Faces*

The transformation from government not designed to serve its customers to one that works tirelessly on their behalf follows a similar path. Let's watch Javier, the head of Name-the-State's

Department of Revenue (DOR), take his people through the seven major milestones that mark the hero's journey to better results:

1. *Call to Action:* Javier decides to transform the DOR into a results-driven organization. He describes his vision of a better future to his leadership team, stressing the gap that exists between where they are now (12 percent customer satisfaction) to where they should be in two years (85 percent).

2. *Road of Trials:* In the beginning, the leadership team resists this strategy, insisting that taxpayers will always hate the DOR, no matter what. Why waste a lot of time and energy making meaningless changes? Javier almost despairs over the team's deep-seated pessimism.

3. *The Supreme Ordeal:* Several members of Javier's leadership team not only bad-mouth the effort, but also quietly sabotage every new initiative. Results decline even further, until it seems that Javier may lose his job before he has a chance to accomplish his mission. Maybe he should fire everybody before the Governor fires him. That's when the team threatens to resign *en masse* if Javier does not stop this nonsense.

4. *Meeting the Mentor:* Struggling with this impasse, Javier shares his frustration with the new Governor, a man who has overseen turnarounds in the private sector and has sworn his commitment to government that works. Armed with a lot of practical advice about overcoming resistance to change, Javier redoubles his efforts. He installs scorecards, provides highly motivational coaching to his key people, and fires Carey, the ringleader of the opposition who refuses to join the cause.

5. *Early, Big Wins:* The scorecards begin to reveal a few major improvements, demonstrating a measureable return on a six-month investment of blood, sweat, and tears. Enthusiasm for the transformation mounts throughout the DOR.

6. *Crossing the Point of No Return:* People at every level of the DOR are "all in," betting their futures on the transformation's initiatives. The scorecards prove that most of the agency's processes have improved dramatically, an accomplishment that engages the commitment and enthusiasm of all employees. Javier marvels that the change effort has taken on a life of its own, accelerating the DOR toward the target of 85 percent customer satisfaction.

7. *Master of Two Worlds:* Two years after the mission's launch, Javier takes his leadership on a weekend retreat. There, they take time to relax and review the journey from lethargic, reactive government to dynamic, results-driven government. Borrowing a notion from Campbell's *The Hero's Journey*, Javier tells the group that they now live as Master of Two Worlds: each of them recognizes the difference between the Old World, in which the DOR's customers hated the organization, and the New World, in which 85 percent of the people who come into contact with the DOR rate the experience as "good-to-excellent."

Javier and his team proved their transformational leadership, not only keeping themselves on the right path (self leadership), but also guiding all of the DOR's people on the journey (leading others) and confronting the day-to-day problems and distractions of organizational life (situational leadership).

Mastering the Five Steps of Transformational Leadership

Whether you're managing your own journey, helping others manage theirs, or tackling all the problems that crop up along the way, you'll find following these problem-solving steps quite useful:

Five Steps of Transformational Leadership

	SELF LEADERSHIP	LEADING OTHERS	SITUATIONAL LEADERSHIP	
1. **O**BSERVE		Collect information on the issue		IN SILENCE
2. **A**NCHOR		Decide what matters with regards to the issue		
3. **D**EFINE		Create a shared understanding of the issue		IN CONVERSATION
4. **D**ECIDE		Coach people to determine actions to take on the issue		
5. **A**CT		Give people the power to solve the issue		

FIGURE 9.3: Transformational leaders benefit from using a conscious model to guide their efforts in addressing the resistance they will inevitably face.

This process works especially well when an organization is mired in a reactive approach and needs to take positive action to get better results. Still, getting people who have become accustomed to reacting to problems, rather than creating conditions in which fewer problems arise, can sometime feel like teaching dinosaurs to dance. Talk about resistance!

Resistance comes in many forms, from active disagreement and even outright rebellion to more passive behaviors, such as failing to complete assignments, inappropriately delegating critical work to others, not showing up to meetings on time, or letting a smartphone or laptop interrupt the work.

Leaders must remain vigilant that they do not unwittingly support any form of resistance and address it head-on as soon as it arises — or as soon as you notice it has arisen. As Kelly Johnston, a senior consultant for our company, Mass Ingenuity, has observed, "Your response to the struggle determines the success of the transformation. As a leader, when you are accommodating the resistance, you could very easily be fueling it. It is not always easy to know when you are encountering resistance, because often it is disguised as questions, missed deadlines and claims 'I don't understand'."

Let's look more closely at how you can conquer resistance by applying the Five Steps of Transformational Leadership to self-leadership, leading others, and situational leadership.

Lead Yourself

"Physician, heal thyself." Before you can effectively lead others, you must successfully lead yourself. You are only human and susceptible to all the negative emotions than arise in a time of upheaval and change. Make no mistake. Transformation *is* an upheaval — an upheaval of the status quo.

It all starts with self-awareness: awareness of your own strengths and flaws, your flickering emotions, and, most importantly, of your internal and external reactions to what other people say and do. Leadership takes more than deep thinking and impeccable logic; it requires an understanding of all the icky, gooey, sticky human stuff at our primal center, where our hardwiring often prompts us to react instinctively to situations. Only when you understand your own instinctive reactions and know how to work with them can you hope to maintain the constancy of purpose you need as you travel the path of the hero. Lose that constancy, and you not only lose your followers, you also lose any chance of effecting lasting change and getting better results.

How would Javier employ the five-step process to maintain his commitment to results-driven leadership? First of all, he would pause in the midst of every challenging situation to weigh his resolve:

IN SILENCE

1. **Observe:** *Collect information on the issue*
   Javier takes his team on a two-day retreat at a state park equipped for such things. Toward the end of the first day, as the team tries to finalize the Department of Revenue's customer satisfaction scorecard, he can see that the group has gotten hung up on problems such as the DOR website — problems that seem overwhelming. A little dialogue unearths deeper reasons behind their frustration. No wonder they feel overwhelmed, with a new legislative session about to begin just as the department faces another round of budget cuts. All that, coupled with the fact that his people have been putting in 50-60 hour workweeks during the hectic tax season, prompts Javier to announce a break from work. "Get outdoors and enjoy this beautiful day," he orders the group. Then he sits down with his second-in-command, Deputy DOR Director Jeanne Hernandez, to confide his growing doubts about the transformation initiative. If he has lost his resolve, how can he possibly lift the team's energy and positive emotions?

2. **Anchor:** *Decide what matters with regards to the issue*
   Jeanne talks about the transformation that has begun. Is this the right time to introduce major changes into a department already running on the ragged edge of exhaustion? Jeanne takes a strong position: "Boss, we know it's the right thing to do. We may be living in the middle of a tornado at the moment, but if we pull this off, there'll be tremendous calm after the storm." One of Jeanne's colleagues, politely eavesdropping on the conversation, agrees:

"You're right. When we get DOR into a streamlined, results-driven operation, people will find lots of reasons to feel great about themselves and our work. We need to remind them of what lies down this challenging road." They strengthen their commitment to the cause and plan to focus on the central issue: keeping their own and everyone else's eyes on the goal.

IN CONVERSATION

3. **Define:** *Create a shared understanding of the issue*
    When Javier reconvenes the meeting the next morning, he tells them the story of New Mexico's Department of Motor Vehicle Division, where Mark Williams turned a desperately underperforming and much-hated agency into a model of efficiency widely praised by its customers and by its national peers:

    "It took less than a year," he says. "Imagine how happy the results made all those people who had been the targets of criticism for so many years."

    Jeanne chimes in with the example of Ford Motor Company:

    "One day working for Ford felt like trudging into a coal mine, the next it felt like mining for gold. We can perform the same miracle here!"

    When Javier asks if everyone in the room shares his renewed commitment, he hears an enthusiastic response. Sensing renewed energy, he feels more optimistic about the transformation himself: "We're all in this together, guys. We've still got a lot to learn."

4. **Decide:** *Coach toward appropriate action on the issue*
    The team acknowledges that Josephina Johnson, the Information Technology (IT) team leader who has been heading up the website overhaul, needs help. It's a massive

undertaking, and it's gotten bogged down as the effort to patch the existing software has created more problems than solutions. She's on board with the program to make the DOR portal user-friendly and efficient, but she has begun to despair over the seemingly insurmountable problems. Javier and the rest of the team rally to her aid, offering personnel and resources that will help her build a system that will show marked improvements on her scorecard. This act of support bolsters Javier's optimism that they really can pull this off.

5. **Act:** *Give people the power to resolve the issue*
   By the end of the second day, the team has renewed its commitment to the cause, devised a plan to get over one major hurdle, and built scorecards that will track performance toward results. Javier leaves them with this thought:
   "Only you have the power to get the results we need. Don't be afraid to do whatever you need to do to make it happen."
   He makes a mental note to follow his own advice.

Javier will need to continue self-managing as he manages others and wrestles with inevitable setbacks. To help him do that, he keeps reminding himself that he must continually address his own resistance, which usually causes self-doubt; his desire for quick, simple answers; and his tendency to postpone addressing problems. During the two-day meeting, Javier dealt with his self-doubt by inviting the counsel of a trusted peer. He dealt with his desire for a quick, easy answer by acknowledging to the team that they were all climbing the same learning curve; and he dealt with both reactions as soon as they arose. Finally, he held himself, not just his team, accountable for results.

Once Javier sharpens his self-management skills, he can do a much better job managing others.

Results-driven leaders encounter their own self-induced resistance. This type of resistance comes in many forms, but most commonly in the form of self-doubt, the need to know everything, and reluctance to face their own doubt.

Here's what we have observed works and doesn't work:

Dealing with Your Own Resistance

MODES OF RESISTANCE	BEHAVIORS	
	SUCCESS RESPONSES	*FAILURE RESPONSES*
Self Doubt		
You wonder if you made the right decision	Seek advice from experienced peers or advisors; read books and articles to increase your knowledge; study examples of bold leadership decisions	Reveal your doubt to your team or organization; ignore your doubts
You worry that you lack the skill to lead a successful transformation	Find a coach to build your confidence; read relevant books and articles to increase your knowledge; publicly acknowledge your need to grow	Let your doubt paralyze your decision; abandon your commitment
Need to Know Everything		
You feel the need to answer every question	Acknowledge your human fallibility; emphasize the need to keep learning and growing	Guess the answers to important questions; fake confidence in your guesswork
Hesitancy in Addressing Resistance		
You avoid conflict and difficult conversations about the project	Engage people in candid private and public conversations; confirm that you expect greater cooperation	Ignore your doubts; expect them to dissipate naturally
You lose your cool and berate yourself	Confront your own doubts directly and positively; do not let your doubt derail your commitment	Let others see your anger; berate yourself in public

FIGURE 9.4: It is very common for leaders of transformational change to experience their own challenges in the form of self-resistance.

Lead Others

A leader not only travels a personal Hero's Journey, but he also helps others navigate their paths to a better future. Doubt and fear lurk around every bend in the road, especially when you and your people are making the pilgrimage from an old-style, reaction-based system of management to one driven by results.

For some people the journey from the old world to the new comes quickly and easily; for others it takes an enormous amount of time and energy. It all comes down to resistance. Those who embrace the new approach will eagerly press forward with the new thinking, while those who doubt and fear it will dig in their heels and refuse to budge. The latter will test even a great leader's patience.

Having put himself through the five-step transformational leader process, Javier applies it, to varying degrees, with each and every one of his people.

IN SILENCE

1. **Observe:** *Collect information on the issue*

   During a tough meeting he has convened to deal with impending budget cuts, Javier takes note of the fact that Sarah, his chief budget officer, thinks that, Josephina, head of the IT group, has been gobbling up far too many resources to fix the website. Their constant bickering has begun to deflate the whole team's mood.

2. **Anchor:** *Decide what matters with regards to the issue*

   Javier has observed that while the two women got along quite well when they began working together, they have somehow drifted into constant rivalry, even over inconsequential matters. Since he values the terrific skills both of them bring to their work, he decides to coach them out of what has clearly become an ongoing turf battle.

IN CONVERSATION

3. **Define:** *Create a shared understanding of the issue*

   Javier conducts separate coaching sessions with each of the women. After letting Sarah vent her frustration, he asks her to list Josephina's strengths as well as weaknesses. Ditto for Josephina. Both lists contain more pluses than minuses. After the individual sessions, he invites them into a small conference room. Before he leaves them alone, he says, "Look, I need you both working at your peak. All this squabbling has not only undermined your own performance, it has brought down the entire team's enthusiasm for our initiative. I'm leaving you here so you can agree on how you plan to resolve this problem. Forget about turf. Focus on results."

4. **Decide:** *Coach toward appropriate action on the issue*
Sarah and Josephina emerge an hour later, laughing at a private joke. "What's so funny?" Javier asks. Josephina just shakes her head and says, "Nothing, Boss. What next?" Javier tells them to think about what they can do in the next full team meeting to show their recovered mutual respect and lift the team's spirits. Sarah suggests a team-building exercise she found in Jackie Barretta's book *Primal Teams*: "You don't need to do anything but bring your bongo drums to the meeting." Bongo drums? Ah well, Javier decides to play along.

5. **Act:** *Give people the power to resolve the issue*
At the next team meeting, Sarah asks if she can take charge. "Certainly," Javier says with a chuckle. "I brought my drums." Sarah and Josephina pass out an assortment of instruments, including a tambourine, a cowbell, and a triangle. They ask Javier to tie their left and right hands together with a bandanna before they stand before a xylophone, each clutching a drumstick in her free hand. "Okay, one-two-three." They launch into a spirited but cacophonous rendition of "Row, Row, Row Your Boat." Soon the whole gang is laughing and banging away like mad.

Suffice it to say, the team gets a big emotional boost from this silly game and soon gets its teeth into all the pesky problems it must solve to get the transformation on track.

Javier deals with other people's predictable modes of resistance the way he dealt with his own. He affirms his belief that the team has embarked on crucial work and sorely needs the whole team performing at peak levels. He also facilitates communication between the rivals, making sure they acknowledge each other's abilities, not just each other's shortcomings. Finally, he increases his own power by giving it away.

Again, the modes of resistance from others are pretty predictable and some responses are far more effective than others.

Leading Others Through Resistance

MODES OF RESISTANCE	BEHAVIORS	
	SUCCESS RESPONSES	*FAILURE RESPONSES*
Discounting the Importance of the Work		
People delegate their work to others and expect others to take accountability for results	Step 1). Clarify expectations privately; seek reasons for the resistance; answer questions clearly and honestly; verify understanding of the expectation; remain positive	Ignore the repeated offenses; accept excuses; keep answering the same questions over and over; make exceptions
People fail to meet deadlines for no good reason	Step 2). State your expectations publicly; verify the expectations; remain positive	
People work too quickly	Step 3). Confide privately the consequences of continued resistance	
People do sloppy work		
People fail to attend critical meetings	Step 4). Follow through on consequences	
People divert attention from the work at hand		
People refuse to engage in difficult conversations		
People refuse help when it is needed		
Discrediting the Approach		
People express confusion	Make sure people receive all of the information and tools they need; explain everything clearly, concisely and compellingly; stress accountability for results	Repeatedly re-explain everything; answer the same questions again and again
People question the process, methods, tools, and consultants	Separate the importance of the work from the processes, methods, tools, and consultants; ask people to look at the substance of the work, not the form	Abandon the process, methods, tools, or consultants because people feel uncomfortable with them

FIGURE 9.5: Part of a transformation leader's job is to help others who are struggling to get on board with the new ways of doing things.

Not all situations lend themselves to happy endings. Sometimes a leader needs to make that most difficult decision of all: removing a talented team member, who has not, for one reason or another, gotten on board with the program. You know it's time to do that when neither multiple coaching sessions nor the encouragement and support of teammates works. Had either Sarah or Josephina proven unable or unwilling to collaborate with each other, Javier would have found himself considering the final option: "I admire your skills and know you will find a way to make the most of them in your next job."

Lead through Situations

When Professor Paul Hersey and leadership guru and author Ken Blanchard wrote *Management of Organizational Behavior* in 1972, they introduced the Situational Leadership theory. The authors argued that when it comes to leadership, "one size does not fit all." Instead, leadership style depends on the task at hand. Thus, effective leaders adapt their style to a specific situation and the different people involved in that situation (Hersey & Blanchard, 2013). One situation, such as the one Javier faced with Sarah and Josephina, may require a soft touch, while one involving continued underperformance demands a firm hand. Fixing a website takes a different approach than engineering an organization-wide transformation.

Daniel Goleman, author of *Emotional Intelligence: Why It Can Matter More Than IQ* (1996), maintains that the ability to incorporate emotional information into your thinking and behavior will help you more effectively adapt your leadership style to differing people and situations.

Javier remembers what it was like working for Henry Phillips, a boss with a hair-trigger temper whose outbursts created havoc on his team. Henry would shout, call people names, and publicly berate them: "You moron! A child could do a better job!" At other times, Henry would act like an indulgent parent, slowly and carefully telling people exactly what he wanted them to do: "Put Tab A in Slot A, then put Tab B in Slot B."

As Javier liked to say, "He displayed the full range of emotional intelligence, from A to B." Javier promised himself he would boost his own EQ.

Goleman defines six styles of leadership, each of which can get results in certain circumstances. The best leaders mix and match and blend these styles:

Six Leadership Styles

STYLE	DESCRIPTION	WHEN TO USE IT	WEAKNESSES
Commanding/Coercive	Dictatorship. "Do what I say"	In urgency -- when time is scarce, and in crisis	Members can feel stifled as they are treated as workers and not asked for an opinion
Visionary/Authoritative	Mobilizes people towards a vision	When a new vision and direction is needed	Lack the ability to help team members understand how they get to a vision or goal
Affiliative	Focuses on emotional needs over work needs	Best used for healing rifts and getting through stressful situations	Confrontation and emotionally distressing positions can be avoided
Democratic	Uses participation, listening to both the bad and the good news	To gain valuable input from employees and to gain buy-in when there is time to do so	Confrontation and emotionally distressing positions can be avoided
Pacesetting	Builds challenging and exciting goals for people	When the team is already highly motivated and competent	Can lack emotional intelligence
Coaching	Connecting corporate goals whilst helping people find strengths and weaknesses, linking these to career aspirations and actions	Coach mentor and develop individuals when they need to build longer term strengths	Can come across as micromanaging

Courtesy of: http://www.educational-business-articles.com/six-leadership-styles.html

FIGURE 9.6: Goleman's Leadership Styles are useful for leaders trying to understand which style of leadership is best in what situations.
Source: educational-business-articles.com

When moving an organization from a reactionary position to a more results-oriented one, leaders can encounter situations that challenge even the most adept and flexible. Situational resistance comes in many forms, from fear of future failure and guilt over past failures to frustration, finger pointing, confusion, and outright sabotage. Whatever the reasons, people often feel the strong gravitational pull of old ways.

Combating resistance taxes even the best leader's skill and patience. The leader must "walk the talk," model new thinking and behaviors, and avoid coming off as an arrogant know-it-all with all the answers to every single question. Otherwise, the troops will grow cynical about the initiative.

Javier knows in any organizational transformation the hero must walk through the Valley of Doubt but never let doubt derail the journey toward results.

IN SILENCE

1. **Observe:** *Collect information on the issue*

   The annual employee engagement survey alarms Javier. Almost a year into implementation of the new results-driven system, employee engagement has actually declined. How could that have happened? The report totally discourages the leadership team. The DOR's Assistant Director for Human Resources, Frank Valli, an early opponent and late adopter of the initiative, mutters, *almost* under his breath, "I told you so."

   "Wait a minute," urges Elizabeth Rowley, the Deputy Director of Administration for DOR and Frank's boss. "If you step back and put this in perspective, I think you'll see a big message to management. People say we are not letting them make the frontline problem-solving decisions we promised they could make without a ton of permissions. Why not?" Frank mutters dissent, but the rest of the team sees the light. "You can't argue with the data," Javier says. "I know we can do a much better job following through on our promise."

2. **Anchor:** *Decide what matters with regards to the issue*
   Javier really wanted to jump down Frank's throat when he heard him say, "I told you so." Instead, he exercises a little restraint, closes his eyes, takes a deep breath, reminds himself to act like a leader, and thinks about the best way to handle Frank's continued resistance. After a few minutes of listening, he decides to use a combination of democratic, commanding, and coaching styles to address the situation.

IN CONVERSATION

3. **Define:** *Create a shared understanding of the issue*
   Javier interrupts the discussion to address the group, avoiding eye contact with Frank. "I'm asking for a time-out here. Before we go forward with this discussion, I want to see a show of hands. How many of us are surprised by the response from our employees?" Everyone raises a hand. He follows with another question. "How many of us believe this is a message that our people expect us to live up to our commitment to delegate more decision making to the frontline?" Everyone raises a hand, except for Frank, who sits with his arms folded across his chest. "Okay, let's talk about solutions." A lively discussion about delegation and trust ensues. Only Frank keeps silent, doodling on a legal pad.

4. **Decide:** *Coach toward appropriate action on the issue*
   Javier lets the team continue the discussion until they have listed a few steps they can take to move more problem-solving skills and decisions to the frontlines. Once again, Javier asks the team to pause for a moment. "Frank, please join me in the hall for a minute." Beyond the earshot of the others, Javier looks Frank directly in the eye and says: "You have opposed this initiative from the get-go. I respect your opinion and always welcome dissenting opinions,

but in this case, your resistance does nothing but get in the way of our solving this current problem. I wouldn't call you out in front of the whole team if you and I had not gone over this issue a hundred times this past year. Perhaps you'd like to take a break, go for a long walk while we continue the meeting, and decide if you want to remain with the team or not. We can find plenty of other important assignments for you." Javier then rejoins the team to explain his brief absence. "Look, guys, we've got a solid team here. Everyone's making huge contributions to the transformation. I appreciate that. Let's keep going while Frank thinks about his continued role on the team."

5. **Act:** *Give people the power to resolve the issue*
   To close the meeting, Javier gives each member of the team the authority to go back to his or her area and take whatever steps they deem necessary to give their people decision-making power: "Be creative. Play with it. Get your people engaged in helping you achieve the objective. We'll reconvene in two weeks to discuss progress and share what worked and didn't work."

Two weeks later, the team reports steady progress on the issue. Frank decides to leave the DOR and find a job with what he calls "a less experimental" part of state government. Javier shakes his hand after their exit interview. "Good luck, Frank. But you must know the whole state's engaged in transformation."

Note the ways Javier tailored his leadership to the situation. He met Frank's resistance head-on; he confronted him in a sensitive and positive way; and he gave Frank a way to save face by letting him gracefully bow out of the team.

In his book *Topgrading: How to Hire, Coach and Keep A Players*, psychologist Brad Smart discusses the traits of top performers and what it takes to attract and keep them in an organization. In the end, he stresses one key leadership trait that will see any leader through the most nettlesome situations: *resilience*.

Here are some of the most common modes of situational resistance and resilient ways you can deal with them:

Leading Through Situational Resistance

MODES OF RESISTANCE	BEHAVIORS	
	SUCCESS RESPONSES	*FAILURE RESPONSES*
Executive Team Holding onto Decision Making		
Executives cling to the need to decide everything	Address the issue directly; stress the value of delegation and the need for decision-making at the lowest possible levels in the organization: provide expert coaching; model effective behaviors	Ignore the struggles of other executives; allow executives to make decisions others can and should make
Burying the Poor Performance		
Executives hide measures that show poor performance	Embrace mistakes and shortcomings; focus on desired results; work to close the gap between performance and desired results; assign appropriate resources to the problem	Ignore the problem; falsify the data; refuse to talk about it; hope it will go away on its own
Ducking Responsibility		
Executives withdraw support because they don't know what to do	Encourage leaders to accept the fact that they will never know it all; guide them through their own self-doubt; seek outside help; patiently persevere	Fill the gap by providing support yourself; let people kick the problem to a higher level; expect time to heal the wound
Reverting Back to Old School Thinking		
Executives slip back to previous programs and ways of thinking	Teach the importance of process; link process improvement to program outputs/outcomes. Sponsor/support cross departmental process improvement	Allow silos that prevent enterprise-wide thinking; Focus on program, rather than process
Expressing Disappointment in People		
Executives criticize people who expect their leaders to walk the talk	Urge everyone to pay close attention to people's feelings and doubts; share the fact that everyone is traveling the same learning curve; model the ability to be good students; admit mistakes; encourage constructive feedback	Encourage everyone not to label people as poor performers and failures; not to tell people they should simply shape up or ship out; insist that the boss knows best
Defining Everything as Strategic		
Executives do not distinguish between routine work and strategic initiatives	Teach the difference between routine work and strategic initiatives; install a clear organizational planning process; assign ownership for each type of work; encourage strategic thinking at all levels	Think the strategy is perfect; disallow input from all levels; ignore the need for strategy to drive toward desired results

FIGURE 9.7: All kinds of things get in the way of advancing a results-driven transformation. Transformational leaders need to address the obstacles in order to keep the change moving forward.

Mastering Resilience

When the going gets tough, the tough get flexible. In the midst of the worst possible news about his company, Ford's Alan Mulally never let his smile fade. His positive attitude and resilience enabled him to stay the course, guiding Ford away from the precipice of bankruptcy. Make no mistake: he got tough when he needed to be tough, but he never let troublesome situations derail his enthusiasm for better results. That inspired his people to teach an ailing elephant to do cartwheels. A young friend of mine would say, "He's got mojo."

Globally respected executive coach Marshall Goldsmith, who has worked with Mulally, offers this advice in his *New York Times* best-selling book, *Mojo, How to Get It, How to Keep It, How to Get It Back If You Lose It*: "Mojo is that positive spirit toward what we are doing now that starts from the inside and radiates to the outside. Our mojo is apparent when the positive feelings toward what we are doing come from inside us and are evident for others to see. In other words, there is no gap between the positive way we perceive ourselves — what we are doing — and how we are perceived by others" (Goldsmith, 2009).

Goldsmith adds four "vital ingredients" that help leaders maintain their resilience:

Identity

Who are you? Look for the answer within yourself, not in the eyes of your friends, colleagues, and family members. Goldsmith argues, "Without a firm handle on our own identity, we may never be able to understand why we gain — or lose — our mojo" (Goldsmith, 2009). Leader, know thyself.

Achievement

What have you accomplished? What have you done to

make a difference in the world? Mojo springs from a track record of achievement. Mojo breeds success. Succeed and you will succeed again (Goldsmith, 2009).

Reputation

What do others think of you? Do they know who you are? Do they recognize your accomplishments? Just as no man is an island, no leader is a mountain unless others see him that way. Goldsmith advises, "It's your coworkers, customers, friends (and sometimes strangers who've never met you) grabbing the right to grade your performance — and report their opinions to the rest of the world." Look at yourself through the eyes of those around you. Honest feedback can keep you honest (Goldsmith, 2009).

Acceptance

What can you change? What can you *not* control? The road to hell is paved with the bones of leaders who reached beyond their grasp, tilted windmills, and tried to stuff a camel through the eye of a needle. Mojo feeds on reality. Accept it (Goldsmith, 2009).

You have probably heard that the Chinese character for the word "crisis" also means "opportunity." Linguists have debunked that myth. Crisis is danger. Period. And resistance is danger. Period. However, the resilient leader manages self, others and situations in ways that turn even the most ardent resistance into opportunity: "Hello, Resistance, my old friend. Good to see you again. Glad to see you brought Opportunity with you." That attitude, as much as any technical knowledge or expertise, will speed you down the path to results.

CHAPTER TEN

A Results Legacy

Sustaining a Hard-Fought Shift

"Knowledge has to be improved, challenged,
and increased constantly, or it vanishes."

~ PETER DRUCKER

Standing in line at a Starbucks in Seattle in 2010, David Giuliani could not help but overhear a loud group of what he
called "old, white, angry men" sitting at a table ranting on and
on about all that is wrong with this country. Giuliani, a serial
entrepreneur with numerous national awards, including National Entrepreneur of the Year in Manufacturing and US Small
Businessperson of the Year, and such household names as Soni-
care® and Clarisonic® to his credit, found the tenor of the conversation distressing.

"You know what's wrong with this country . . . blah, blah,
blah . . . healthcare . . . blah, blah, blah . . . President Obama . . ."
raged the men, shaking their fists and jabbing their fingers into
the air at some imaginary culprit.

"And what's wrong with this country," David muttered to

himself, "is people sitting around and complaining and doing nothing about it."

Ten seconds later something clicked in David's brain. While he felt irritated by the disgruntled men at the nearby table, did he love his country more than they did? He recalled the epiphany. "There's no difference really between those who just complain about this country and don't do anything about it, and those who quietly stand in line and don't do anything about it."

That pivotal insight prompted David to join forces with Howard Behar, retired president of Starbucks, to found the Washington Business Alliance (WaBA) a year later. While most such business organizations lobby for the benefit of private enterprise, Giuliani and Behar set a far broader mandate for WaBA. "Business at-large benefits from living in a better place and better state, better managed and governed," explained Giuliani. "When I say governed, it's not necessarily government. It's how we govern ourselves. And how we define who plays what roles."

WaBA not only plays an active role as a stakeholder in government that works, it is also bringing others to the table with Plan Washington, an initiative that promotes a broad base of stakeholder collaboration. In this chapter we will look at how business leaders can help sustain The Results Revolution, as well as other factors that support the hard-fought shift to government that works:

- The effective use of big data
- Legislation that supports the executive branch's agenda
- Leadership structures that maintain a focus on the operations of government
- The maturation of a results-driven management system
- Automation of performance management

There's no point in engineering a revolution if you cannot sustain it far into the future. You're not just fixing broken government; you're establishing a legacy of effectiveness and efficiency that will benefit the customers of government far beyond your tenure. And that takes more than a little hard work. As David Giuliani came to understand as he listened to those angry critics decrying the failures of government, it takes "all hands on deck" and no small amount of hard work, patience, and perseverance.

Building a Positive Business Alliance

Giuliani thought of WaBA as a convener. "Probably our most important ongoing function, most significant contribution, is the collecting and distributing of information, building relationships, spotlighting best practices, and praising the great work being done. We supply information to the press and also the Internet audience that shows all the work being done."

Giuliani sees WaBA as a group of concerned businesspeople who strive to "lift the spirits" of those who deliver and receive government services.

That does not mean WaBA only fulfills a public relations function. It also prods government to look beyond superficial quick fixes. Take the debate in Seattle over a proposal to hike the minimum wage to $15 per hour. While politicians argued the merits of this simple idea, the larger and more complex problem, the virulent spread of poverty, went unheeded. A Band-Aid would not cure a problem that requires a deep systemic overhaul, and perhaps some radical surgery.

Giuliani wanted officials to tackle that problem with more creative solutions. "For the most part workforce development is relegated to government to supply people with skills helpful for getting jobs. Why not turn that around? Why not have businesses become the primary developer of talent within its current employment ranks as well as outside?" To do that Giuliani favored tightly focused certification programs where people learned valuable new skills with which they could actually lift themselves out of poverty. That approach could build a stronger relationship between business and government.

The self-described "happy guy" who grew irritated with do-nothing critics believes in the power of strong relationships. He often cites University of Washington's John Gottman's studies on marriage when he talks of the role of positive energy in bringing people together. Good work matters; so do-good cheerleaders. "It takes a ratio of 4-or-5 to 1 positive to negative to keep a personal relationship healthy. The same is true in society. Organizations grow well when there is positive energy supporting that which is going well."

WaBA's Plan Washington provides a bold and comprehensive long-term strategy for a stronger relationship between the business community and the State of Washington. With the express intention of pulling together a diversity of organizations to address societal needs, the plan resembles the Oregon Business Council's (OBC) groundbreaking collaboration with state government that resulted in the Oregon Business Plan. Annually, under that organization's president, Duncan Wyse, OBC convenes a major summit conference where the who's who of business and government take a hard, fact-based look at the state of the state. (You can find out more about the plan at www.oregonbusinessplan.org).

WaBA's Giuliani, author of more than a dozen patents in the private sector, described how his organization does something similar. "We apply known successful business methods to the broader issue of society and how we govern ourselves. If you and I are going to do something together, for example form a corporation, we have to agree on what we're going to get done as part of our passion and persistence." To apply a businesslike approach to public sector problems, Giuliani begins with clearly stated goals for the state of Washington, based on extensive stakeholder interviews and workshops. Plan Washington strives for top 10 percent state performance on such issues as economic development, education, the environment, governance, health and transportation.

The plan includes a comprehensive set of metrics and targeted results, showing the state's ranking in everything from average commute time, to digital government leadership, to higher education funding per student, to the quality of drinking water, and to the level of economic innovation funding.

From the plan introduction (www.planwashington.org/plan-washington):

Successful enterprises confront challenges by charting a vision, setting goals, implementing smart strategies, and delivering results. Washington State can be most successful by applying this approach to its most pressing economic, social, and environmental problems.

PLAN Washington is a goal-based framework to create economic prosperity and a high quality of life for all residents by the year 2025. This is the first annual edition. More importantly, PLAN Washington is a process of learning, collaborating, innovating, activating, and getting results. It's all about achieving our goals.

PLAN Washington is an initiative of the statewide and non-partisan Washington Business Alliance. It reflects over two years of engagement with diverse business, government, and community stakeholders, and research into best practices by issue committees.

The plan focuses on six key topic areas: economic development, education, environment, governance, health, and transportation. Some topics will be saved for later, such as non-transportation infrastructure and social services. Year 2025 goals are supported by strategies and carefully vetted metrics. The target year is far enough away to allow time to meet the goals but soon enough to compel concentrated action.

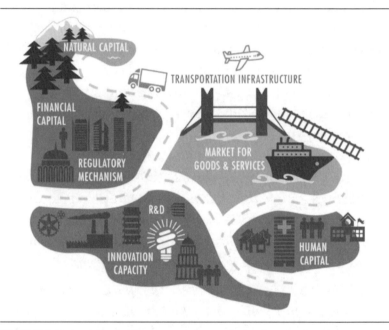

FIGURE 10.1: Washington Business Alliance's view of the factors that play a role in a vital society. Source: Washington Business Alliance

The alliance based PLAN Washington on several basic assumptions:

1. Businesses play an integral role in the community and know that their success depends on effective stewardship of natural and human assets.

2. Government must work with limited funds and should invest its money wisely.
3. Good governance and accountability for results requires accurate, transparent, and meaningful data.
4. Government must involve all relevant stakeholders in order to come up with solutions to challenges that cross conventional boundaries.

The Plan's founders realized that success depended on the inclusion of a broad range of stakeholders. In that same spirit of cooperation, it included teams of business leaders from among its 100 member companies, each working to develop goals and create/assemble the necessary elements of the plan. For each goal the teams offered specific strategies, metrics, and recommended actions. WaBA also partnered with such organizations as the Center for Accelerating Innovation, The Russell Family Foundation, and Governor Inslee's Results Washington effort.

Giuliani and his team applied extensive entrepreneurial experience to the Plan. "We have to get clear on how we're going to do it. Long term, short term. How we're going to measure our success. How we see ourselves in the world around us. What assets we have and how we leverage them. How we finance what we need to do. That kind of strategic approach to getting things done wins. That's how businesses do it. So let's take that and apply it to the bigger opportunity."

When Giuliani spoke about his personal belief in giving back to society, he quoted Margaret Mead from memory, "Never doubt that a small group of thoughtful, committed citizens can change the world; indeed, it's the only thing that ever has." That's a wonderful sentiment. But exactly how do you do it?

Turning Big Data Into Large Opportunities

In recent years businesspeople have fallen in love with Big Data. But what, exactly, does the term mean? Basically, people use this buzzword to describe a massive volume of data, both structured and unstructured, that grows so quickly it exceeds current processing capacity. If you can harness it to some extent, however, you can use it to improve operations and make faster, more intelligent decisions. Transformed into information, Big Data can unlock the secrets hidden in the vast stores of bits and bytes collected by state government.

Connect the Dots

Just as businesses can use Big Data to boost the bottom line, government can access it to get better results. Better results naturally flow when you improve operations and make smarter decisions. Think of Big Data as the trillions of stars dotting the night sky. That's a lot of little sparkles. If you start connecting those dots, you start to see some pictures: the Big Dipper, Orion, Ursa Major and Minor. Government collects trillions of bits and bytes of data. If only it could connect all the dots and see the pictures they contain, it could do a better job meeting society's challenges. It could see and deal with the hidden patterns that cause environmental hazards, unintended pregnancies, high rates of child and spousal abuse, too many infant mortalities, the epidemic of obesity, alarming numbers of traffic fatalities, unacceptably low math scores, increases in the number of high school dropouts, and the outbreak of gang violence.

Here's a perfect example. The State of Louisiana had been operating clinics in locations where officials assumed they could best serve mothers at risk of delivering low-birth weight babies by opening clinics. Lauren Bennett, a product engineer at ESRI (Environmental Systems Research Institute), the highly respected global geographic information systems company, recalled what happened when officials looked at the hard data. "So they did a bunch of spatial analyses to see where the low birthrate babies actually were. What they learned when they looked at the live birth records spatially was that they could target certain neighborhoods that needed clinics the most, and make a bigger impact."

By connecting the dots and turning the raw data into information, officials saw the need to shift dollars to where they would better satisfy the need for care. "And what's great is that there are less low-birth weight kids being born in the state now than just a few years ago," said Bennett, a Ph.D. candidate in information systems and technology at Claremont Graduate University when we talked with her.

Doug Robinson, executive director of the National Association of State Chief Information Officers (NASCIO), sees all hard data, big and small, as a major asset for any organization. "Data is a strategic asset if you're looking at better decisions, better outcomes and better results. I would also argue personally that the tools for visualizing data are high on the list of ways to make that data useful for policymakers. I don't think that raw numbers are going to do it." In other words, dots don't matter unless you connect them so people can see the connections clearly.

Paint a Picture

You can connect them a lot of different ways: pie charts and other diagrams, performance scorecards, easily accessed dashboards, and all other forms of delivering accessible and downloadable data. When a picture emerges, it becomes a magnet for investment; when it doesn't, people put their dollars elsewhere.

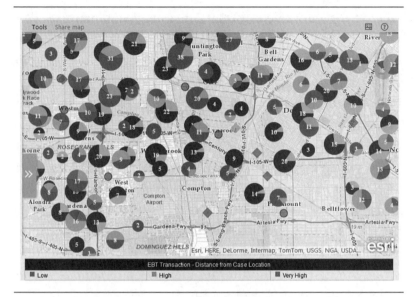

FIGURE 10.2: Geographic visualizations of data such as this screenshot from ESRI (normally in color) help transform large data sets into actionable information.
Source: ESRI

ESRI's Bennett agreed. "You don't have to be a rocket scientist to understand a histogram or to understand a bar chart of the values that you're looking at. The same goes for a map. They add context to the data, which is critical because nothing happens in a vacuum." She champions the use of spatial analysis techniques (such as hot spot maps) to enhance people's ability to see the relationships in large and diverse data sets. As an example, she cited the analysis performed in order to understand the relationship between a major drought and agriculture jobs. In the end, officials could *see* the connection.

NASCIO's Robinson shared Bennett's enthusiasm, and the two also shared the same word of caution. You can install an array of gigantic servers and fill them with data, but *high volume* and *high variety* alone do not automatically answer all your questions. "The states have data stored across multiple systems and multiple formats and multiple agencies, but it's dirty and it's messy," Robinson said. The data can only be useful if it's cleaned up and put in some sort of order — and that's a big job. Bennett suggested anyone interested in trying to understand just how big the job is should simply look at the struggles of data. gov, a federal attempt to address the big data opportunity.

Robinson speaks at many conferences and often tells audiences that states collect much of their data to meet federal requirements. "These things have rolled downhill for 30 years from the federal government," Robinson said. His association represents a total of 54 US territories and states. In most cases, the Federal Government never applied a set of standards across its agencies, which created a mish-mash of data. "There are some pretty significant hurdles that have to be overcome. And most of those are around governance and organizational dynamics and change management."

As if that's not enough of a battle, two other major issues make matters even more complicated: the long-standing reluctance of agencies to share data with each other (hello, silos) and the dangers associated with violating the right to privacy (good morning, eavesdropping on telephone calls).

How would Robinson solve those problems? "I would create a body, I would create a group that could discuss these issues and look for an opportunity." He described how Indiana took on one challenge at a time. Instead of trying to take advantage of the Big Data opportunity statewide, officials first tackled a single policy issue — low-birth weight babies and infant mortality. "They are trying to reduce infant mortality because they have one of the highest infant mortality rates in the country," he said. "And the governor and others are asking, 'Why?'" To find the answer, they used graphic visuals and connected the dots.

Create Context

A good picture deserves a great frame, a context in which it makes sense to people. In the case of government's vast collection of data dots, policy provides the frame, answering the questions, "Why are we doing this? What does this all mean to our citizens?" The best policy statements energize those who must turn the data into information. They also set frameworks for cooperation with stakeholders, such as legislatures and the business communities.

As results-driven leadership teams create outcome and process measure scorecards for their dashboards, and as problem solving teams search for data that may reveal root causes of problems, you want to make sure everyone understands the context and addresses only the truly relevant data. For instance, we worked with Bryan Irwin, the enterprise performance manager for Washington State's Department of Corrections, to develop guidelines and worksheets and what Irwin called "counting rules" to ensure the collection of pertinent and accurate data. According to Irwin, "Counting rules define the measure like a recipe defines the ingredients and instructions necessary to create an award-winning cake every single time."

His worksheets, assigned to the various agency executives who owned particular measures, included the measure's name, description, purpose, connection to other related measures, category (cost, quantity, quality, or time), as well as its counting rules, data sources, frequency, and time rules. The worksheets included performance targets and spaces for ranking performance (red, yellow, green) with respect to the targets.

When agencies start viewing the same old data they have always collected through the focused lens of policy, they quickly see that an awful lot of it is unreliable and/or not terribly relevant to the problem at hand. Source A gathers one set of numbers, source B a different set, and Source C yet another. Try connecting all the dots when one third of them lie outside the frame and one third of them don't belong in the picture at all. Imagine what can happen in a department of corrections where officials want to see data on inmate-on-staff assaults. The stats vary wildly from one facility to another because staff was not working with a common definition of "assault."

Customer portals, such as a single sign-in site for business customers, demonstrate the power of connecting data in the service of customers. It's not an easy thing to do, but both Michigan's Governor Rick Snyder and Colorado's Governor John Hickenlooper of Colorado believe it's essential to supporting a healthy business climate.

Robinson believes the portals require total accuracy and reliability of all data and information. "You usually would have what I call one version of the truth," he told us. This applies to a seemingly small bit of data, such as a citizen's correct name. When the Department of Revenue recognizes a citizen as John Q. Public, while the Department of Motor Vehicles only responds to J.Q. Public, and the Registrar of Voters only accepts John Quentin Public, Junior, you're going to end up with one very confused, frustrated, and probably angry citizen on your hands.

As Robinson said, "You have to get the agencies to agree in the end to trust it." ESRI's Bennett concurred, "The real bummer is we've got so many people working hard on the exact same thing." This underscores the fact that everyone must make sure the "exact same thing" means the same thing to everybody, from the Governor to a citizen trying to renew a driver's license. It also means that a consistent context will allow Louisiana and New Mexico to learn what Mississippi and Montana are doing to increase literacy rates.

Big Data, little data, it doesn't matter. Consistency, accuracy, and relevance should rule the day. Otherwise, government will not work the way everyone wishes it would. Results will slip further and further from our grasp.

Passing Results-Driven Legislation

Many states have passed and signed into law legislation that promotes effectiveness and efficiency in state government. Most of these laws, though well intentioned, have not achieved their goal. For example, states requiring agencies to apply for the Baldrige Quality Award can easily lead to compliance for compliance's sake as the agencies reluctantly drop customer-focused work to complete the necessary paperwork. Both quality of service and any chance to win the award fall by the wayside. Oregon's Senate Bill 676 proved an exception to the rule. It resulted from an unusually high degree of cooperation between the executive and legislative branches. Strongly supported by Oregon's Chief Operating Officer Michael Jordan, the legislation encompassed the principles of results-driven government: transparency, accountability, priorities, and measurement.

It read in part:

> *The Legislative Assembly believes that the state government must allocate its resources for effective and efficient delivery of public services by:*
> - *Clearly identifying desired results;*
> - *Setting priorities;*
> - *Assigning accountability; and*
> - *Measuring, reporting and evaluating outcomes to determine future allocation.*

Fred King, Chair of the Committee that brought forth the legislation, loved the way it turned out. "It was truly a collaborative effort. And it was what propelled the state's forward commitment to results-driven management and outcome-based budgeting."

King said the committee got the job done because it drew together the right stakeholders: union representatives, legislators, the executive branch, and the private sector. He credited chief sponsor Senator Frank Morse for making it happen. Oregon Senate President Peter Courtney agreed, calling Senator Morse "a great statesman and perfect Oregonian." Senators Vicki Berger, Richard Devlin, Betsy Johnson, Chris Telfer, Jackie Winters, and representatives Peter Buckley, Paul Holvey, and Dennis Richardson also played a major role in getting the law approved.

Tennessee also passed results-driven legislation in the form of the historic T.E.A.M. Act (Tennessee Excellence, Accountability, and Management), which Governor Bill Haslam (R) initiated, sponsored and signed into law in 2012. Tennessee's Department of Human Resources Commissioner Rebecca Hunter praised the way it drove results. "The TEAM Act transformed the state of Tennessee's employment practices, which was really the start of changing our state government from one based on seniority to one based on performance."

A number of pressing issues drove the need for the legislation, including an archaic state law that provided employees a property right to the position they held. This made it virtually impossible to reward good performance and address performance deficiencies. When Governor Haslam came into office, he asked each cabinet member to conduct a top-to-bottom review of his or her organization's performance. At the same time, an extensive survey resulted in some 700 suggestions for helping the state operate more efficiently. Both fact-gathering efforts shed light on the fact that antiquated employment practices stood in the way of Haslam's goal to introduce results-driven practices in Tennessee.

Rebecca Hunter helped uncover the facts. "The Deputy Governor at the time, Claude Ramsey, and I went on an employee listening tour, visiting the four largest cities in Tennessee to hear from our employees. We asked for suggestions on how we could recruit and retain the best and brightest employees."

Knowing that the state faced the potential of a huge wave of pending retirements throughout the ranks of state employees, as much as 40 percent by 2020, Hunter saw a big opportunity for installing more effective employment practices. "The purpose of the TEAM Act was what we called the three R's: recruit, retain, and reward the best applicants and employees based on performance and equal opportunities, but free from coercive political influences." Among other outmoded practices, the state eliminated the practice of "bumping." When a reduction in force occurred, an agency was required to maintain longer-tenured employees, based solely on seniority, often displacing a less-tenured employee, regardless of performance, skills, or ability.

The new approach to employment also eliminated the damaging influence of political appointments because it required that appointees bring relevant education and experience to a given job. In order to emphasize talent over political loyalty, the state has revised over 70 percent of its job descriptions, specifically identifying the knowledge, skills, abilities, and competencies required for each position. Updating these job descriptions increased the state's ability to recruit highly qualified candidates. The law also required that Tennessee adopt compensation structures that reflected performance, and the state is currently developing a market- and performance-based pay plan.

As a result of the legislation, the Department of Human Resources gained control over leadership development (see Chapter 6). "We are all approaching leadership and development with the same mindset," says Hunter. "And all that learning is aligned with the Governor's vision and priorities." To further this alignment, the department created a statewide learning and development council. Bringing the agencies together to see they all have a common desire to learn and grow and to drive that within their agencies has been really encouraging to everyone involved in training and development."

Perhaps most importantly, Tennessee's TEAM Act enabled a performance management system that connects the work of the agencies and their employees directly to the Governor's goals in specific and measurable ways. It's a more state-of-the-art business approach, Hunter told us. "The State has begun looking at things from an enterprise perspective and not just from our own silos. There are now sub-cabinets. For instance, there is a children's services cabinet, a public safety cabinet, and a shared services cabinet."

Governor Haslam advanced the idea of thinking about government as an enterprise when he created the position of Chief Operating Officer for the state, something only Oregon had done before. When the Governor appointed a 37-year veteran, IBM executive Greg Adams, to the post, he said that Adams would concentrate his efforts on the "effective and efficient" operation of state government. "Now that I have been here two-and-a-half years, I realize one of the things that's hardest for me about being Governor is I can't spend the time I would like to with each department."

Hunter commented on the impact of having a Governor who understands the importance of all employees having alignment to his vision and priorities. "Having the SMART [specific, measurable, attainable, realistic, and timely] goals for each employee, including cabinet members, has been a huge part of obtain-

286 | GOVERNMENT THAT WORKS

ing that alignment. If you're going to move to a performance-based culture, you've got to make sure that your process is objective."

More states will surely follow the lead. Surveys conducted by the National Conference on State Legislatures show state legislators display a strong interest in using performance measures to understand and evaluate the effectiveness of state programs. This approach especially benefits newly elected legislators because it emphasizes the purpose of programs. Measures also tell you what's working and what's not working. And that helps you manage outcomes much more effectively.

Creating a Sustainable Management System

Matt Power, who ran StateStat for Governor O'Malley, talked about the importance of a sustainable management system. "Anyone who gets the keys to this multi-billion corporation called Maryland is going to want to know how it's actually functioning. People always ask me, 'Are you worried they'll cancel the program in the next administration?' It's pretty hard now for a governor to walk in and say, 'you know, I don't really care how many prisoner-on-staff assaults we had last year. I don't care how many non-fatal shootings happened last month'."

Power believes the stakeholders who access online scorecard data would raise a political ruckus if a new administration did not display the measures. The scorecards reveal results-driven management at work, but that's just one of the many factors that sustain such a system.

When you decide to build a good management system, you need to do it right. You can't do it overnight. After all, you're dealing with an incredibly complex enterprise that resists even the smallest change. Rather than asking, "How quickly can we complete the necessary changes?" ask, "How can we make the changes stick? How can we make them the very foundation of our organization's culture?"

As experienced business executives sometimes put it, management is a journey, not a destination. Think of delivering results as *your* destination. You can never do it perfectly. But you can get closer and closer to what you envision, and what you envision as possible is inspired by what you have accomplished.

The ongoing journey involves both the quantity and the quality of the actions people perform. They must do a lot of work, and they must do it well. One without the other will always cause a crash.

The management system must allow for the right quantity of quality actions by those accountable for achieving the goals set by the Governor. The most effective ones rely on mechanisms that work to improve fundamentals, achieve breakthroughs, monitor performance, and solve problems. They use mechanisms like scorecards not just to review improvement, but also to drive behaviors that lead to breakthroughs and innovative solutions. "Aha, the number of service complaints has dropped only five percent. What more can we do to knock it down 10 more points?"

The answer involves another mechanism, the organization's guidelines and methodology for solving problems. The problem solvers gather, analyze, and present the relevant data so anyone from the Governor to the statehouse janitor can understand it, perhaps using histograms and Pareto charts. As structured problem-solving protocols become common practice in the organization, they become almost second nature to everyone who works there. What becomes second nature (i.e., "the way we do things around here") shapes the organization's culture.

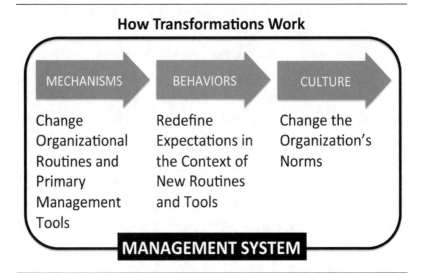

FIGURE 10.3: Culture changes as an indirect result of new management routines where the desired behaviors are modeled and repeated until they become a part of the organization's culture.

A sustainable management system and a new organizational culture come only after a lot of practice. That's how you develop any new habit — you do it, as Malcolm Gladwell has suggested, 10,000 times. It works best if leadership employs the classic PDCA cycle (Plan/Do/Check/Adjust) over and over again. A successful transformation employs that cycle to push the change through three distinct phases:

Develop: Install the mechanisms; establish new routines for doing the work.

Deploy: Apply the new routines throughout the organization.

Embed: Ensure that people consistently display the new behaviors.

You can't just mandate the desired change from the top. You must gather input from the people who actually do the work, because they know it better than you ever will. Rather, you establish the framework for the new behaviors and invite people to figure out how to do their work more effectively and efficiently. That's the only way you can get them to buy into the transformation. A bunch of people cannot shed a lot of unhealthy weight unless they commit to the goal with all their hearts and choose the methods they know will work best for them.

Leaders do not singlehandedly change the world — they manage the changes others must make in order to fashion a better world. For leaders in state government, change management is Job One. Our consulting group recommends a specific change management approach known as ADKAR (Awareness, Desire, Knowledge, Ability, and Reinforcement). Developed by Prosci®, this approach helps you progress smoothly through the Three Phases of Change Management: preparing for, managing, and reinforcing the change (Prosci, 2014). This applies to every change you want to make, from a little tweak in a small agency (such as installing a scorecard) to a huge shift throughout the whole organization (such as adopting Lean techniques in all agencies).

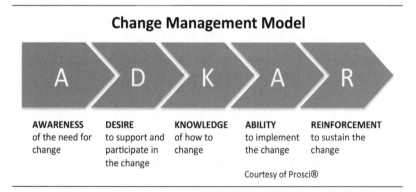

Change Management Model

AWARENESS	**DESIRE**	**KNOWLEDGE**	**ABILITY**	**REINFORCEMENT**
of the need for change	to support and participate in the change	of how to change	to implement the change	to sustain the change

Courtesy of Prosci®

FIGURE 10.4: Successful change requires leaders to consciously manage the change. The ADKAR model is considered by many to be the best-in-class for change management.

Once you have chosen to plant a change, you need to prepare the soil for it during Phase One. To do that, you must communicate it clearly, concisely, and compellingly to everyone it will affect. In the case of a new scorecard, you may only need to present and explain it once. For something more massive, such as installing Lean techniques, you might assign some homework, asking people to read one of the excellent books on the subject and discuss it in study groups over a 12-week period.

After you have successfully communicated the change, you can move to Phase Two and start managing the change. This includes everything from continued communication to project management, training, and pilot programs, all of which can play a key role in teaching people about the change, motivating them to embrace it, and providing them with the skills they need to make it happen.

Phase Three, reinforcing the change, can involve everything from acknowledging and rewarding people who behave and act in ways that accomplish the change to promoting those who can lead others further down the path toward the intended transformation. All along the way, you must reinforce the fact that improvement never sleeps. Everyone must remain alert for breakthroughs and innovative solutions every minute of every working day.

Can you do all this in a month? Perhaps, if it's a small change. Big ones can take many months, even years before the required mechanisms, behaviors, and ultimately the culture change.

Automating Performance Management

Technology can help speed things up, and the technologies themselves can shape the way we think and act and work. Our laptops, desktops, tablets, and smartphones put LinkedIn, Twitter, selfies, Instagram, texts and voice and FaceTime chats at our fingertips. Everyone can communicate with everyone else, and they can do it NOW. Why not harness that incredible power in the service of The Results Revolution?

Rapidly advancing technology can accelerate and embed results-driven government. When a state's management system is automated, people can easily and quickly access vital data on agency and personal performance. Few evolving technologies offer as much promise as cloud computing, which can store a vast amount of data without cluttering and slowing down physical computer systems — and give anyone with a password access to it from anywhere. It's like a huge warehouse in the sky. Whatever the particular hardware (tablets and smartphones) or software (operating systems geared to cloud storage and advanced networks), technology can help you take advantage of at least five elements that contribute to results-driven government: near real-time scorecards, automated workflow, project management, knowledge access, and virtual collaboration.

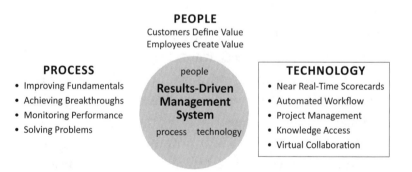

FIGURE 10.5: Technology that enables the management system both speeds its adoption and increases the ability to sustain it over time.

Design Near Real-Time Scorecards

As measures and the measurement processes mature, give

people ready access to the data that can drive improvement. This allows managers, the people who do the work, top leadership, and, in many cases, the general public to see what progress an agency is making toward its primary goals. Scorecards not only display data — they also connect stakeholders with the effort to deliver on the promise of government that works. On the surface, scorecards seem like little more than tracking devices, but, in fact, they incorporate the most fundamental aspects of a sustainable management system: an emphasis on results and continuous improvement, measurement, clear and concise communication, ownership, transparency, and accountability.

With well-designed scorecards in place, everyone from the Governor to a data entry clerk at the Department of Revenue and a taxpayer knows the score and can see what it will take to win the game. If a measure falls below expectations, instant access to this fact sounds a call to action. Workers devise innovative solutions to solve the problem or blast apart the bottleneck. Performance improves. Everyone wins.

Automate Workflow

Online tools such as Lean A-3 forms, problem-solving templates, data gathering sheets, team charters, and planning tools automate workflow and sustain practices. Whether you're performing a background check on an applicant for a sensitive job or seeing real-time data generated by the inspection of an underground storage tank, you can now use mobile devices to gain almost instant access to that data. Performance data can automatically migrate to scorecards. Now the management system becomes a living, breathing, constantly evolving organism that both drives relentlessly toward better results and reinforces them.

Once again, the organization benefits from more open communication, more complete transparency, and more positive accountability. Most importantly, however, automation gives people the data they need to solve problems. When you get right down to it, that's what life in results-driven government is all about.

Introduce Project Management Techniques

A tremendous body of knowledge and a vast array of skills and tools have amassed around the use of state-of-the-art project management techniques. A brief tour of the website maintained by the Project Management Institute (PMI) will reveal just the surface of that ocean (visit www.pmi.org). Scorecards and automation can help project managers and their teams keep important initiatives on track, on time, and on budget. Needless to say, PMI's best practices promote transparency and accountability in the drive toward exceptional results (Project Management Institute, 2014).

Project tasks and timelines land directly on their owners' performance pages, enabling a clear view of exactly what people need to do and when they need to do it. Visibility of problems spurs corrective action to get the work back on track, often with much-needed breakthroughs and innovative solutions.

Allow Easy Access to Knowledge

A dozen years ago the phrase "knowledge management" joined the Buzzword Hall of Fame. Academics heralded it as the next big thing, computer and software companies rushed to feed the demand for knowledge management tools, and executives around the world jumped on the bandwagon. Eventually the brouhaha died down and the very real need for more effective and efficient knowledge management went largely unmet. All the while, however, data and information, the parents of knowledge, kept expanding exponentially.

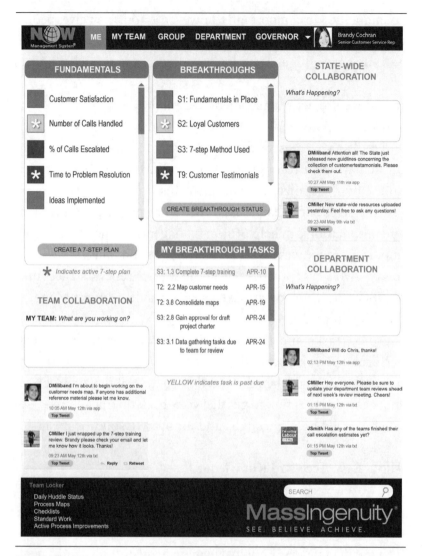

FIGURE 10.6: An integrated performance portal such as this one being developed by Mass Ingenuity will enable a more accelerated and sustainable implementation of a results-driven management system.

Enter social media. Facebook and Twitter and Linked-In and Instagram, not to mention smartphone texting and FaceTime, have made it possible for users to share data and to share it *now*. Bill and Bonnie can use it at school. George and Sandy can use it at home. Sean and Elisa can use it at work. Why can't the Governor and the Secretary of Transportation use it? The use of social media on the job, often discouraged or limited by managers, offers government a huge opportunity to make knowledge easily accessible to everyone who wants or needs it.

Imagine a manager in the Department of Transportation using the agency's equivalent of a Facebook page to broadcast important developments on a major project. The site includes a scorecard and dashboard accessible to state workers and the general public. The DOT manager also tweets a link to the dashboard and announces its availability on Linked-In. Transparency grows alongside its twin sister, accountability. With a little imagination, you can envision a limitless number of possibilities for harnessing social media in the service of results-driven government.

Enable Virtual Collaboration

Technology also enables collaboration among people who work at different locations. Given the importance of constant communication and teamwork, online virtual collaboration tools such as Dropbox, Flow, Skitch, Google Hangouts, and Microsoft's SharePoint make it possible for workers in Boston, Springfield, Worcester, and Lakeville to readily engage. These are examples of products that enable people to work together without being together. Not only does this promote full engagement in improvement efforts — it also gives managers a powerful change management tool.

New technologies will come along in the future. State leaders should keep their eyes open for ones they can deploy as weapons in The Results Revolution.

Taking Time to Get It Right

Mark Twain once apologized for a longwinded letter he had written to a friend, saying, "I would have made it shorter, if I'd had the time." You could say the same about a management system: "I would have made it more sustainable, if I'd had the time." You need to take the time. A sustainable management system won't grow overnight. It can only grow, thrive, and take root after a lot of work, tears, and heartache. It won't ever become perfect, but nothing will move you closer to exceptional results than a well-crafted, sustainable management system.

CHAPTER ELEVEN

Recommendations

Winning The Results Revolution

"Educate and inform the whole mass of people...
They are the only sure reliance for the
preservation of liberty."

~ THOMAS JEFFERSON

Heather Adams leans back from her monitor, smiling as she recalls meeting her soon-to-be boss Bob Tomkins at a training session conducted a few years ago by Department of Health Services. Bob had advised his naive young colleague to dampen her enthusiasm and learn how to "go along to get along." She has never forgotten the words that made her heart sink: "Once you get used to the way we do things around here, you'll see that it's better not to mess with the status quo. Look around you. Most of these people have died inside." That was before the Governor launched a Results Revolution.

Now, some four years later, she looks at the clock and notices it's almost noon. Time to head to the lunchroom where DHS will throw a party honoring Bob's retirement after 26 years of service to his beloved state.

Heather, once Bob's protégé and now a highly respected regional supervisor, has agreed to say a few words about her mentor. After all, the two of them have fought side-by-side to help transform DHS from a reactive bureaucracy with unknown results to a vibrant, results-driven organization that has become the envy of its counterparts across the nation.

When the crowd has taken the last bite of the potluck lunch, Dr. Jane Koponen, Director of the DHS, rises from her seat and strides over to the folding table piled with funny cards, gag gifts, and a big chocolate sheet cake. The group listens intently as the Director shares a few highlights of Bob's career. She teases him about the time four years ago when he had to drop out of a watercolor class in order to earn a black belt in Lean. Finally she presents Bob with a plaque thanking him for his dedicated service to DHS, the state, and its citizens.

Now it's Heather's turn to say a few final words.

"Bob," she begins with a big smile, "Do you remember the first time we met at that training class for the field staff and I suggested we develop a checklist app to help manage our field people's workloads?"

Bob leans back in his chair, shaking his head and chuckling, as if to say, "Ouch!"

"I have to admit that at the end of *that* day I had decided that going to work for the state was a colossal mistake! I wished I had become a soldier in the Tony Soprano family, driving a garbage truck." That brings a laugh from the audience. "But I'm glad I stayed. Just a few weeks after that fateful meeting the Governor and our Director set us on a path that has made it possible for all of us to do what we love to do, and that is help the people in our state live better lives. They saved us from Zombieland, where people are dead inside."

Heather proceeds to tell the group how she and Bob led a

series of major process improvement efforts in DHS, and have just rolled out a major new breakthrough app that will improve service and cut costs. "Who can ask for more than that? It happened because our people are so totally engaged in efficiently and effectively serving our customers. We have such talented and committed people here, and they all deserve an award like this." She holds up the plaque for everyone to admire.

Everyone's eyes turn to the now-tearful Bob. "Speech! Speech! Speech!" they cry. He reluctantly stands to a round of hearty applause.

"Thanks, Heather. I must say you were one big pain in the rear end when I first met you. So passionate but such a smarty-pants, still wet behind the ears. But I've got to admit your can-do attitude woke me up and made me think about why I had gotten into public service in the first place. You taught me that I was not really dead inside, just numbed by all the 'business as usual' that had turned DHS into a bureaucratic dinosaur. We have the Governor and Dr. Koponen to thank for helping us teach that dinosaur to dance."

Other states are teaching their own dinosaurs to dance by joining The Results Revolution. It's never too late. Any state or state agency can begin today. It just takes a commitment to change "business as usual" by transforming the fundamentals of the game. Only if you change the game can you change the results.

Government that works depends on the basic, no-nonsense principles we have discussed in this book. These principles have already helped many states develop the best practices for delivering better and more cost-efficient service to their customers. Those practices create a culture of transparency, accountability, and sustainability.

In this chapter, we summarize the principles and best practices we have discussed throughout this book. We give you recommendations you can use wherever you are in your own Results Revolution — whether you are just deciding to join, have already created a results-driven culture, or are anywhere in-between.

Implementing Your Own Results-Driven System

In the Introduction we set the stage for this book by describing Thomas Jefferson's firm belief in the power of the states to create a perfect union. If you're thinking about joining The Results Revolution, but have not taken the first step toward government that works, you might take Jefferson's advice to heart: "Do you want to know who you are? Don't ask. Act! Action will delineate and define you."

Or maybe you have joined The Results Revolution already. Jefferson would applaud.

You know you have built a results-driven management system when:

1. The leaders model transparency and accountability with every word and action
2. Managers/supervisors spend their time coaching, not bossing
3. Every employee sees how their work connects to the organization's goals
4. Every employee can define their customers and what their customers value
5. Every employee routinely and effectively solves problems and improves processes
6. Processes flow efficiently and effectively because the organization has dismantled the silos that breed bureaucracy and prevent communication
7. Units deliver initiatives on spec, on time, and on budget

8. The organization conducts routine business reviews at every level in order to drive candor, accountability, and collaboration
9. Decisions and solutions depend on timely and accurate hard performance data, data that has been turned into information through charts, graphs, and maps
10. Performance measures ensure continuous improvement

These practices must become second nature throughout the organization. As one agency leader told us, "We knew we had made the transition when we stopped talking about it as a management system and just began to see it as how we run the department."

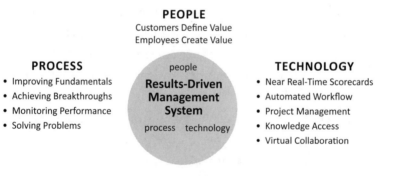

PEOPLE
Customers Define Value
Employees Create Value

PROCESS
- Improving Fundamentals
- Achieving Breakthroughs
- Monitoring Performance
- Solving Problems

people
Results-Driven Management System
process   technology

TECHNOLOGY
- Near Real-Time Scorecards
- Automated Workflow
- Project Management
- Knowledge Access
- Virtual Collaboration

FIGURE 11.1: Installing a Results-Driven Management System requires the achievement of levels of maturity in people, process, and technology, all focused on the desired results of the organization.

That's a crucial point. As you begin the transformation effort you must stop thinking about the work as a collection of initiatives (scorecards, Lean/process improvement, employee engagement, improved customer experiences, etc.) and start thinking about it as a fundamental shift in the way you manage. You are not installing various practices; you are building a *management system.* By adopting a systems perspective leaders can provide the proper context for change. That context focuses everyone on doing their work in a way that gets results for the customer.

An effective system integrates people, process, and technology. It applies to each agency and the state as a whole.

Implementing Your Transformation in Phases

Whether you have just begun a transformation effort or have progressed well along the path toward delivering better results to your customers, you will want to keep in mind the three major phases of any successful change initiative:

PHASE ONE: *Lay the Foundation* (Timeline: 3-6 Months)

1. Build a Governor's Fundamentals Map (mission, vision, values, key goals, outcome measures, core processes, and process measures) and the scorecards that measure progress. The governor and his key leaders participate directly in this task.
2. Select three agencies with highly respected leaders who will engage their teams in building agency level Maps.
3. Connect the Governor's and agency Maps.
4. Identify and create charters for three cross-agency breakthroughs aligned with governor's policy agenda.
5. Install a project management process to guide the transformation.
6. Develop and initiate a change management/communication/stakeholder plan.

PHASE TWO: *Deploy the System* (Timeline: 12-24 months)

1. Communicate the governor's map to agency leadership.
2. Rollout the governor's scorecards complete with performance ranges (red/yellow/green) and performance targets.

Once measures become stable and reliable, give the public easy access to them.

3. Communicate the initial three agency Maps within the agencies.
4. Rollout the agency scorecards, cascading them to all teams and individuals. Once you stabilize the outcome measures, make them public.
5. Establish Governor's Quarterly Target Reviews.
6. Institute initial agency-level Quarterly Target Reviews.
7. Set expectations for the agencies to create aligned Fundamentals Maps, develop scorecards, and institute regular business reviews.
8. Deploy cross-agency breakthrough teams to pursue charters aligned to the governor's policy agenda.
9. Redefine the role of leaders and managers; launch comprehensive leadership and management training programs to enable leaders and managers to work successfully in the world of results-driven government.
10. Select a common problem-solving model and a philosophy for engaging employees in improving process and outcome measures. Set up learning experiences where improvement teams learn how to solve real problems and deliver real results.
11. Rollout a comprehensive change management/communication/stakeholder strategy. Include recognition/celebration programs to acknowledge successful innovation.

PHASE THREE: *Embed for Sustainability* (Timeline: 24-48 months)
1. Keep pushing the transformation to ever lower levels until it touches every employee.
2. Continuously improve measures as learning drives better understanding.

3. Communicate, communicate, communicate.
4. Continue development of leaders and managers.
5. Automate the system to make data immediately available to everyone; use information systems to turn the data into information.

States and agencies that have adopted this approach, or a variation of it, have established a number of best practices that help deliver exceptional results.

Eight Best Practices of Results-Driven Government

There's a lot to be learned from the experiments going on across the nation. All eight of these best practices are being followed somewhere, but no state has yet to combine them all. When it happens, you will see the most successful implementation. Recommended best practices:

1. **Appoint a Chief Operating Officer**
   In most states the Governor's Chief of Staff oversees both policy and operations. Each of these potentially full-time jobs requires a particular set of skills. Imagine that the Governor serves as Chairman of the Board. Few, if any, Chairmen of a multi-billion dollar enterprise would assign the roles of Chief Executive Officer and Chief Operating Officer to the same person. Few Chiefs of Staff bring state-of-the-art operations management experience to their jobs. That's why it makes sense to set up a new position. A highly skilled Chief Operating Officer should possess the skills it takes not only to oversee day-to-day operations, but also to shoulder responsibility for a major transformation initiative.

2. **Make the Transformation Job One**

   Government employees can get so busy putting out daily fires that they see a major change effort as nothing but an added burden. Yes, the transformation will take even more blood and sweat, but it should not cause tears to flow. Stress how much more smoothly the work will flow after the transformation, when a results-driven management system will help people do their jobs more efficiently and effectively. Life will only get sweeter.

3. **Hold every employee accountable for results**

   Routine Business Reviews should measure progress and emphasize accountability for improvement. Use your business reviews to follow-up rigorously and relentlessly on progress toward pre-established goals. Consider centrally tracking action items the way Maryland does (see Chapter 7). Maryland nicely balances effective follow-up with support to remove obstacles on the path to results. Never forget that accountability does not mean punishing people for performance that is below expectation; it means encouraging and educating people to fix their processes so they can deliver better results.

4. **Build a shared-interest partnership with the Legislature**

   Our system of checks and balances prescribes certain responsibilities for each branch of government. Since major transformation inevitably requires new or amended laws or the elimination of outdated laws, the executive branch must engage the Legislature in the process. Ignore the lawmakers, and you risk their opposition to elements of your drive toward results-driven government. The more you can educate the Legislature about the value of installing a more effective and efficient management system, the more they will trust and support the changes you need to make. Involve the Legislature by inviting their representatives to participate as stakeholders in the development of the state's goals and its outcome measures. This cements shared-interests at the outset.

5. **Lead from the front**
    Many strong executives like to delegate almost everything to subordinates. That works fine with tactical decisions on the battlefield, but not with the strategic decisions that set the course for the troops. Leaders should not show up only at the important meetings with their briefing packets and staff in tow. The Governor and agency heads must exercise strategic leadership throughout the change effort, attending and actively participating in all top-level business reviews to make it clear how much the work matters to them. Transformation involves steep learning curves for everyone, including senior leadership. Embrace the curve!

6. **Drive out fear**
    Frightened people duck and cover. Nothing can more quickly thwart any change effort than the natural fear any change ignites in the human brain. Anticipate and prepare for fear, working tirelessly to communicate the benefits of the change for all concerned, from the people who do the work to the citizens who receive the results of that work.

7. **Celebrate success**
    Take time to celebrate improvements. Praise innovation. Honor the innovators. Cheer results. Reward and promote those who add great value to the transformation. Don't wait to throw a party at the end of a quarter, but generously pass out congratulations whenever someone does something exceptional, something that models the new

results-focused behaviors. Nothing more surely reinforces the behaviors you want people to bring to their work.

8. **Emphasize *Why* We're Doing *What* We're Doing**

When people are fighting the hard day-to-day battles, it's easy for them to lose sight of the reason they joined the revolution in the first place. Leaders must frequently remind their people that they're deploying the weapons of results-driven management to reach an all-important goal of better results for the citizens, better results for the state. That's both their rallying cry and their banner: RESULTS! Always put it in human terms, stressing the satisfaction Bob the Department of Motor Vehicles agent and June the Department of Revenue customer service rep get from delighting John and Jane Q. Public. Transformation takes heart, not just brains.

Life in government can get extremely hectic, especially when serious problems rise to the attention of the voting public. The need to address such issues makes it hard for executive branch leaders to concentrate fully on engineering a results-driven transformation, but concentrate they must. In fact, they must pay as much attention to it as they do any major emergency.

Matt Gallagher, who helped Governor O'Malley set up and run both CitiStat in Baltimore and StateStat in Maryland, appreciated the challenge. "Bringing your management team together on such a regular basis, having such structured discussions about performance and then displaying that performance with maps, charts, and graphs, which tell a story about that performance, it's very impactful. People learn in different ways. People adapt in different ways, and when you have these meetings, these very dynamic meetings, in the case of Baltimore and the State of Maryland, they were important in bringing about improvement."

Talk about concentration. Gallagher has sat in on more than a thousand Stat reviews during his career. He advises leaders to buy in or go home. "Most people will tell you executive buy-in is critical." That applies to every agency and department head as well. But then, Gallagher warns, leadership must go further and obtain buy-in throughout the organization.

To Gallagher, real buy-in becomes obvious when the departments begin to do more than gather and report data. You know it's happening when you see people discussing the meaning of all the raw data, looking for problems and solutions to problems they detect. That's what Gallagher and the Governor were always looking for.

The Stat programs instituted under Governor O'Malley have won widespread admiration, but even the most ardent admirers do not find it so easy to follow suit. Gallagher told us that over the years he and his teams entertained countless visits from local, state, federal, and even international governments interested in the techniques. Few, however, were willing to take them home and make them work in their own organizations, especially the real-time conversation about what isn't working or what isn't getting done. They miss some of the subtle but powerful aspects of building government that works, like letting the risk of imperfection and struggle be a source for innovation and inspiration.

"But we're not looking for staged meetings, we're looking for give and take, we're looking for a free-flowing discussion," said Gallagher. "We want people to come in and know their data. That's what we always wanted them to do. We wanted them to demonstrate that they were using this information to manage."

In many ways, Maryland set the standard for transparency and accountability, as well as the standard for a number of the other eight best practices. The lessons learned from their experiments will benefit every warrior who joins The Results Revolution.

CHAPTER 12

Conclusion

Joining the Voices for the Common Good

"Darkness cannot drive out darkness; only light can do that.
Hate cannot drive out hate; only love can do that."
~ MARTIN LUTHER KING, JR.

I wrote this book not as someone with extensive involvement in politics but as a business executive and an American who believes in the transformative power of results. As a veteran of the business world, I know government and the citizens it serves can benefit from a sharp focus on getting results. I believe this will restore our nation's position of global leadership.

In the early part of this new century many Americans became increasingly disillusioned with "business as usual" at all levels of government. Many vented their frustration in rancorous and unproductive debates assigning blame for broken government, arguing that only their ideology could fix it. I worry that the argument has become so strident and contentious that we could easily pass a point of no return.

Fortunately, new heroes have emerged to set the ship of state on a better course, among them Governor Rick Snyder of Michigan and Governor Martin O'Malley of Maryland. This book concludes with some of their personal thoughts about that new direction. But first, let me share a story.

Reclaiming Our Voice and Our Common Interest

In October of 2013 during a layover in Houston, I learned that our Congress would not approve a budget and that a government shutdown was only hours away. I was in a shoeshine stand and asked the fellow polishing my shoes what he thought of this debacle. He erupted with a startling degree of anger.

"They sit in their big offices acting like kings and queens with no consideration for the impact of what they do to us paupers," said this hardworking, middle-aged man. "What they are doing has a huge impact on me and my family, but they simply don't care."

His frustration with government leaders made me think of Thomas Jefferson witnessing the French Revolution. The people had grown so enraged by the excesses of the governing monarchy that they had resorted to violence in order to get their voices heard. They spoke with weapons more dangerous than words. Could this happen in modern-day America? Could angry citizens get so fed up with the excesses and inadequacies of government that they would attack with bullets rather than ballots? The image, though farfetched, frightened me.

I went out on a limb and told the fellow about my current work, helping state government leaders join a non-violent revolution that aimed at getting the sort of results he wished his government could produce. "Believe it or not, I've met a lot of dedicated and hardworking public servants, from Governors to clerks in the Department of Motor Vehicles who not only share

your frustration but have begun to do something about it."
Again, he surprised me. He nodded thoughtfully as he listened
to my words.

When he finished his work, I paid him for a job well done.
Before I walked away, he took my hand in his and offered a
quiet prayer that I was right, that government could and would
deliver on its promise of the American dream for him and his
children.

Whenever I grow frustrated with what can seem like an almost
impossible task, replacing "business as usual" with government
that works, I remember the shoeshine man's prayer. He's the
customer. He's why I do the work I do. Him, his children, and
of course my children.

I have chosen to get involved with state government because
I think most citizens feel closer to it than to the federal government in Washington, DC. They come into contact with state
government every day in so many ways, from the pothole on the
highway that the Department of Transportation should have
fixed to the schools that are falling short of educating children
to the highest standards on earth. If one state transforms its
delivery of such services with results-driven government, that
would be good. If six states do it, that would be even better. But
if 50 states do it, then we could really have a (peaceful) revolution
on our hands. Then, with luck, the transformation might trick-
le down to counties and towns and flood up to the federal level.

It all starts with government leaders and workers listening to
the voices of the people, to the customers who expect more from
elected and appointed officials. I feel quite fortunate that during
my travels I have met and spent time with two leaders of The
Results Revolution who know how to listen to the voice of the
shoeshine man.

Meet Governor Rick Snyder of Michigan

When Michigan Governor Rick Snyder testified before a Congressional Committee on the Workforce Investment Act, he made a startling suggestion. As he told us later, he invited Congress to strike a deal with Michigan: "You have a federal deficit. You've got big financial problems. Cut my budget in this area [workforce investment]. I'm willing to have you come and cut my budget, but here's the deal. We'll agree on four or five individual metrics looking at the situation as a whole. I said, cut my budget by 25 percent or even a third, but get rid of all the overhead, all the prescriptive stuff. Get rid of that and we'll be ahead. We'll both be ahead."

By "all the prescriptive stuff" he meant the mountain of rules and regulations and the miles of bureaucratic red tape that made it impossible to get the best possible results from workforce investment programs. He figured his state could get better results out of 45 federally supported workforce investment programs if the federal government would simply get out of the way, and that they could get those results with less money.

When he spoke with us in his Detroit office, he offered this insight. "It's all about inputs, it's not about results." He meant that the federal government collected a lot of data about a program, such as how many people participated in it and how much it cost, but never measured outputs (i.e., results). Did participants land better jobs? Did they improve their financial position in the community? Did they get off welfare?

Results matter to Governor Snyder, a former business executive, venture capitalist, lawyer, and accountant. His perspective on the proper role of government grew out of an environment in which you judge success by measuring the bottom line, not from one where you define it in terms of how well you amass and retain power.

His views did not always sit well with his new colleagues in state government. "When I did my first State of the State address, I put up a dashboard of metrics. I said, 'Here's a bunch of measurements about how the state's doing, I'm going to talk about them every year.' It was interesting to see all the criticism that I got from the political world. They said, 'You're nuts. Why would you ever publish a bunch of measurements? Why would you do something like that?'"

None of the skepticism deterred him from his dedication to installing more accountability, transparency, and a focus on results through every leader, department, team, and individual working for the state of Michigan. Doing that meant much more than applying a more businesslike approach to government; it meant fundamentally rethinking the purpose of government.

"I ask people, when is the last time you sat down and had a thoughtful discussion about why government exists," he told us. "I didn't know what I thought, but then when I became Governor, it became readily apparent that no one had had that discussion in a long time. The default setting for people in the construct of the political world was that it was about taking money from someone and giving it to someone else. And that's wrong."

Snyder's business experience told him that if an organization never pauses to think about why the business exists, it won't exist for long. To drive home his point, he cited the state's Pathways to Potential program in which caseworkers support children in 90 schools in Detroit and another 180 statewide. He asked the big "why" question.

"Why do you do your casework in a situation where someone [a student] has to take two or three city buses to some bland government office and wait in line to be serviced? That's not customer service."

Customer service? Officials had not thought in those terms before. But they did not resist the obviously good idea that they visit the students, rather than the other way around. "So we placed a whole bunch of them out in these schools, and now they've gone to the customer, which are mainly the kids in those schools and their families. That's customer service."

The change got better results and ended up costing less. "My goal is when you conceive of the amount of taxes you pay, [you want to know] that you have paid for the *right* amount of government." That attitude flies in the face of "business as usual," where it's all about amassing power. Bigger is not better, Snyder insisted. Better is better.

How do you make government better? You look for ways to improve effectiveness and efficiency. "Michigan is one of the most diverse states by far," explained Snyder. "We're a bigger state geographically and a bigger state population than most people recognize. And we're extremely diverse. You're sitting here in downtown Detroit, but I can take you an hour [beyond the city limits], and you'll see horse and buggy signs on the road."

How, Snyder wondered, can state government best serve such a sprawling and diverse clientele? To answer that question the Governor asked the state's 20 departments to bring him their maps of the state and show him their regions. When he put them all together, he saw a complicated overlapping mess that looked like a "spaghetti bowl." No departments organized themselves into the same regions.

"It's nuts," said the Governor. "And talk about a classic case of people trying to resist. We got everything from, 'We've done this for 100 years, and we can't change' to sort of a 'dog-ate-my-homework' kind of excuse. And so I said, I don't care, change your lines."

Snyder wisely saw his job not as changing a cog here and a

wheel there, modifying this or that law or changing a regulation, but changing government's basic culture. He needed to get the elephant of government bureaucracy dancing like a ballerina. And that's no small task. The key, to Snyder's mind, was an emphasis on what he called relentless positive action.

"You just keep on coming back to it. I've seen it everywhere from people who are fairly senior who say, 'Look, I've been doing this all my life, and it doesn't make any sense.' Other people just say, 'We're going to wait him out, even if it's 4 years or 8 years.' And so far that hasn't worked out so hot for people."

Once all of the state's departments began serving the same set of 10 economic regions, they could finally share data. The old silos gave way to collaborative problem solving. Instead of the occasional "treaty negotiation" between different departments, the state adopted a master agreement approach that covered 80 to 90 percent of the interagency agreements and honored federal privacy requirements.

Governor Snyder, a firm believer in total transparency, has championed a single sign-in system where citizens and businesses can log into one site and seamlessly access any state service they need. Without the matching regions, data-sharing agreements, common formats for reports, and a consistent set of tools, that could not possibly happen.

"Everyone likes change until it affects *them*. I appreciate that; I won't minimize that, because it's hard. But it's done in the context of what's the best for all of us in the long term. And again, if you're going to institutionalize best practices and a results focus, you need a longer horizon. And that is one of the challenges, sometimes to get the results you want, you're not going to see it for some time. You have to have that conviction to measure enough outputs . . . to see you're on a positive path. And that's part of the patience it takes."

Given Snyder's background in the world of technology, he often thinks of changing a culture in terms of what he calls "the tech adoption curve." It starts with a few early adopters, grows quickly with fast followers, and eventually attracts the laggards. That's why he likes to "go with the pace of the fastest runner." If you let those who embrace the change set the pace of adoption, you will get everyone on board much more quickly.

It also takes leadership. "You have to set the tone at the top, and you have to live what you're doing. So that's where I did the dashboard, because I wanted to show that I'm not asking anything of them that I'm not willing to do myself. That's part of good leadership."

The Governor's fact-based, results-oriented leadership has the Legislature on board as well, and not just members of his own party. Both sides have come together to pass an incredible number of important bills with a supermajority of both parties. With performance back in the picture, results trumped rhetoric.

Governor Snyder suggests that Michigan's track record of success can inspire other states to follow suit. "We had our economy go broke because we were so successful we didn't have to change," he said about the once-prosperous region that fell on hard economic times with the decline of the auto industry in the 1970s. With results at the center of the agenda, with government paying closer attention to the voice of the "customer," and with a dedication to the common good, Michigan government has brought the state and a bankrupt Detroit back from the dead.

"We'd been too successful [in Detroit's heyday]. We just rode a good thing into the ground. And our country has similar attributes because it hasn't acknowledged that our government needs to change the way it does things. And we spend too much time arguing with ourselves instead of recognizing that, gee, we're all Americans."

Meet Governor Martin O'Malley of Maryland

I met with Maryland's Governor Martin O'Malley in the Maryland State House, which had served as the temporary capital of the nation from 1783-84. His words uncannily spoke to the issues raised by the man in the shoeshine stand. "I think ideology, fear, rhetoric, spin, all perpetuate the notion that our government can't work and will never work. I think the only way to overcome that is to tell a larger story, and a story that is built on facts of achievement and accomplishment of results."

Like Rick Snyder, Governor O'Malley preferred results to rhetoric, but he believed that the future of the states and the country boils down to people, not a bunch of numbers and statistics. Government, he told us, should create a world ". . . where people can give their children better lives." The shoeshine man would applaud that sentiment.

"There are many of us who are concerned that our best days are behind us, rather than ahead of us, and that somehow we aren't going to be able to give our children better futures with better opportunity." Facts matter, but measures that reveal poor performance should drive improvement, not despair. "I think you have to acknowledge the negative perception, but then appeal to the belief that we're stronger together." United, we stand; bickering, we fall.

Governor O'Malley trusts the next generation of American leaders to put results before rhetoric. "This new generation that is quickly becoming part of the electorate might be called the 'show me' generation. They want their servant leaders to show them where their dollars are being spent, to show them how their dollars are being spent. In other words, are we making progress towards our goals? 'Show me.'" How better to show them than by giving them the facts and performance measures that indicate whether or not government is listening to their voices and fulfilling their expectations?

O'Malley's political career began with his election to the Baltimore City Council in 1991. In 1999 he ran as the only Caucasian candidate for mayor in the predominately African-American city. He won the general election with 90 percent of the vote, and then won re-election in 2003 with 87 percent of the vote. O'Malley's platform stressed crime reduction, installing CitiStat, and leveraging that methodology across city government during his two terms as mayor. As Mayor and later as Governor, O'Malley entertained many curious visitors from around the world who wanted to see for themselves how the Stat method actually worked.

That interest delighted O'Malley. "I think there is an emerging desire throughout the country for a government that is visible, transparent, and performance-measured. Mayors have always had an advantage because they produce services that are more readily visible to the eye. But that should tell state and federal leaders they should also embrace this new form of leadership."

With something mundane and clearly visible, such as trash pickup and potholes, city leaders can easily see what's working and not working. As you progress up the food chain to state and federal government, however, it gets harder and harder to witness results and performance gaps firsthand. That fact argues that state government leaders listen even harder to the voices of their citizens and measure more carefully whether or not they are truly serving the common good.

"We can't continue to have a great government, and we can't continue to have a great country unless we're able to make our government work." He pointed out that earlier generations believed in a shared platform for success and the idea that hard work and smart work would create a better world for their children and grandchildren. O'Malley thinks we must recapture that "can-do" optimism.

"I see the emergence of a new way of governing. It's happening across the country, and it's emerging from our city centers and our metropolitan governments . . ." He sees it going viral, eventually affecting each and every state in the union. "It's casting aside the old ways of political parties and hierarchy of bureaucracy. Instead, with the use of technology, geographic information systems, 311 call centers, and big data it's a new way of continually asking the question, 'Is it working?'"

Governors Snyder and O'Malley both see measurement as a key component of the transformation from rhetoric to results because measurement answers questions with cold, hard facts. When government workers see the facts, they can see the gaps, and when they see the gaps, they can improve performance. In this way, facts drive innovation. That sounds a lot less like business as usual and much more like a new era of entrepreneurial behavior in government.

"It's that common platform that everyone can see and measure and evaluate . . . and be a part of it if they choose." In a world governed by the common good, collaboration rules and compartmentalized silos that thwart sharing disappear. "The key, the greatest improvement in government, I think, is through better coordination, cooperation, and collaboration."

Once again, facts rule the day. The latest technologies, from cloud computing and social media, to geographic information systems, big data, and mobile devices, empower collaboration in the interest of the common good. They also give citizens a voice.

Transparency grows naturally in such an environment. "Data allows you to make better decisions based on fact and not on hunch. But the Internet and GIS also give us the ability to lay that decision and that process wide open for all the citizens to see in a way that we've never been able to do in the history of democracies on the planet. There was always a much greater element of trusting the leader or the leader having an information advantage where he or she knew about something 6 months before the public."

This brought the Governor back to the young people of America, as he noted their comfort with technology and their expectation that they can communicate with anyone, anytime, anywhere. "And when they see their bank, their retailer, their taxi service is able to use the Internet and these common platforms to be more individually responsive to them as consumers, they aren't accepting excuses about why their government can't be a part of it."

Younger people also live in a smaller world than their grandparents, one in which everyone and everything is part of a great big system. "On the one hand, the reaction on the surface of the separatist and even the secessionist is to separate away from. On the other hand, you see this desire for closer connection coming up in the next generation. This one movement for connection, and this other movement for separation, I think, are coming out of a greater yearning for control of our own destiny. [Governor] John Hickenlooper [of Colorado] has said that collaboration is the new competition. There's an ability to share information that comes from collaboration and performance."

The country has reached a pivot point where it can either go down the current path to increasingly combative debate over ideological correctness, or it can take the path to renewal and renaissance. Governor O'Malley hopes we choose the latter and regain "that sense the founders always had that history was watching."

He has dedicated his political career to serving the common good in a way that history will record in a positive way. "I've been motivated in my service by three common beliefs. One is the belief in the dignity of every individual. Second is the understanding that whether we like this or not, we're all in this together. Personally, I like that. And third, each of us plays a role in forming, strengthening, and advancing the common good we share. I think it's the politics of the common good that people are yearning to hear right now. It expresses itself in phrases like, 'We have to get things done again as a people. We need leaders who can get things done. We need to learn how to talk to one another so that we can get things done.'"

Getting things done means solving some real and pressing problems with innovative solutions and breakthroughs that would astonish our grandparents and will delight our grandchildren. "We are the greatest problem-solving people ever brought forth on the face of the planet. We are at the tip of what Teilhard de Chardin described as an ascending area of human development. And that's our gift, not just to our kids and theirs. It's a gift that can heal this very challenged world of ours."

Choosing Results Not Sides

Both Governors O'Malley and Snyder, not to mention Governors Hickenlooper, Haslam, Inslee, and Kitzhaber and other state government leaders, hear the voices of the people and the clarion call for results-driven government. They choose to set aside partisan squabbling and gridlock. They choose measurable results over hollow rhetoric.

These leaders deserve recognition for their efforts to transform state government, and so do the tens of thousands of public servants engaged in better serving the common good. They labor at every level of government, from the frontline service agent at the Department of Motor Vehicles to the state trooper working overtime to save lives by getting drunken drivers off the road. Behind the scenes, less visible public servants work diligently to remove waste from mundane processes. Their work ranges from speeding the processing of invoices and background checks of teachers to providing healthy meals to inmates of correctional facilities and helping taxpayers receive credits for installing energy-efficient heating and cooling systems.

Every single citizen can join The Results Revolution by standing up and speaking out to make sure those who work in state government will hear their voices and strive even harder to serve the common good. I wrote The Results Pledge because I believe it represents the sentiments of those involved in The Results Revolution. Whether you work in government or not, you can take the Results Pledge here or online at www.resultsamerica. org/pledge.

The Results Pledge

Whereas, I believe in these United States of America, and hold as precious the sentiments Abraham Lincoln expressed at Gettysburg in 1863: *"A government of the people, by the people and for the people shall not perish from this earth."*

Whereas, I believe we as a nation have lost our way, and that as a citizen I have the sacred duty to speak for the betterment of our Union.

Whereas, increasingly our political system does not serve the people, but instead has degenerated into a circular world of ideological rhetoric that serves *only* the desire to get elected and re-elected in order to maintain or accumulate power.

Whereas, I believe our government can, should, and must work for the common good.

Whereas, I believe the mission of our Government is to make this Nation better, and that our Nation should lead the world with:

- The best-educated people
- The most innovative and prosperous economy
- The safest place to live, work, and raise a family
- The most responsible sustainability practices
- The healthiest and fittest people
- A second-to-none infrastructure
- A government respected for its efficiency and effectiveness

Whereas, these goals can be best achieved by a Government that thrives on being transparent, efficient, effective, and accountable to its citizens, routinely publishing its results in scorecards that demonstrate its progress.

Whereas, henceforth our Government shall function for the purpose of achieving RESULTS, and that we shall elect and appoint as our government leaders those people who demonstrate actions that achieve the results we as a nation hold dear.

Therefore, I sign **The Results Pledge** with the very words used by the signers of our founding Declaration of Independence, in order to demonstrate the strength of my resolve: *"And for the support of this Declaration, with a firm reliance on the protection of divine Providence, we mutually pledge to each other our Lives, our Fortunes and our sacred Honor."*

Whether you work in government or not, you can sign the Results Pledge by signing here or online: _____

To sign online visit: www.resultsamerica.org/pledge.

APPENDIX A

MVD Customer Bill of Rights

The staff of the Motor Vehicle Division is pleased to welcome you to MVD. We are committed to providing outstanding service – *every customer, every transaction, every time.*

All customers conducting business with the Motor Vehicle Division have these rights:

◆ **Prompt, friendly, and courteous service.**
When interacting with MVD employees you have the right to consistent, timely, accurate, confidential, efficient, and professional service.

◆ **The first name of your MVD Customer Service Representative.**
You're our guest today. You should know who is helping you.

◆ **Professional, knowledgeable assistance in answering questions.**
Our staff should be able to answer MVD-related questions accurately, or direct you to a specialist to obtain more detailed information.

◆ **Service that is free from unlawful discrimination.**
MVD prohibits discrimination by its employees and contractors on the basis of race, ancestry, color, religious affiliation, national origin, age, mental or physical ability, gender, sexual orientation or political beliefs.

We value your feedback and will respond promptly to your suggestions, comments, or complaints.

If we haven't met your expectations, please ask for the manager at this office. Or you can contact the MVD director at:

Motor Vehicle Director
P.O. Box 1028
Santa Fe, NM 87504-1028
mvd.director@state.nm.us

NEW MEXICO

APPENDIX B

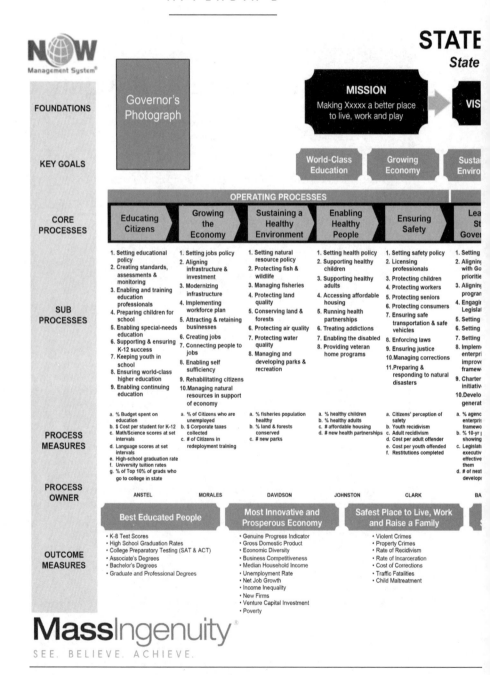

NOW Management System®

STATE
State

MISSION
Making Xxxxx a better place to live, work and play

VIS

FOUNDATIONS

Governor's Photograph

KEY GOALS

World-Class Education | Growing Economy | Susta Enviro

OPERATING PROCESSES

CORE PROCESSES	Educating Citizens	Growing the Economy	Sustaining a Healthy Environment	Enabling Healthy People	Ensuring Safety	Lea St Gover
SUB PROCESSES	1. Setting educational policy 2. Creating standards, assessments & monitoring 3. Enabling and training education professionals 4. Preparing children for school 5. Enabling special-needs education 6. Supporting & ensuring K-12 success 7. Keeping youth in school 8. Ensuring world-class higher education 9. Enabling continuing education	1. Setting jobs policy 2. Aligning infrastructure & investment 3. Modernizing infrastructure 4. Implementing workforce plan 5. Attracting & retaining businesses 6. Creating jobs 7. Connecting people to jobs 8. Enabling self sufficiency 9. Rehabilitating citizens 10. Managing natural resources in support of economy	1. Setting natural resource policy 2. Protecting fish & wildlife 3. Managing fisheries 4. Protecting land quality 5. Conserving land & forests 6. Protecting air quality 7. Protecting water quality 8. Managing and developing parks & recreation	1. Setting health policy 2. Supporting healthy children 3. Supporting healthy adults 4. Accessing affordable housing 5. Running health partnerships 6. Treating addictions 7. Enabling the disabled 8. Providing veteran home programs	1. Setting safety policy 2. Licensing professionals 3. Protecting children 4. Protecting workers 5. Protecting seniors 6. Protecting consumers 7. Ensuring safe transportation & safe vehicles 8. Enforcing laws 9. Ensuring justice 10. Managing corrections 11. Preparing & responding to natural disasters	1. Setting 2. Aligning with Go prioritie 3. Aligning progran 4. Engagin Legislat 5. Setting 6. Setting 7. Setting 8. Implem enterpri improve framewo 9. Charter initiativi 10. Develo generat
PROCESS MEASURES	a. % Budget spent on education b. $ Cost per student for K-12 c. Math/Science scores at set intervals d. Language scores at set intervals e. High-school graduation rate f. University tuition rates g. % of Top 10% of grads who go to college in state	a. % of Citizens who are unemployed b. $ Corporate taxes collected c. # of Citizens in redeployment training	a. % fisheries population healthy b. % land & forests conserved c. # new parks	a. % healthy children b. % healthy adults c. # affordable housing d. # new health partnerships	a. Citizens' perception of safety b. Youth recidivism c. Adult recidivism d. Cost per adult offender e. Cost per youth offended f. Restitutions completed	a. % agenc enterpris framewo b. % 10-yr p showing c. Legislati executiv effective them d. % of next developi
PROCESS OWNER	ANSTEL	MORALES	DAVIDSON	JOHNSTON	CLARK	BA

	Best Educated People	Most Innovative and Prosperous Economy	Safest Place to Live, Work and Raise a Family	
OUTCOME MEASURES	• K-8 Test Scores • High School Graduation Rates • College Preparatory Testing (SAT & ACT) • Associate's Degrees • Bachelor's Degrees • Graduate and Professional Degrees	• Genuine Progress Indicator • Gross Domestic Product • Economic Diversity • Business Competitiveness • Median Household Income • Unemployment Rate • Net Job Growth • Income Inequality • New Firms • Venture Capital Investment • Poverty	• Violent Crimes • Property Crimes • Rate of Recidivism • Rate of Incarceration • Cost of Corrections • Traffic Fatalities • Child Maltreatment	

MassIngenuity®
SEE. BELIEVE. ACHIEVE.

To see this map in detail visit: www.resultsamerica.org/govmap

E NAME

Slogan

ION

VALUES

How We Operate
- Transparency and Accountability
- Operating as a Single Enterprise
- Shared Leadership through Demonstrated Collaboration

What We Ensure
- Fiscal Stability and Sustainability
- Equity for All Citizens
- Opportunity for Prosperity

STATE FLAG

nable nment	Healthy Citizens	Safe Place to Live	Efficient & Effective Government

EFFICIENT & EFFECTIVE GOVERNMENT PROCESSES

ding ate nment	Managing Performance	Managing Finances	Attracting & Developing Staff	Leveraging Technology	Procuring Goods & Services	Managing Assets & Shared Services
direction g strategies vernor's s g policy with n delivery ng the ture budget policy HR policy IT policy enting an ise continuous ement ork ing statewide es ping the next ion of leaders	1. Setting operating policy 2. Establishing State outcomes & targets 3. Establishing Agency outcomes & targets 4. Selecting major initiatives 5. Reviewing agency performance against outcomes 6. Reviewing initiative performance against project targets 7. Driving corrective actions when plans fall short of targets	1. Forecasting revenue 2. Budgeting 3. Monitoring budgets 4. Accounting 5. Monitoring revenue streams 6. Capital planning 7. Managing & monitoring capital spending 8. Financing 9. Auditing	1. Setting Human Resources policy 2. Staffing and workforce planning 3. Developing the organization/training 4. Supporting employee performance management 5. Administering classification 6. Administering compensation 7. Administering benefits 8. Administering retirement benefits 9. Managing compliance 10. Managing employee relations	1. Setting & Monitoring Standards 2. IT Strategic planning & management 3. Gaining agreement on service levels 4. Managing business/ service relationships 5. Managing service operations 6. Managing the data center 7. Managing service lifecycle 8. Delivering IT applications 9. Managing IT projects 10. Managing technology suppliers	1. Setting procurement policy 2. Identifying services/ goods best contracted 3. Developing service agreements 4. Identifying qualified sources for goods/ services to acquire 5. Providing procurement services 6. Managing contract risk	1. Setting capital asset policies 2. Planning capital improvements 3. Managing capital projects 4. Managing fleets 5. Managing shared equipment 6. Managing shared services & resources 7. Managing facilities 8. Managing communications
ies implementing se improvement rk plan metrics progress ure's rating of e branches ness in engaging -gen leaders in ment program	a. % State Outcomes on target to plan b. % Agency outcomes on target to plan c. % Initiatives on-time, budget & deliverables	a. Revenue collected as a % of forecast b. Budget performance to actual by agency c. Actual Capital spending vs. budget d. Bond ratings	a. % of positions filled in <60 days b. % performance reviews completed on time c. % of employees citing pay as reason for leaving d. % of employee engagement e. # Training hours per employee f. Cost per retiree to administer benefits	a. % IT budget to revenue b. % external customer satisfied c. Average time to respond d. % uptime e. % projects on time f. % IT staff turnover g. % business continuity plan current h. Information security risk rating	a. Days from inception to RFP issuance b. Days from inception to contracting c. $ per contract to let d. % Vendor performance to contract	a. % Capital Projects on time & budget b. $ per square foot to operate office space c. $ per mile to operate state fleet d. # Days to lease office or other space
RKER	JACKSON	MOORE	GUY	DOOLITTLE	FRANKLIN	HAGAR

Most Responsible Sustainability Practices	Healthiest and Fittest People	Second-to-None Infrastructure	Government Respected for Efficiency and Effectiveness
• Renewable Energy • Carbon Dioxide Emissions • Water Quality • Air Quality	• Cost of Healthcare • Rate of Obesity • Quality of Health • Infant Mortality Rate • Rate of Uninsured • Smoking • Workplace Injury • Quality of Life and Happiness • Food Insecurity	• Infrastructure Index	• Government Debt • Citizen Tax Burden • Unfunded Pension Liabilities • Federal Dependency • Credit Rating • State Employees • Financial Transparency • Government Use of Technology • Results Champions • Open Data Access • Government Spending

APPENDIX C

LEAD Tennessee Core Competencies

Competency and Definition	Behaviors
Lead an Organization: Guides overall strategic and operational direction	
Customer Focused *Places the customer at the center of strategic and operational planning*	1. Clearly identifies the full range of customers to be served 2. Follows through on commitments 3. Identifies and monitors customer metrics to improve performance 4. Anticipates and responds to changing and evolving customer needs
Innovation *Demonstrates flexible thinking while producing creative thought processes; open to suggestion to others*	1. Offers and unique ideas 2. Demonstrates value to teams and organizations by providing original thought and connections to ideas outside own area of focus 3. Demonstrates enthusiasms and support of innovative initiative by others 4. Balances perspective and forward thinking
Mission-Driven *Demonstrates through actions, absolute clarity as to the purpose of the organization*	1. Ensures the organization has a relevant mission that instills a sense of purpose 2. Demonstrates focus on mission, goals, and priorities of the organization when making strategic decisions 3. Clearly communicates the organization's mission to others 4. Balances daily operational responsibilities while implementing long term mission-critical strategies
Lead People: Enables others to achieve high performance and full potential	
Courageous *Demonstrates understanding of concerns; takes responsibility and addresses them with fortitude and composure*	1. Clearly identifies tough feedback situations and demonstrates ability to give feedback in a timely and effective manner 2. Addresses issues and challenges with the appropriate persons and takes responsible risk 3. Ensures controversy, misperception, and misunderstandings are quickly addressed and reconciled 4. Leads with a strong sense of courage through the uncertainty, making bold transformational changes 5. Demonstrates the ability to effectively manage conflict
Talent Focused *Demonstrates the ability to create an environment that encourages outstanding individual performance for each employee*	1. Demonstrates a commitment to the development and success of the employees who are tasked with implementing and executing results by providing work challenges and opportunities for growth 2. Motivates other to perform at their best 3. Utilizes effective strategies to facilitate change initiatives and to overcome resistance to change 4. Creates an environment that attracts highly talented, engaged, and productive employees 5. Provides ongoing coaching and mentoring opportunities in an effort to promote continual learning and growth for employees

Chart Continues

Lead Self: Expands depth and breadth of capability	
Self-Management *Actively works to continuously improve, deploy strengths and compensate for weaknesses and limits*	1. Has a clear understanding of personal opportunities for improvement; capitalizes on personal strengths 2. Establishes networks to stay active in the business of the organization and to stay abreast of trends 3. Continuously seeks opportunities to improve both professionally and personally 4. Seeks out experiences that challenge perspective or provide an opportunity to learn new things 5. Demonstrates the ability to adapt and navigate change within the organization
Integrity *Takes responsibility for personal actions, follows through on commitments, and instills confidence that all words and actions are the truth*	1. Can be relied on to tell the truth regardless of the circumstances 2. Does not blame others 3. Ensures alignment between words and actions 4. Acts in the best interest of others and for the greater good of the organization
High Performing *Sets a high standard that represents the organization in the best light to both internal and external customers and produces results that exceed expectations*	1. Uses strong, well-rounded written, and oral communication skills in a variety of situations 2. Collaborates with managers, co-workers, peers, and external stakeholders to gain cooperation 3. Utilizes the mission of the organization to evaluate options and identify those that are most likely to move the business forward 4. Identifies top talent to grow a culture of high performance 5. Establishes clear expectations for self and others to achieve goals

APPENDIX D

NOW Management System
Leadership Requirements

CAPABILITIES

1) Skills

    a) Communication (planning, messaging, timing, delivery) and influencing others

    b) Problem solving - root cause, fact based, disciplines and methods to
-       i) Drive for facts (vs. opinion)
-       ii) Innovation

    c) Self-awareness

    d) Change leadership
-       i) Define the social good to inspire people
-       ii) Promote a shared vision of the future
-       iii) Engage respected leaders
-       iv) Create agenda for personal change
-       v) Promote reinforcing actions
-       vi) Lead organizational communications

    e) Team leadership
-       i) Helping people through fear
-       ii) Relationship building
-       iii) Understanding people and personalities
-       iv) Coaching
-       v) Delegating

    f) Creating safe environment

2) Aptitudes

    a) Curiosity and learning

    b) Servant leadership and teacher

    c) Passion and enthusiasm

    d) Optimism and resiliency

    e) Envisioning the future

3) Values and Beliefs

    a) Belief in employee engagement

    b) Continuous improvement

4) Qualities/Reputation

    a) Trustworthy

    b) Credibility

    c) Accountable

Chart Continues

5) Experience
  a) Managing significant organization change
  b) Leading leaders
  c) Problem solving - root cause, fact based, disciplines and methods
  d) Working with consultants, leveraging externals
  e) Failures they can learn from

6) Domain Expertise/Knowledge
  a) LEAN, Six Sigma, performance improvement, TQM, metrics
  b) Their business, context, industry

NOW SYSTEM EXPECTATIONS

1) Business Maturity

  Decision making, problem solving, accountability, communications, acumen, experience

2) Set Team Expectations. Hold self and team accountable
  a) Healthy effective decision making model
  b) Start / end the meeting (set the tone)
  c) Model healthy conversation and communication

3) Articulate the "why", make the case for change
  a) Be on the same page with us (both in and outside of meetings)
  b) Set and clarify priorities across business and MS

4) Lead the Changes
  a) Lead organization communications
  b) Lend their authority to the project
  c) Set direction and pace; bring energy
  d) Articulate stakeholder management approach, process, communication
  e) Walk the talk re change and lead the team through change

5) Manage external environment
  a) Explain agency interfaces with governor, legislators, peers, sec of state, treasurer, media
  b) Explain risk management profile and process for responding to risk

ORGANIZATIONAL EXPECTATIONS

1) Lead the change
  a) Get the desired results
  b) Set the stage
  c) Support
  d) Vision and direction
  e) Deal with the "we be here when you are gone" phenomena
  f) Demonstrate commitment and follow through

2) Lead the change team
  a) Make my life better - help with WIIFM (what's in it for me)
  b) Don't hand the project over to the consultant
  c) Address road blocks in a timely manner
  d) Be present
  e) Provide ways for the team to feel and be successful

3) Resource allocation, meet financial goals

APPENDIX E

Links of Interest

John M. Bernard
 Twitter: @johnmbernard
 LinkedIn: John M. Bernard
 Facebook: MassIngenuity
 Email: jbernard@massingenuity.com

Governor's Map: www.resultsamerica.org/govmap

Oregon Youth Authority Map: www.resultsamerica.org/oyamap

Government That Works: www.resultsamerica.org/book

Mass Ingenuity: www.massingenuity.com

Results America: www.resultsamerica.org

10-Year Plan for Oregon: http://resultsamerica.org/fX2Y

Maryland StateStat: http://resultsamerica.org/1nCu

Washington's TVW: http://resultsamerica.org/D8fe

Harvard Business Review: http://resultsamerica.org/R8be

Oregon Business Plan: http://resultsamerica.org/Esu7

WBA's Plan Washington: http://resultsamerica.org/wV8H

Project Management Institute: http://resultsamerica.org/vSD6

The Results America Pledge: www.resultsamerica.com/pledge

APPENDIX F

Recommended Reading

- *Good to Great* (Jim Collins)
- *Mojo* (Marshall Goldsmith)
- *What Got You Here Won't Get You There* (Marshall Goldsmith)

On Personal Growth and Development
- *7 Habits of Highly Effective People* (Stephen R. Covey)
- Myers/Briggs Type Indicator
- *Strengths Finder* (Tom Rath)

On Teamwork
- *The Five Dysfunctions of a Team* (Patrick Lencioni)
- *Crucial Conversations* (Kerry Patterson, Joseph Grenny, Ron McMillan, Al Switzler)
- *Primal Teams* (Jackie Barretta)

On Process Improvement
- *The Toyota Way* (Jeffrey Liker)
- *Lean Thinking* (James P. Womack and Daniel T. Jones)
- *The Goal* (Eliyahu M. Goldratt and Jeff Cox)
- *Managing to Learn* (John Shook)

On Performance Management and Measurement
- *Performance Management* (Aubrey C. Daniels and James E. Daniels)
- *The Balanced Scorecard* (Robert S. Kaplan and David P. Norton)
- *Checklist Manifesto* (Atul Gawande)

On Government
- *The Rule of Nobody* (Phillip K. Howard)
- *The Performance Stat* Potential (Robert D. Behn)

ABOUT RESULTS AMERICA

Results America is a non-partisan, non-profit organization dedicated to spreading the word about results-driven government. A single mission guides our work: demonstrating that an unrelenting focus on results will do more than anything else to fulfill the promise of America. Results America fulfills this mission not only by disseminating information about the results revolution taking place in the state government, but also by offering practical tools that will help other revolutionaries replace political rhetoric with the results we Americans expect from our government.

The results revolution has already begun in states and state agencies across America, where responsible government leaders understand that they must improve the services they deliver with fewer resources. They can only do that if they create more efficient and effective management systems.

Our Four Basic Goals

To Inspire Leadership: Encouraging bold actions grounded in sound management practices

To Accelerate Success: Teaching best practices for achieving greater effectiveness and efficiency

To Connect Like Minds: Expanding a community of government officials and workers dedicated to delivering results to their customers

To Encourage Transparency and Accountability: urging officials and workers always to tell the truth and take full responsibility for results

Visit the organization at www.resultsamerica.org

ABOUT THE AUTHOR

John Bernard currently consults with state government leaders on the transformation to results-driven government. Bernard has authored two books on designing state-of-the-art management systems, the best-selling *Business at the Speed of Now* (Wiley, 2012) and *Government That Works, The Results Revolution in the States* (Results America, 2015).

In the early 1980s Bernard began studying, writing about and implementing the concepts of Dr. W. Edwards Deming and Toyota. One of the pioneers who introduced Lean thinking to American business, he founded and serves as Chairman of Mass Ingenuity, a Portland, Oregon based consulting firm that focuses on helping state government become more efficient and effective. He also co-founded Results America, a not-for-profit organization dedicated to promoting and installing best-practice, results-driven management systems in government.

For the past thirty years Bernard has been inspiring organizational leaders to rethink how they run their organizations. A forward-thinking business executive and consultant, he ardently challenges conventional management philosophy, and over the past twenty-five years has been fine-tuning a system of management that eliminates the gap between what leaders say they want to achieve (rhetoric) and what employees actually deliver (results). His philosophy stresses total transparency, full accountability, and innovative problem solving at every level of an organization.

His hands-on management experience spans the full spectrum of leadership responsibilities, from starting, running and building an entrepreneurial organization, to serving as a senior vice president of a multibillion-dollar financial services company with responsibility for the performance of thousands of employees. At Omark Industries, Electro Scientific Industries, Floating Point Systems, and StanCorp Financial Group, he worked in such far-ranging areas as high-tech manufacturing, communications, strategic planning, operations, information technology, marketing, and quality assurance. In his consulting practice, he has offered expert advice to Nike, Baxter Healthcare, Kaiser Permanente, Tektronix, PacifiCorp, and Standard Insurance, and more than one hundred other companies around the world.

Most recently, he has been advising a number of Governors and state agency leaders on adapting best management practices to the public sector.

To contact John Bernard for public speaking engagements or consulting services, please visit: www.massingenuity.com or email him at jbernard@massingenuity.com

REFERENCES

All links provided were active at the time the book went into production.

Action Learning Associates (2014). Reg Revans - action learning pioneer. Retrieved September 2, 2014, from http://www.actionlearningassociates. co.uk/regrevans.php

Americashealthrankings.org. (2014). Smoking Nevada Rank: 18. Retrieved from http://www.americashealthrankings.org/NV/Smoking

Balancedscorecard.org. (n.d.). The Deming Cycle. Retrieved from http:// balancedscorecard.org/Resources/Articles-White-Papers/The-Deming-Cycle

Barretta, J. (2014). *Primal Teams: Harnessing the Power of Emotions to Fuel Extraordinary Performance. AMACOM Books.*

Behn, R. (2014). *The PerformanceStat Potential: A Leadership Strategy for Producing Results. Brookings.*

Bernard, J. (2012). *Business at the Speed of Now: Fire Up Your People, Thrill Your Customers, and Crush Your Competitors* (pp. 196-197). Wiley.

Bunkley, N. (2007, January 25). Ford Loses Record $12.7 Billion in '06. *New York Times. Retrieved August 22, 2014, from http://www.nytimes. com/2007/01/25/business/25cnd-ford.html?_r=1 &*

Bureau of Economic Analysis. GDP by State. (2014, June 11). Retrieved from http://www.bea.gov/newsreleases/regional/gdp_state/gsp_ newsrelease.htm

Campbell, J. (2008). *The hero with a thousand faces* (3rd ed.). Novato, Calif.: New World Library.

Carey, M. (2013, May 1). Counting Regulations: An Overview of Rulemaking, Types of Federal Regulations, and Pages in the Federal Register. Retrieved from http://fas.org/sgp/crs/misc/R43056.pdf

Casear, S. (2014, April 28). California's high school graduation rate passes 80% for first time. Los Angeles Times. Retrieved from http://www.latimes.com/local/la-me-grads-dropouts-20140429-story.html

Center for Digital Government. (2012). The Government Dashboard. Retrieved October 28, 2014, from http://statestat.maryland.gov/documents/CDGgovtDashboard.pdf

City of Seattle. (2014). Data.seattle.gov. Retrieved July 15, 2014, from https://data.seattle.gov

Congressional Budget Office. (2014). CBO Estimate of Discretionary Appropriations for Fiscal Year 2014, Including H.R. 3547, the Consolidated Appropriations Act, 2014, as Posted on the Website of the House Committee on Rules on January 13, 2014. Retrieved from http://cbo.gov/sites/default/files/cbofiles/attachments/hr3547.pdf

DeCarlo, N. (2007). *The complete idiot's guide to lean six sigma.* Indianapolis, IN: Alpha Books.

Florida Advanced Technological Education Center. (n.d.). Awards Organizations. Retrieved April 28, 2014, from http://fl-ate.org/about_us/docs/State%20Quality%20Award%20Organizations.pdf

Ford Motor Company. Investor Relations. (2014). Retrieved October 28, 2014, from http://corporate.ford.com/our-company/investors

Fortune. Fortune ranks the World's 50 Greatest Leaders. (2014, March 20). Retrieved October 28, 2014, from http://fortune.com/2014/03/20/fortune-ranks-the-worlds-50-greatest-leaders/

Gallup. (n.d.). State of the American Workplace. Retrieved April 8, 2014, from http://www.gallup.com/strategicconsulting/163007/state-american-workplace.aspx

Goldsmith, M., & Reiter, M. (2009). *Mojo: How to get it, how to keep it, how to get it back if you lose it.* New York: Hyperion.

Goleman, D. (2005). *Emotional intelligence: Why it can matter more than IQ.* New York: Bantam Books.

Governing. (November, 11 2013). The Unintended Consequences of Improvement. Retrieved April 28, 2014, from http://www.governing.com/columns/smart-mgmt/The-Unintended-Consequences-of-Improvement.html

Harrington, H. (1987). *Poor-quality cost*. New York: CRC Press.

Harvard University Kennedy School of Government. (2014). Oregon Benchmarks. Retrieved from http://www.innovations.harvard.edu/awards.html?id=3634

Hersey, P., & Blanchard, K. (2013). *Management of organizational behavior: Leading human resources* (10th ed.). Boston: Pearson.

Hoffman, B. G. (2012). American icon: *Alan Mulally and the fight to save Ford Motor Company*. New York: Crown Business.

Holden Leadership Center. (n.d.). Retrieved October 28, 2014, from http://leadership.uoregon.edu

Hoover, J. (2010, March 12). Data, Analysis Drive Maryland Government. Retrieved October 28, 2014, from http://www.informationweek.com/software/information-management/data-analysis-drive-maryland-government/d/d-id/1087551?

If Japan can – why can't we? [Motion picture]. (1980). United States: NBC.

Kouzes, J., & Posner, B. (2009, January). To Lead, Create a Shared Vision. Retrieved October 28, 2014, from http://hbr.org/2009/01/to-lead-create-a-shared-vision/ar/1

Kouzes, J., & Posner, B. (2012). *The Leadership Challenge: How to Make Extraordinary Things Happen in Organizations* (5th ed.). Jossey-Bass.

MacDonald, H. (2010, February 17). Compstat and Its Enemies. Retrieved May 30, 2014, from http://www.city-journal.org/2010/eon0217hm.html

Maryland Baystat. (2014). Retrieved October 4, 2014, from http://baystat.maryland.gov

National Association of State Chief Information Officers. (2014). Retrieved October 28, 2014, from http://www.nascio.org

New York Times. To Restore New York City; First, Reclaim the Streets. (1990, December 30). *New York Times*. Retrieved February 13, 2014, from http://www.nytimes.com/1990/12/30/opinion/to-restore-new-york-city-first-reclaim-the-streets.html

Office of the Governor of Maryland. (n.d.).Biography of Governor Martin O'Malley. Retrieved October 28, 2014, from http://www.governor.maryland.gov/biography.html

Perry, J. Measuring Public Service Motivation: An Assessment of Construct Reliability and Validity. *Journal of Public Administration Research and Theory*. 6.1 (1996): 5-22. Web. 8 Apr. 2014.

PLAN Washington. (2014). Retrieved October 28, 2014, from http://www.planwashington.org

Politifact. Leonard Lance claims federal tax code contains 4 million words, is 7 times as long as Bible. (2013, April 15). Retrieved from http://www.politifact.com/new-jersey/statements/2013/may/02/leonard-lance/leonard-lance-claims-federal-tax-code-contains-4-m/

Project Management Institute. (n.d.). Retrieved October 28, 2014, from http://www.pmi.org

Prosci. Change Management Learning Center - Prosci. (n.d.). Retrieved October 28, 2014, from http://www.change-management.com

Results Washington. Prosperous economy. (2014). Retrieved August 12, 2014, from http://www.results.wa.gov/what-we-do/measure-results/prosperous-economy

Results Washington. Sustainable energy & a clean environment. (2014). Retrieved August 12, 2014, from http://www.results.wa.gov/what-we-do/measure-results/sustainable-energy-clean-environment

Rivenburgh, D. (2013). *The New Corporate Facts of Life: Rethink Your Business to Transform Today's Challenges Into Tomorrow's Profits*. AMACOM.

Rosenthal, B. (2012, November 29). Inslee picks Renton schools chief Mary Alice Heuschel as chief of staff. Retrieved October 28, 2014, from http://seattletimes.com/html/politics/2019793520_heuschel30m.html

Senge, P. (2006). *The fifth discipline: The art and practice of the learning organization (Rev. and updated. ed.)*. New York: Doubleday/Currency.

Standish Group, The. (2009). CHAOS Report.

State of Michigan. Reinventing Performance in Michigan. (n.d.). Retrieved August 22, 2014, from http://www.michigan.gov/lara/0,4601,7-154-10573_66085---,00.html

State of Michigan. (2014). Measuring Michigan's Performance. Retrieved October 28, 2014, from http://www.michigan.gov/midashboard

State of Oregon. (n.d.). 2011 Senate Bill 676. Retrieved October 28, 2014, from https://olis.leg.state.or.us/liz/2011R1/Downloads/MeasureDocument/SB0676/Enrolled

State of Tennessee. (April 24, 2012). Haslam Signs TEAM Act Into Law. Retrieved October 28, 2014, from https://news.tn.gov/node/8718

State of Washington. (2011). Executive Order 11-04 Lean Transformation. Retrieved August 15, 2014, from http://www.governor.wa.gov/office/execorders/eoarchive/eo_11-04.pdf

State of Washington. (2013). 2013 Lean Conference. Retrieved August 4, 2014, from http://www.results.wa.gov/what-we-do/apply-lean/2013-lean-conference

Sullivan, G. (2014, August 12). How Colorado's teen birthrate dropped 40% in four years. Retrieved October 28, 2014, from http://www.washingtonpost.com/news/morning-mix/wp/2014/08/12/how-colorados-teen-birthrate-dropped-40-in-four-years/

US Census Bureau. (n.d.). 2012 America Community Survey. Retrieved April 23, 2014, from http://www.census.gov

US Census Bureau. (n.d.). Census of Governments: Government Employment and Payroll. Retrieved from https://www.census.gov/govs/apes/

US Census Bureau. (2013, September 17). Income. Retrieved July 2, 2014, from https://www.census.gov/hhes/www/income/data/index.html

US Environmental Protection Agency. (2014). Inventory of U.S. Greenhouse Gas Emissions and Sinks 1990-2012. U.S. Environmental Protection Agency, Washington, D.C. April 2014. EPA 430-R-14-003

US Geological Survey. Fact Sheet 102-98 - The Chesapeake Bay: Geologic Product of Rising Sea Level. (1998, November 18). Retrieved October 28, 2014, from http://pubs.usgs.gov/fs/fs102-98/

Usgovernmentspending.com. Government Debt Chart: Wyoming 1992-2015. (2014). Retrieved from http://www.usgovernmentspending.com/spending_chart_1992_2015WYp_H0c%22

Washington Business Alliance. (2014). An Introduction to PLAN Washington. Retrieved October 28, 2014, from http://www. planwashington.org/plan-washington

Washington State Correctional Industries. (2014). Retrieved October 28, 2014, from http://www.washingtonci.com

Washington State Department of Transportation. (2013). 2013 Annual Collision Summary: Preliminary. Retrieved September 5, 2014, from http://www.wsdot.wa.gov/mapsdata/collision/pdf/PreliminaryAnnual CollisionSummary2013.pdf

Wikipedia. (2014, October 27). Rick Snyder. Retrieved October 28, 2014, from http://en.wikipedia.org/wiki/Rick_Snyder

Wikipedia. (2014, October 27). Systematic inventive thinking. Retrieved October 28, 2014, from http://en.wikipedia.org/wiki/Systematic_ inventive_thinking

Young, Z., Reddehase, S., & Comer, E. (2011). Lessons Learned: Phase 2 Prototype Development and Technical Notes. *Texas Student Data System*, NA. Retrieved October 8, 2014, from http://www.ptsteams. com/lessons_learned.pdf

INDEX

A

A3, 221
abortions, 157
abuse, 158, 216, 276
accountability, 4, 14, 20, 22-24,
   35, 46, 109, 112-113, 126,
   129-131, 142, 145, 146, 147,
   151, 163, 185, 186, 188, 190,
   192-193, 195-196, 201,
   204-209, 213, 219, 237, 241,
   245, 275, 282-283, 292, 293,
   295, 299, 300, 301, 305, 308,
   313, 335, 337
   accountability and transparency,
   22, 46, 109, 113, 188, 201,
   241, 313
Accountability, seven steps to
   true, 207-209
Adams, Greg, 167, 285
ADKAR, 289
Administrative Services, Oregon
   Department of, 144
Aerne, Melissa, xx
agriculture, 185-186, 195, 278
Agriculture, Washington Department of, 137
Alabama, 39
Alaska, 4, 25, 61
Albuquerque, NM, 176
alcohol, 171
Aljets, Paul, xxii
Allard, Claire, xix, 126, 128-129,
   131-132, 246, 247

Allen, Patrick, xix
American College of Obstetri-
   cians and Gynecologists, 156
America Global Rankings, 93
American Indian Tribes, 173
Annenberg, Walter, 38
Apple, 13
Arizona, 64
Armbruster, Danielle, 231
Arwood, Steve, 90-92
Ash Center for Democratic
   Governance and Innovation,
   186
Asian Pacific American Affairs,
   Washington State Commission
   on, 195
assault, 22-23, 68, 281
inmate-on-staff, 281, 286
associate's degrees, 85
AtlantiCare, 38
automakers, 240

B

bachelor's degree, 85, 238
Baird, Rich, xix, 125
Baldrige National Quality Award,
   38-39, 282
Baltimore, MD, 119-120, 153,
   307, 318
Barber, Ted, xxi
Barker, Christine, xxi
Barretta, Jackie, 33, 236, 258,
   333, 339
Batiste, Chief John, 170

Baugh, Cyndee, xx
BayStat, 120, 186, 189, 191, 209, 341
Beck, Sharon, xx
Becker-Green, Jody, xx
Behar, Howard, xxvii, 270
Behn, Robert D., 186, 187, 334
Bennett, Lauren, 276-279, 281
Benson, Bobbi, xxi
Bergen, Jean, xx
Berger, Vicki, 283
Bernard, Ashley, xxii
Bernard, Christian, xxii
Bernard, Ed, xxi
Bernard, Erin, xxii
Bernard, Jacqueline, xxii
Bernard, Jim, xxi
Bernard, Joe, xxi
Berntsen, Teresa, xx
best practices, xvii, xxv-xxvii, 5, 35, 83, 85,101, 190, 204, 237, 271, 273, 293, 299, 304, 308, 315, 335
big breakthroughs, 155
big data, 77, 270, 276, 279, 281, 319
big lean, 225, 226
birth control, 155-156
birth records, 277
birth weight, 158, 276, 277, 279
birthrate, 277
Black, Jennifer, xx
black belt, 28, 168, 298
Blanchard, Ken, 260
Blount International, 102
BlueCross BlueShield, 175
Bodek, Norman, 101
Boeing, 95, 239
Bonaparte, Napoleon, xxiv
Bonetto, Mike, 141

Bonlender, Brian, xx, 196-198
Boston Marathon, 159
Boston, MA, 177, 295
brainstorm, 47, 74, 190, 192, 222
Bratton, Bill, 23, 24
breakthroughs
    purpose statement, 160
    seven phases, 160-161
    types of, 159
British Broadcasting Corporation, 38
Buckley, Peter, 283
Buffett, Warren, 239
build vs. buy, 235
Burckle, Ed, 174-176
burglary, 22, 23, 68
Business at the Speed of NOW, xxvi, 8, 50 ,66, 71, 337
Butler, Kathleen, xxi

C

cabinet, 19, 54, 55, 134, 174, 191, 227, 283, 285
Calcutta, 21
California, 64, 84, 211
Calley, Brian, 89-92, 132
Campbell, Joseph, 248-250
Canby, OR, 16, 17
Capps, Lindsey, xix
carbon dioxide emissions, 84, 85
Carlsbad, NM, 27-31
Cascading, 41, 47, 147, 205-206, 303
Cause and Effect Diagram, 222
Centers for Disease Control and Prevention, 156
Chafee, Lincoln, 25
Chamber of Commerce, Seattle, 140

Chandler, Melanie, 203
change management, 46, 53-54, 56, 131, 177-183, 279, 289, 295, 302-303
Checksheet, 222
Chesapeake Bay, 119, 185, 186, 192
Chief Budget Officer, 257
Chief Economist, 240
Chief Learning Officer, 166, 168
Chief Medical Officer, 157
Chief of Staff, 190
Chief of Staff, 141, 190, 304, 342
Chief Operating Officer, 15, 17, 21, 81, 101, 141, 144, 167, 200, 282, 285, 304, 332
child maltreatment, 85
Child Welfare Services, 4
CitiStat, 119-120, 153, 307, 318
Citizen Tax Burden, 86
Claremont Graduate University, 277
Clarisonic, 138, 269
Clark, Jim, xxi, 225
Cleary, Paul, xix
Cleveland, Mark, xxi
ClimateStat, 189
Clontz, Jon, xix
cloud computing, 291, 319
Coleman, 225
College Preparatory Testing, 85
Collins, Jim, 333
Colorado, xxvii, 4, 39, 51-52, 55-57, 155-158, 161, 183, 281, 320, 343
Colorado Teen Pregnancy, 155-162
results, 156-157
Commerce, Washington Department of, 137, 195, 196, 198

CompStat, 22, 23-24, 77, 100, 119, 187, 341
CompStat NYC crime statistics, 22-24
Congress, US, 310, 312
Constitution, US, 18, 60
contraceptives, 156, 161
COO (see: Chief Operating Officer)
CORE (see: Customer Outcomes Reengineering)
core competencies, 328
core processes, 45-46, 146-147, 149, 151, 302
Cornell University, 28
Correctional Industries, Washington State, 230
Corrections, Oregon Department of, 57, 211-212, 214-215, 230, 237
Corrections, Washington Department of, 230, 280
cost of corrections, 85
Courtney, Peter, 283
Covey, Stephen R., 333
Cox, Jeff, 333
creativity, 34, 73, 106, 120, 211, 224, 228-229, 232, 234
crime, 21- 24, 67-68, 79, 84-85, 90, 100, 119, 153, 188-189, 318
cross-agency breakthrough, 302-303
Cunningham, Richie, 240
customer
customer needs, 36, 73, 146
customer outcomes, 29, 41
customer expectations, 35, 111, 124
customer feedback, 36, 114

customer satisfaction, 4, 41-42, 76, 227-228, 244- 245, 249, 250, 253

customer service, 12, 40, 62, 103, 132, 168-169, 171, 247, 307, 313-314

customers define value, 73, 102-104, 116, 291, 300-301

Customer Outcomes Reengineering, 41

D

Damon, Perrin, xx

Damron, Darrell, xx

Daily Management, 221

Daniels, Aubrey C. & Daniel E., 333

dashboard, 77- 80, 126, 127, 129, 245, 277, 280, 295, 313, 316

data

data access, 78, 86

data analyst, 78, 204, 292

data gathering, 56, 292

data sharing, 79, 315

Davis, Sutter, 38

Dawson, Pete, xx

daycare, 90

DeCamp, Joe, xx

de Chardin, Teilhard, 321

Deal, Nathan, 25

debt, 62, 84, 86

DeCarlo, Neil, 222

decision-making, 20, 47, 203, 264

Declaration of Independence, xxiii, 323

deficit, 67, 174, 187, 242, 312

Delaware, 61

Deming, W. Edwards, 7, 9, 38, 115, 220, 337

Democrats, 4

Denver Health Medical Center, 52

Detroit, 312-314, 316

Devlin, Richard, 283

Dexter, Tim, xxi

DHMC (see: Denver Health Medical Center)

died inside, 2, 297

digital government, 77-79, 273, 340

Dillon, Sharon, 172

District of Columbia, 61, 169

DMAIC, 221

donation, 156, 161

Doolittle, Beth, xxi, 178, 180-183

Dorn, Randy, 172

Downton Abbey, 193

driver's license, 43, 82, 211-212, 216, 281

Dropbox, 295

drought, 278

DRS (see: Retirement Services, Washington Department of)

Drucker, Peter, 80, 108

drugs, 171

E

early adopters, 41, 316

Ecology, Washington Department of, 137

Education Agency, Texas, 78, 79

Education, Colorado Department of, 57

Education, Oregon Department of, 144

Effectiveness Gap, 143

ELT (see: Enterprise Leadership Team)

Emotional Intelligence, 236, 260

Emotionally Intelligent Team, The, 236

employee engagement (see engaging employees)

employees create value, 72-73, 102-104, 116, 194, 291, 301

employment, 13, 163, 224, 235, 272, 283-284

Employment Security Department, Washington, 195

engaging employees, xxiv, 8, 22, 28, 35-37, 40, 47, 92, 101-108, 131, 132, 147, 178, 211, 224-225, 232, 241, 262, 303

engagement, level of, 182

Enterprise Leadership Team, 144

Environmental Protection Agency, 119

Environmental Quality, Oregon Department of, 144

Essential 48 Outcome Measures, 84-87

ESRI, 276, 278, 281

F

Facebook, 294, 295

FaceTime, 291, 294

fear, 9, 30-34, 51, 71-73, 108, 113, 204, 212, 217, 231, 236, 243, 256-257, 262, 306, 317

Federal Dependency, 86

federal government, 25, 61-62, 279, 308, 311-312, 315, 318

Feldhausen, Mark, xx

Ferguson, Kelly, xxi

Fifth Discipline, The, 93-94, 342

Financial Institutions, Washington Department of, 195

Financial Management, Washington Office of, 137, 195

Financial Transparency, 86

Firkins, Tammy, 134

Fish and Wildlife, Washington Department of, 137

Fitzpatrick, John, xix

Five steps of transformational leadership, 251

Five Whys, 221

Florida, 39, 197

Ford Motor Company, 7, 107-108, 112, 115, 239, 240, 241-243, 254, 266

Fortune Magazine, 52, 239

Founding Fathers, 60, 323

Four elements of a shift to results, 35

Franklin, Benjamin, 61

French Revolution, xxiv, 310

Frost, Dorothy Teeter, xx

Frost, Marcie, xix, xx, 134

Fundamentals, improving, 109-116. 287-291, 301

Fundamentals Map, 46, 48, 145-147, 149, 150, 152, 213, 302-303

Summary explanation of elements, 146

G

Gabow, Patti, 52, 55

Gallagher, Matt, 307-308

Gallup, 8

Gateway, 125

Gawande, Atul, 333
GDP (see: Gross Domestic Product)
Gebhardt, Bob, xx
Gemba, 221
Genuine Progress Indicator, 195-198
geographic information systems, 277, 319
Georgia, 25, 39
Gettysburg, 322
GIS (see: geographic information systems)
Giuliani, David, xxi, 138, 269-273, 275
Giuliani, Rudy, 21-24
Gladwell, Malcolm, 288
Glausi, Wally, xxi
Global Rankings, America, 93
Goal Council, 171, 194-198
Golden, Nancy, xix
Goldratt, Eliyahu M., 333
Goldsmith, Marshall, 266-267, 333
Goleman, Daniel, 236, 260-261
Google, 3, 31, 217, 295
Gottman, John, 272
Governing Magazine, 6
Governor's Map, 150-152, 326-327
government
    shutdown, 310
    government, reactionary system of, 75-77
    government, results driven (see results-driven government)
    government, results focused (see results-focused government)

GPI (see: Genuine Progress Indicator)
Graduate and Professional Degrees, 85
Green, Senator Mark, 20-21
Gregoire, Christine, 134, 227
Grenny, Joseph, 333
Grinnell, Karen, xxi
Grondel, Darrin, 169, 172, 173
Gross Domestic Product, 84, 85, 196, 197, 198
Guy, Jody, xxi

H

Hamilton, Alexander, xxiii
Hammond, Joni, xix
Hanson, Bill, xx
Harra, Scott, xxi
Harrington, H. James, 10
Harvard Business Review, 244
Haslam, Bill, 25, 163, 168, 283-285, 321
Hawaii, 61
Health Authority, Oregon, 144
healthcare, 21, 38, 86, 141, 158-159, 161, 174-176, 183, 269, 338
Henry Ford Health Center, 38
Herbert, Gary, 25
Hernandez, Jeanne, 253
Hero's Journey, 248-250, 256
Hersey, Paul, 260
Heuschel, Mary Alice, xix, 133-134, 139-140, 342
Hewlett-Packard, 102
Hickenlooper, John, xx, 52-53, 281, 320-321
Hill, Steve, xix
Hillsboro, OR, 63

Histogram, 222
Hoffman, Suzanne, xix
Holden Leadership Center, The, 235
Holliday, Trish, xix, 162-164, 166-168
Holvey, Paul, 283
Honeywell Federal Manufacturing and Technologies, 38
Hoshin Kanri, 221
Houston, TX, 310
Howard, Aaron, xxi, 133
Howard, Phillip, 334
Hughes, Marcia, 236
Human Resources, Tennessee Department of, 163, 165, 168, 262, 283-284
Human Services, Michigan Department of, 89
Human Services, Oregon Department of, 44, 71, 144
Hunter, Rebecca, xix, 163, 166-168, 283-285
Hussein, Sadaam, 20-21

I

IBM, 10, 285
Idaho, 61
Iles, Cathy, xx
Illinois, 64, 69
implementation, 18, 20, 30-31, 56, 159, 164, 262, 294, 304
improvement zone, safe, 214-217
Indian Affairs, Washington Governor's Office of, 195
Indiana, 25, 279
Inslee, Jay, 25, 133-134, 136, 138, 172, 193-194, 227, 275, 321

Instagram, 291, 294
Intel, 63
internet, 176, 271, 319, 320
intrauterine devices, 156
Iowa, 39
Irving, TX, 39
Irwin, Bryan, xx, 280
IUDs, (see: intrauterine devices)

J

Japan, 7, 9, 38, 101-102, 105, 220
Jefferson, Thomas, xxiii-xxiv, 61, 300, 310
Jensen, Hollie, xx, 134, 227-229, 230
Jeske, Ken, xix
Johnson, Betsy, 283
Johnson, Dacia, xix
Johnson, Michelle, xx
Johnson, Nathan, xx
Johnston, Kelly, xxi, 252
Jones, Daniel T., 333
Jordan, Michael, xix, 15-18, 20-21, 81, 141-144, 282
Judicial Branch, 214

K

Kaiser Permanente, 338
Kaizen, 220-223
Kaizen Blitz, 221
Kanban, 220
Kaplan, Robert S., 333
Kastama, Isaac, xxi
KATA, 220-221, 231
Kelley-Siel, Erinn, xix
Kennedy School of Government, 81, 187

Kennedy, Robert, 243
King, Fred, xxi, 282-283
Kitzhaber, John, 17, 25, 141,
  144, 321
Klingler, Greta, 158, 161
Kohler, Pat, xx, 171-172, 229
Koponen, Jane, 298, 299
Koponen, Libby, xx, xxi
Korthuis-Smith, Wendy, xix, 134,
  193-194, 196, 198-199, 200
Kouzes, James M., 243, 244, 341
Kuhn, Russ, xx
Kulongoski, Ted, 213

L

Labor and Industries, Washington
  Department of, 195
Lakeville, MA, 295
Lanham, Julia, xix
LARC (see: Long-acting Reversible Contraceptives)
Lauer, Matt, 90
Lead Tennessee, 162-169
  competencies, 165, 328-329
leading others, 259
leadership
  leadership strategy, 187
  leadership development,
    164-165, 167-168, 284
  leadership style, 260-261
  leadership summit, 166
  leadership team, 43, 55, 107,
    122, 144-145, 147, 150,
    178, 181, 187, 217, 229,
    249, 262, 280
  leadership, transformational,
    253
Leadership Challenge, The, 243

Lean, 7, 10, 13, 15, 24, 28, 36,
  39, 41, 44-46, 51-57, 67,
  71-72, 74, 91, 101-102, 132,
  134, 142, 160, 194-195, 199,
  209, 218, 221-232, 235-236,
  289- 290, 292, 298, 301, 333,
  337, 340, 343
lean environment, 136-137,
  198, 342
lean initiatives, 39, 54, 57, 224,
  227, 236
lean management, 13, 74
lean maturity, 223
lean philosophy, 71, 195, 230
lean principles, 199, 227
lean process improvement, 46,
  222-223, 301
lean projects, 51, 55, 134, 227
lean techniques, 39, 41, 51,
  160, 289, 290
lean terminology, 221
lean thinking, 224, 333, 337
lean tools, 44, 226
lean training, 52, 91, 132, 229
lean transformation, 227, 343
Lean Conference, Washington
  State, 227
Legislative Branch, 30, 96-97,
  214, 282
legislators, 27-28, 47, 75, 213,
  283, 286
legislature, 56, 63, 75, 82, 96,
  131, 144, 171, 174, 280, 286,
  305-306, 316
Leitch, Kari, xx
Lencioni, Patrick, 333
Levi Strauss, 180
liberals, 4
Licensing and Regulatory Reform,
  Michigan Department of, 90, 189

Licensing, Washington Department of, 171-172, 229
Liker, Jeffrey, 333
Lincoln, Abraham, 322
literacy rates, 281
living conditions, 2, 197
Lockheed Martin, 38
Long-acting Reversible Contraceptives, 156, 158, 161
Lord of the Rings, The, 220
Lottery, Oregon, 144
Louisiana, 276, 281
Lovas, Lou, xxii
Loveall, Heidi, xx, 134
Lucas, Susan, xx

M

MacArthur, Douglas, 7
MacDonald, Heather, 24
MacGlashan, Sue, xx
Madison, James, xxiv
management, traditional, 8, 10
management, results-driven (see results-driven management)
Manhattan Institute, 24
Maple, Jack, 23, 24
Martin, Julie, xx
Martinez, Susana, 25, 29, 43
Maryland, xxvii, 4, 25, 65, 77- 79, 84, 100, 119-122, 133, 152-53, 185-190, 192-193, 196, 209, 286, 305, 307-308, 310, 317, 332, 340, 341-342
Maryland's SMART Goals, 121-122
mass customization, 12, 103
Mass Ingenuity, xxiv, 5, 133, 144, 149, 178, 205, 207, 225, 252, 294
mass production, 12, 103

Maynard, Gary D., 79
McConnon, Dan, xx
McFadden, Joan, xxi
McMillan, Ron, 333
Mead, Margaret, 275
measure types defined, 83
measures
  agency, 83
  cost, 83
  governor, 83
  outcome measures, 45, 47, 83-84, 135, 137, 146-147, 195, 202, 205, 302-303, 306
  process measures, 45, 110, 146, 204, 205, 214, 303
  performance measures, 110, 142, 286, 301, 317
  quality, 83
  quantity, 83
  societal, 83
  time, 83
media, 34, 75, 82
median household income, 84, 85
Medicare, 216
meeting memo, 189, 190, 192
Mellon, Phyllis, xix
Merkel, Angela, 239
Michigan, xxvi-xxvii, 4, 8, 25, 83, 89-92, 124-127, 129-133, 142, 188, 245, 247, 310, 312-314, 316, 343
Michigan's Dashboard, 127-129
Michigan's Office of Good Government, 131-133
Miller, Sarah, xix
mission, 21, 28-29, 39, 40-41, 45-46, 55, 57, 81, 93, 101, 122, 125, 135, 146, 148, 151, 179, 206, 217, 227, 237, 245, 249, 250, 302, 323, 335

Mississippi, 281
Mojo, 266, 267, 333, 340
Montana, 61, 281
Moore, Tom, xxi, 205, 207
Morales, Emery, xxii
Morales, Ryann, xxii
Morales, Sawyer, xxii
Morrow, Mitch, xix
Morse, Frank, 283
Morse, Lyle, 230, 283
Motor Vehicle Division, New
  Mexico, 16, 27, 42, 57, 254
Motor Vehicle Division, New
  Mexico, 27-31, 34-35, 37,
  39-43
Muda, 220, 221
Mulally, Alan, 107-108, 115,
  239-244, 266
Myers/Briggs Type Indicator, 333

N

National Association of State
  Chief Information Officers,
  277-278, 341
National Conference of State
  Legislatures, 63, 269, 286
Natural Resources, Washington
  Department of, 192
NBC, 7, 90
Nebraska, 61
Nestle Purina Pet Care Co., 38
Neuroscience, 10
Nevada, 61, 84
New Mexico, xxvii, 16, 25, 27,
  30, 35, 37, 39, 42-43, 57, 61,
  83, 174-175, 183, 254, 281
  New Mexico MVD rating
    system, 42

New Mexico Healthcare, 174-177
New York, NY, 21-24, 67, 84,
  99, 100, 119, 187, 266
Newell, Kaylyne, 134
Nike, 180, 338
Niswender, Larry, xix
North Dakota, 61
Norton, David P., 333
NOW Management System, 100,
  144, 164, 200, 225, 330
  performance portal, 294
NYPD, 23, 24, 100

O

Obama, President, 269
OBC (see: Oregon Business
  Council)
Oklahoma, 25
O'Leary, Joe, xix
Omark Industries, 101, 102, 338
online, 41, 42, 138, 152, 189,
  196, 286, 292, 295, 322
operating processes, 31, 147-149,
  151
  table of typical, 148
Oregon, xxvii, 4, 17, 44, 46, 59,
  63-64, 81-82, 100, 133,
  141-145, 150, 152, 188, 196,
  209, 211, 213, 216, 238,
  282-283
Oregon Benchmarks, 81-82, 142
Oregon Business Council, 272
Oregon Business Plan, 272, 332
Oregon Correctional Enterprises,
  144
Oregon Senate Bill, 676 282
Oregon 10-year Plan, 144, 332
Oregon Youth Authority, xxiv,

44-45, 48, 50, 57, 144-145, 213, 238

Oregon Youth Authority Fundamentals Map, 48-49

outcome-based management, 204

Outcome Measures, Essential, 48, 87

outcome measures (see measures, outcome)

owners, 146, 200, 208, 224, 293

OYA, (see: Oregon Youth Authority)

O'Malley, Martin, 25, 65, 119-120, 133, 153, 185-186, 191, 286, 307-308, 310, 317-321

P

PacifiCorp, 338

Pacholke, Dan, xx

Pack, Barry, xix

Padilla, Demesia, 29, 43

Pakseresht, Fariborz, xix, xxiv-xxv, 44-46, 213

Pannkuk, Pam, 134

pareto, 222, 287

Parks and Recreation Commission, 137

Parks and Recreation Commission, Washington, 137

Parnell, Sean, 25

Patterson, Kerry, 333

PDCA (Plan, Do, Check, Adjust), 115-116, 288

Pedersen, Dick, xix

PerformanceStat Potential, The, 187

performance portal, 294

Perry, James L., 3

PERS (see: Public Employees Retirement System)

Peters, Colette, xix, xxiv-xxv, 44-45, 211-214, 216-217, 237-238

Peterson, Lynn, 172

Pette, Sharon, xx

Pewaukee School District, 39

Plan Washington, 138, 270, 272-273

Playboy Magazine, 38

Poka-Yoke, 220, 221

Pollution Liability Insurance Agency, 137

Pope, Sarah, xix

Portland, OR, 17, 101, 337

Posner, Barry C., 243, 244

poverty, 5, 85, 158, 161, 179, 271, 272

pregnancy, 155-158, 161-162, 183, 276

Presbyterian Healthcare, 175

PricewaterhouseCoopers, 125

Primal Teams, 236

problem solving, 36, 47, 77, 105, 114-115, 192, 198, 222-223, 225, 233-237, 251, 262, 280, 287, 292, 303, 315, 321, 337

problems-solving burst, 12-week, 233

process improvement maturity, 223

process map, 56, 114, 222

process measures, (see measures, process)

Project Management Institute (PMI), 293

Prosci, 289

Public Employees Retirement System, Oregon, 144, 200,

202, 204, 215
public health, 25, 155-157, 162
Public Health and Environment,
  Colorado Department of, 155,
  157-158, 161
public interest, 3, 36, 62, 63, 66,
  67, 218
public safety, 5, 68, 78, 79, 100,
  126, 242, 285
Public Safety, Maryland Department of, 78
public servants, 6, 7, 8, 10, 18,
  52, 82, 104, 106, 109, 114,
  132, 163, 214, 216, 220, 244,
  310, 321
Puget Sound Partnership, 137
Putintsev, Vitaly, 204

Q

QTR (see: Quarterly Target
  Reviews)
quality of health, 86
Quarterly Target Reviews, 47, 50,
  112, 200-205, 207, 208, 303
Quigley, Kevin, 172

R

Ramirez, Chris, 134
Rankings, 93
rape, 22, 67
Rath, Tom, 333
Rawson, Brian, 79
Reagan, Ronald, 38
recidivism, 69, 85, 238
ReEntryStat, 189
Regulatory Innovation and
  Assistance, Washington Office
  of, 195

Reinventing Performance in
  Michigan, 90-91, 343
Renton, WA, 342
Republicans, 4
resistance, 47, 75, 77, 239-243,
  248-252, 255-267
results
  results revolution, xxiii-xxvii,
    30, 228, 300, 322, 337
  results champions, 86
  results-focused government, 3,
    76-80, 225
  results-driven government, xxi,
    5, 30, 35, 108, 144, 173,
    199, 209, 214, 225, 250,
    282, 291, 293, 303, 304-311
  results-driven management, xix,
    5, 9, 10, 103, 109, 116, 123,
    145, 159, 178, 214, 217,
    225, 270, 283, 286, 300,
    301, 307, 337
  results cycle, 19
  results, four elements of the
    shift to, 35
  results wheel, 73
Results-Driven Management
  Purpose Statement, 109
  Improving Fundamentals,
    110, 123
  Achieving Breakthroughs,
    111, 160
  Monitoring Performance, 113,
    188
  Solving Problems, 114, 213
  Model, 116, 145, 291, 301
Results Washington, 133-141,
  171, 193, 194-196, 198, 227,
  275
  Goal Map, Sustainable and
    Clean Energy, 138-139

Results America, 5, 49, 84, 152, 322, 326, 332, 335, 337
Results Pledge, The, 322, 323, 332
Retirement Services, Washington Department of, 134
Revans, Reginald, 232
Revenue, Colorado Department of, 56
Revenue, Washington Department of, 195
Revolutionary War, xxiii-xxiv
Rhode Island, 4, 25, 62
Richardson, Dennis, 283
Rickard, Matthew, 204
Roberts, Jack, xix
Robinson, Doug, 277-279, 281
Rodeman, Steve, xix, 200-203
Ross, James, xix
Rossman, Jaime, 198
RPM (see: Reinventing Performance in Michigan)
Rule of Nobody, The, 94, 334
Run chart, 222

S

Safe Improvement Zone, 214, 216
Saiki, Clyde, xix
Salem, OR, 46, 211
Saxton, Rob, xix
Scatter diagram, 222
Scherzinger, Jim, xix
scorecards, 4, 21, 29, 35-37, 77, 80, 82, 107, 112, 126, 128, 130, 142, 147, 204, 241, 245-246, 250, 253, 255, 277, 280, 286-287, 289-293, 295, 301-303, 323

scorecards, red/yellow/green, 37
scorecards, near real-time, 291
Seattle, WA, 78, 133, 269, 271
Senge, Peter, 93, 94
Seven Deadly Sins of Waste, 11, 219
Seven goals for a state, 65
Seven-Step Problem Solving, 221-223
Shewart, Walter A., 115
shoeshine, 310-311, 317
Shook, John, 333
Shumlin, Peter, 25
silos, organizational, 72
situational resistance, 265
six leadership styles, 261
Six Sigma, 28, 39, 101, 142, 221-223, 229
smoking, 84, 86
Snell, Michael, xx
Snohomish County, 170
Snyder, Jon, 172
Snyder, Rick, xxvi, 8, 25, 89, 124-126, 130-132, 188, 245-247, 281, 310, 312-317, 319, 321
Sobanet, Henry, 51-56
Sonicare, 138, 269
Sony, 7
South Dakota, 62
Southwest Airlines, 43
Spencer, Lisa, xix
Sponsoring change, 177-183
Springfield, MA, 295
stakeholders, 16, 18-19, 20, 28, 64-65, 82-83, 145-146, 149, 164, 172-173, 178, 181, 183, 218, 270, 273, 275, 280, 283, 286, 292, 302-303, 306
StanCorp Financial Group, 338

standard work, 221
Starbucks, xxvii, 227-228, 269, 270
state employees, 31, 86, 132, 176, 218, 284
State Farm Insurance, 173
State Hospital, Oregon, 144
State Patrol, Washington, 169-171
State Penitentiary, Oregon, 214
State Treasury, Oregon, 144
StateStat, 77, 84, 122, 190, 332, 341
StatReviews, 189
Stein, Beverly, xxi
Stillings, Rebecca, xx
Straight, Jean, xix
StudentStat, 189
Sun Microsystems, 180
supporting processes, 148-149
    table of typical, 149
sustainable energy, 136, 137, 194, 198, 342
Switzler, Al, 333
System, Government as a, 94-101
Systemic Inventive Thinking, 73-75

T

Tacoma, WA, 134
Target Zero, 169-173
    results, 170
Taxation and Revenue, New Mexico Department of, 29
TEAM (Tennessee Excellence, Accountability, and Management) Act, 168, 283-285
teamwork, 131-133, 200, 295, 333
technology process, 94, 96, 97

teen pregnancy, cycle of, 162
teen pregnancy results, Colorado, 156-157
Tektronix, 338
Telfer, Chris, 283
Tennessee, xxvii, 4, 20, 25, 39, 83, 152, 162-169, 183, 284-285, 343
    Lead Tennessee (see Lead Tennessee)
Total Quality Management, 222
Tomich, Zach, xix
Toussaint, Angela, xx
Toyota Way, The, 94
Traffic Fatalities, 69, 85, 169-170, 172-173, 179, 276
Traffic Safety Commission, Washington, 169-170, 172-173
transformation model, 288
Transformation leadership, 251-252
Transportation, Washington Department of, 195
TSC (see: Traffic Safety Commission, Washington)
TVW, 196, 332
Twain, Mark, 61, 296
Twitter, 294
Tyranny of the urgent, 124

U

University of Cambridge, 232
University of Oregon, 235
University of Washington, 272
US Army Armament Research, 39
Utah, 25
Utilities and Transportation Commission, Washington, 137

V

Valley of Doubt, 248, 262
values, 45, 72, 108, 141, 146, 237, 302
Vermont, 25, 62, 196
VetStat, 189
vision, 45, 130, 135, 146, 237, 242-245, 273, 302
visual management, 221
visualizations, geographic, 278

W

WaBA (see: Washington Business Alliance)
Warick, Jim, xx
Warne, Jack, 101
Warner, Bernard, xx
Washington, xxvii, 2, 4, 25, 39, 64, 82, 84, 100, 133-139, 152, 169-172, 183, 188, 193-196, 198, 209, 227, 229, 230, 270, 272-273, 275, 280
Washington Arts Commission, 195
Washington Business Alliance, 138, 270-275, 344
Washington Federation of State Employees, 199
Washington, George, xxiii-xxiv
Washington State Association of Counties, 172
Washington State Correctional Industries, 230
Washington State Lean Conference, 227
Washington Traffic Fatalities, 170
waste, 7, 9-12, 36, 41, 52, 56, 72, 77, 102, 104, 109, 110, 114, 124, 145, 211-215, 217-222, 224, 228, 231, 237, 249, 322
Waste, Seven Deadly Sins, 11
West Virginia, 62, 170
Wiesman, John, 172
Williams, Mark, 16, 27-30, 37-41, 43, 254
Wise, Tristan, 134
Wolk, Larry, 157, 158
Womack, James P., 333
Worcester, MA, 295
workflow, 222, 291, 292
Workforce Investment Act, 312
Wyoming, 61, 82, 84
Wyse, Duncan, 72

Z

Zars, Janet, xx
Zombieland, 298